T3-BOD-421

Library of
Davidson College

AMERICAN ORIENTAL SERIES

VOLUME 66

ISLAMIC REVOLUTION AND HISTORICAL MEMORY

An Inquiry into the Art of ᶜAbbāsid Apologetics

AMERICAN ORIENTAL SERIES

VOLUME 66

EDITOR-IN-CHIEF

ERNEST BENDER

EDITORS

PAUL W. KROLL DAVID I. OWEN JEANETTE A. WAKIN

AMERICAN ORIENTAL SOCIETY

NEW HAVEN, CONNECTICUT

1986

ISLAMIC REVOLUTION
AND HISTORICAL MEMORY
An Inquiry into the Art of ʿAbbāsid Apologetics

BY

JACOB LASSNER

AMERICAN ORIENTAL SOCIETY
NEW HAVEN, CONNECTICUT
1986

909.09
L347i

Copyright © 1986
BY AMERICAN ORIENTAL SOCIETY

PHOTOTYPESET BY EISENBRAUNS
WINONA LAKE, INDIANA, UNITED STATES OF AMERICA
1986

ISBN 0-940490-66-8

AEG-1322

In Memory of Samuel Maslansky

CONTENTS

PREFACE

Following three decades (A.D. 718–47) of clandestine revolutionary activities, the descendants of the Prophet's uncle, al-ᶜAbbās, coopted a provincial insurrection, overthrew the regime that had displaced the Prophet's family from power, and established a political order that endured for half a millennium. The compelling story of the ᶜAbbāsids and their revolution is described in rich detail by various writers of the Middle Ages. However, the historical and belletristic texts are at best problematic for they preserve echoes of a carefully articulated bias favoring the new dynasts. Indeed, the portrayal of men and events is so patently tendentious that at times it raises doubts concerning the basic historicity of specific episodes, if not the larger events that frame them. Scholars seeking a more accurate view of the ᶜAbbāsid ascendancy are enjoined to recognize the difficult sources and analyze them, balancing imagination and boldness with no small measure of caution. As with other dramatic episodes of early Islamic times, the ᶜAbbāsid revolution represents, above all, a problem of medieval historiography.

At first, my intention was to write still another descriptive history of the revolution, albeit a version of events that gives greater recognition to complex textual issues. However, the total absence of archival materials with which to balance distortion precluded any such treatment of the subject. What finally emerged was a series of discrete but related studies. These retain the narrative mode but, I hope, less of the tendentiousness that often marks a continuous narrative of events. Divided into three parts, the studies consist of an introduction to the analysis of ᶜAbbāsid historical texts, labeled prolegomena, and two segments devoted to case studies. The first of these segments deals with the past as invented history; the second attempts to rediscover the broad outlines of a history that might have been.

Viewed as a whole, the monograph has several foci. The main thrust of the investigation is to demonstrate how apologists for the ᶜAbbāsid house discovered, embellished, and often invented the past to enhance the public image of patrons whose credentials to rule were found lacking. In this respect, *Islamic Revolution and Historical Memory* is about early Islamic apologetics and the art of historical writing. It is, however, also a work of modern historiography; for the intention is to record the rise of the ᶜAbbāsids in a fashion consistent with what J. H. Hexter called "doing history"—in this case, a concern for ways of interpreting a fragmented, highly contrived, and at times opaque record of events and persons, far removed in time and place. Finally, there are matters of wider interest. One speaks here of the ᶜAbbāsids and their revolution, but what is said of them may apply in some manner to other public figures and to the events of other eras. For, more generally, this is a study of how medieval Muslims understood historical processes and forged historical traditions in a traditional and highly lettered environment.

The skeletal structure of the investigation began with a series of papers presented to the American Oriental Society. Some of the papers were then reworked into articles that were subsequently "leaked" before the completion of this volume. Such articles that have already appeared have been duly noted in the bibliography. Needless to say, the final shape of this book reflects directly the critical discussion generated by these earlier efforts. A number of colleagues expressed interest in this project at various stages of its preparation. Expressing gratitude to all of them would require a statement of unmanageable length, but I would like, nevertheless, to single out those whose encouragement and advice were invaluable. My colleague at the Institute for Advanced Study, T. H. Breen, of Northwestern University, was an ideal sounding board for roughly hewn ideas during many impromptu conversations and, as always, Moshe Sharon of the Hebrew University was a learned critic during our many discussions of *ᶜAbbāsīyāt*. Leonard Tennenhouse, Kenneth Walters, Jonathan Marwil, and Rudi Lindner read and reread various segments of the text and offered important stylistic suggestions. Thanks are also due my secretary, Susan Sage, who interrupted her career as a budding poet to type successive drafts of the manuscript.

A grant from the National Endowment for the Humanities made it possible for me to spend a fruitful year at the Institute for Advanced Study. During that time I also enjoyed the privileges of a Visiting Research Scholar at Princeton University. I wish to acknowledge the faculty and staff of both institutions, especially Bernard Lewis, who went out of his way to make me feel like a true *ben bayit*, while extending to me the benefit of his vast erudition. Above all, I am indebted to my wife, Phyllis, as always, a source of encouragement and unusually good counsel.

FOREWORD

Contemporaries referred to the advent of the ᶜAbbāsids as the *dawlah*, a word Arabic lexicographers endowed with a wide range of meanings, including a "turn" that signifies changing times or fortunes. For the new dynasts and their followers, *dawlah* meant, more specifically, victory over their predecessors, the house of Umayyah, and, concurrent with that triumph, the formation of an entirely new order.[1] Advocates of the ᶜAbbāsids thus heralded radical and far-reaching changes as shifting political currents caused the foundations of Umayyad rule to collapse. The new Commander of the Faithful was not seen as carrying on in the tradition of his predecessors. The *dawlah* was no rebellion of ambitious kinsmen in search of personal gain; nor was it a coup of restless praetorians seeking their own aggrandizement. No parochial interests were championed. No simple rotation of palace occupants was anticipated. Eagerly awaited by a significant cross-section of Islamic society, the onset of ᶜAbbāsid sovereignty was looked upon by contemporaries as a substantive break with the immediate past.[2]

Broadly speaking, the expectations of dramatic change were fulfilled by events carefully orchestrated by the emergent dynasts. The exemplary fashion in which the new caliphs attempted to eradicate the vestigial traces of Umayyad rule had been unprecedented in the experiences of the Faithful. Whether one speaks of new

[1] See B. Lewis, "Islamic Concepts of Revolution," 25–26 and his "On Revolutions in Early Islam." See also *EI*² s.v. Dawla.

[2] Conceptually, scholars of the ᶜAbbāsid revolution have made little headway since the pioneering works of Van Vloten and Wellhausen in the nineteenth century. (See G. van Vloten, *De Opkomsi der Abbasiden in Khurasan* and his *Recherches sur la domination Arabe, le chiitisme et la croyances messianiques sous le khalifat des Omayyades*; J. Wellhausen, *Das Arabische Reich und sein Sturz*; and more recently C. Cahen, "Points de vue sur la révolution abbāside.") Only M. Sharon and T. Nagel have shown any significant appreciation for new historical methods based on a detailed understanding of textual problems. (See Sharon's doctoral dissertation in Hebrew, "ᶜAlīyat ha-ᶜAbbāsim la-sh-shilṭōn," and the revised translation of the first part of this work, *Black Banners from the East*. Regrettably this last work appeared too late to be integrated into the text. Also T. Nagel, *Untersuchungen zur Entstehung des abbasidischen Kalifates*.) However, the latter's scholarly interests have shifted to other subjects, and Sharon's longer work, written in Hebrew, remains inaccessible to a larger community of Islamists. Generally speaking, the highly tendentious ᶜAbbāsid traditions continue to vex modern scholars. The most reliable of several recent surveys is at best conventional in its analysis of a historiography that is complex and elusive. (See F. Omar, *The ᶜAbbāsid Caliphate 123–70/750–86*, especially 12–137. This work is essentially a shortened version of his *al-ᶜAbbāsīyūn al-awāʾil*; H. Kennedy, *The Early Abbasid Caliphate*, esp. 35–46; D. Dennet, "Marwān b. Muḥammad and the Passing of the Umayyad Caliphate.") Other

networks of social relationships, a complete overhaul of the military structure, innovations in provincial administration, or the creation of a highly centralized and massive bureaucracy, encased by monumental architecture and reflected in lavish court ceremonial, the changes instituted by the ᶜAbbāsids represent an ambitious departure from both the style and substance of Umayyad rule.[3] In this sense, Arabic *dawlah*, derived from a root meaning "to turn" or "come about" is the semantic equivalent of the English word "revolution" which, since the time of the Renaissance, has come to denote political upheaval as well as rotation.

The far-reaching changes, which completely overturned the existing political and social order, tend, however, to mask another meaning of *dawlah*, a meaning which extends beyond the semantic range of revolution when it is used as a political term. As regards the ᶜAbbāsids, *dawlah* had the additional nuance of an historical process that had come full turn. There is, perhaps, no text where this signification is explicit, but it is implied everywhere in the historiography of the period where the victory of the Banū ᶜAbbās is embellished with apocalyptic symbols and heralded as a return to the halcyon days of early Islam. Seen from this perspective, the great upheaval occasioned by the ᶜAbbāsid revolution was actually a restorative process. For all the emphasis on radical change, the central theme of ᶜAbbāsid propaganda was the regeneration of Islamic society by returning to the ethos of an earlier age when the Prophet himself guided the Community of the Faithful. In such fashion, the nostalgic memories of a not so distant past were instrumental in shaping the political outlook of Muslims during the formative years of the ᶜAbbāsid regime.

Even as they promoted the onset of a new era, apologists for the recently established dynasty focused their attention on events of earlier times. Beginning with a survey of the pre-Islamic age, and continuing through the revolution, they carefully searched the past record for inspiration, guidance, and above all, evidence of their patron's legitimacy. Arguments thus linked the forebears of the ᶜAbbāsids, and also those of their opponents and would-be opponents, to events of dramatic importance that were indelibly etched in the historical consciousness of contemporary Muslims. It was intended, of course, that the performances of the ᶜAbbāsid ancestors should be

---

works, more ambitiously conceived, tend to accept the medieval sources at face value and give rise to interpretations marred by excessive license. Note M. Shaban, *The ᶜAbbāsid Revolution*. The title is somewhat misleading as most of the book treats Arab settlement in Khurāsān; also his *Islamic History: A New Interpretation*, v. 1. See also E. Daniel, *The Political and Social History of Khurāsān Under Abbasid rule 747–820*, esp. 13–100. Daniel argues vigorously and with much learning, although he does not read the sources with enough circumspection. Similarly, M. Azizi, *La domination arabe et l'epanouissment du sentiment national en Iran*, 2–127, and G. H. Sadighi, *Les mouvements religieux iraniens au IIᵉ et au IIIᵉ siècles de l'hégire* which have a distinct pro-Iranian bias.

[3] Unfortunately no lasting historiographical monument extolls the virtues of the Umayyad house. Some residual views of an Umayyad historiography are scattered in different kinds of sources, but there is no early chronicle written from their perspective that is available to current scholars.

seen as authentic models of proper moral and political behavior, and conversely that the ancestors of their opponents should be found lacking. In such fashion, the past became the standard by which the chroniclers of the Banū ᶜAbbās measured the family against its principal rivals and interpreted the dynasty's rise to power for contemporaries and generations of Muslims yet unborn.

The paradigm inspired by the dynastic historians was, in essence, quite simple: the ᶜAbbāsid family was made the most fitting analogue to their kinsman, the Prophet, and the recently proclaimed revolutionary age was heralded as a return to the days of the proto-Islamic community. The ᶜAbbāsid era was seen as the mirror image of a time when God's Messenger presided over the affairs of the Muslims. The Prophet's authority had been unquestioned among his Muslim contemporaries, and the community (*ummah*) of his time was characterized by an Islam as yet unsullied by internal political strife. In any event, this was the idealized view of Prophet and *ummah* that shaped historical consciousness for successive generations of Muslims. But history often has a way of creating difficulties for those who invoke it on behalf of a partisan cause. The ᶜAbbāsid performance during the Umayyad interregnum—the ninety years in which the Prophet's family had been displaced from the leadership of the community—was unimpressive and elicited caustic comments from those who put a high premium on principle and personal courage. As a result, the revolutionary record of the ᶜAbbāsids often had to be rewritten, or, at the least, reinterpreted to make it consonant with the ideals and circumstances of an earlier age. More recent times were therefore recorded as if they were the exact images of the historic past. As one might expect, the perceptions occasioned by this revision of history ultimately blurred, and sometimes obliterated, distinctions between generations and events.

Citing the past to legitimate present and future is commonplace; in this instance, circumstances forced the dynastic chroniclers to go a step further in their appeal to history. When the analogy to the past was clumsy, that is, when the evidence that could be drawn from historical precedents was inconclusive if not totally inappropriate to contemporary ᶜAbbāsid claims, the apologists for the ruling house simply reversed the historiographical process. Returning to earlier periods, they again rewrote history; however, this time, they recorded the past as a back projection of more current events. As a result, critical moments of Islamic experience were idealized and then recorded as distant echoes of one another. At times, accounts of diverse periods are almost indistinguishable. The *dramatis personae* are interchangeable and their utterances tend to be variations of one another. The labels and organizational structures of loyal followers are almost, if not in fact, identical. Even the description of the external forces that shaped ᶜAbbāsid policy produces a sense of déjà vu. Complex realities were thus endowed with a compelling though highly artificial sense of symmetry. It was as though the apologist *cum* historian threw stones into the troubled waters of history and created with each toss perfectly concentric circles. Again and again basic patterns were made to repeat themselves. In account after account, almost without variation, there are specific links, sometimes real, but often contrived, between the formative stages of Islam and later developments of political and religious importance.

One should not be misled by the concurrent privileging of past and present. Earlier images and forms, particularly those which conjured up powerful memories, were sometimes recreated in real life. If, for example, modern readers note obvious similarities in the ᶜAbbāsid effort to overthrow the Umayyads and the Prophet's struggle against the Umayyad forebears, the oligarchs of Mecca, it is because ᶜAbbāsid operatives deliberately imitated the past in choosing their slogans, in constructing their revolutionary apparatus and, more generally, in establishing an agenda for action.

Imitating the past was not an exercise in which historical memories were cynically distorted and presented to a gullible public for political gain. To retrace the steps of the Prophet had an almost magical quality. A former truth proclaimed was a truth recreated; the strategies which led to previous triumphs were considered guarantees of future success. It was as though invoking memories of the past were sufficient to overcome the most discouraging of contemporary obstacles. This need to emulate God's Messenger was deeply embedded in the consciousness of contemporary Muslims and was endorsed by a broad cross-section of society including the main rivals of the ᶜAbbāsid dynasts in the post-revolutionary age.

Unlike those opponents who stressed the efficacy of bold rebellion and even martyrdom, ᶜAbbāsid apologists tended to be circumspect when applying the lessons of history. Given their patrons' low profile during the long years of clandestine struggle, the dynastic chroniclers sought images from the past that accentuated the need for prudent behavior. Patience was a virtue they readily proclaimed. They pointed out that the Prophet, and more particularly his less fortunate followers, had been subjected to numerous indignities over an extended period of time before the historic migration to al-Madīnah. Even then, the Prophet did not initially call for a military campaign against the oligarchs of his native Mecca. Such a request of his new supporters would have been inappropriate and counter-productive considering the preponderance of power that his opponents, the ancestors of the Umayyad dynasts, could bring to bear against them. A politically astute observer knows how to delay gratification and design a policy that discourages risky ventures for the sake of long range gains. The Prophet understood the value of quiet overtures and secret meetings. The description of the extended negotiations with the Medinese prior to his migration would seem to be emblematic of that. In any event, these negotiations apparently served as a model for later descriptions of various ᶜAbbāsid meetings during the clandestine phase of their struggle.

There was no denying, however, that it was the military challenge that brought the oligarchs of Mecca to their knees and the Prophet to power. The ᶜAbbāsid propagandists were therefore in a quandary. Caution had its place, but memories of active resistance to an unwanted and illegitimate authority roused great fervor within the broad community of the Faithful. The ᶜAbbāsid leadership would not have been well served if their official chroniclers pictured them as less willing than others to rise up against the descendants of the Prophet's enemies. A delicate balance was therefore required of ᶜAbbāsid apologetics. The dynastic propagandists argued that the family leadership had indeed challenged the Umayyads politically, and on occasion had actually paid the price for confronting the ruling regime, but, as did the Prophet, they sought to temper their resistance with caution until that proper moment when militant action toppled the usurpers from power. However well conceived, their arguments often strain credulity. Once the sources are exposed to meticulous examination, it becomes increasingly clear that the revolutionary struggle depicted in the ᶜAbbāsid historical traditions is the struggle that should have been, rather than the struggle that was.

Modern scholars who would use the ᶜAbbāsid traditions as historical documents are obliged to ask what can be learned from this tendentious literature, particularly as there are no archival documents against which to check accounts. How can texts so contrived be made to shed light on the ᶜAbbāsid rise to power, especially on the decades when revolutionary activity was confined to clandestine operations? Inherently troublesome, the ᶜAbbāsid sources tend to be most problematic in describing the earlier phases of the revolution, because the initial silence concerning ᶜAbbāsid claims and the slim record of their resistance called for greater denial, more forced explanations, and even more elaborate inventions.

Readers strongly influenced by a positivist outlook will, no doubt, prefer a comprehensive study of the revolution—the sort of study that is based on a thick description of historical processes. However, with the data currently available, it is improbable that anyone can write a detailed narrative history, let alone describe the larger story of the ᶜAbbāsid rise to power. One can paraphrase the apologists as a matter of course and follow the loose chronology suggested by the annals, but only naive readers willing to accept traditions at face value, or those compelled to argue on behalf of parochial interests, are likely to undertake or sanction such an effort.

Nonetheless, much can be learned from these difficult accounts, were historians willing to shift the initial focus of their investigation. Rather than start with recorded events as if they represented actual states of the past, scholars would do better to reconstruct the intricate process by which events were perceived and then recorded for political purposes. Retrieving the past from ᶜAbbāsid historiography is to retrieve officially sanctioned views—not history as it was, but as it was understood. And yet, one can never quite escape grappling with the past as it actually might have been, for contrived as they are, the ᶜAbbāsid traditions are not entirely self referential. Embedded in the tendentious accounts of former times are echoes, however faint, of real events. How that reality was transformed into an idealized view of the past is the major concern of this work.

PART ONE: PROLEGOMENA

Apologetics, Historical Writing, Interpreting the Past

PROLEGOMENA: APOLOGETICS, HISTORICAL WRITING, INTERPRETING THE PAST

> What is in agreement with it [i.e., the Qurʾān] is from me, whether I have, in fact, said it or not.
>
> Attributed to Muḥammad the Prophet

Imbedded in narratives describing the advent of ʿAbbāsid rule are texts and fragments of texts reflecting a well-conceived apologia on behalf of the regime. When taken as a whole, this material represents the echo of sustained and sophisticated efforts to legitimize the ʿAbbāsid Caliphs and their forebears by creating for them a past that transmuted historical realities. The need for this revision would have been self evident to all who promoted ʿAbbāsid claims. Despite their impressive revolutionary triumph, the Banū ʿAbbās, especially the Manṣūrid line which dominated the dynasty, failed to win universal acclaim. Embarrassing questions were raised about their earlier reluctance to confront a usurpative Umayyad regime on the field of battle; and related to these queries, doubts were expressed concerning the specious and shifting claims on which ʿAbbāsid rulers and would-be rulers based their authority. Above all, supporters of the regime must have sensed the danger that important constituencies within the newly established realm would become disaffected and turn to others, better qualified and better known, for political and spiritual leadership. At the least, the early splintering of ʿAbbāsid support would have impeded the process of transforming the new polity from a loosely formed revolutionary movement into a widely recognized state of imperial pretentions.

Paradoxically, the ʿAbbāsids had become prisoners of a revolutionary tradition which they themselves had spawned. Critical to their movement's survival had been the clandestine nature of its operations. For many sympathizers of the revolutionary cause there had been no visually identifiable leadership, and more startling yet, no clearly proclaimed ideology. It was not until the investiture of Abū al-ʿAbbās, the first Caliph of the realm, that the broad coalition of revolutionaries discovered the identity of their hidden leader and the specific basis of his claims to rule. There was, to be sure, an inherent logic to the dual policy of enforced secrecy and restrained activity. It shielded the leading ʿAbbāsids from reprisals by the political authorities during the earlier phases of the clandestine struggle, and when the rebellion was openly proclaimed, rallying behind an unknown leader enabled revolutionary agitators to attract wide support among highly diverse groups. With success, however, came formal exposure. When finally compelled to shed their anonymity, the ᶜAbbāsid family became the object of public scrutiny and invidious comparison. The low political profile that had protected their interests so well now served to underscore what might have been perceived in certain quarters as a conspicuous passivity to Umayyad misrule. Worse yet, it implied the reluctant acceptance of an illegitimate regime.

A. POLITICAL ALIGNMENTS AND POTENTIAL CHALLENGES

By any yardstick of comparison the ᶜAbbāsid record of open resistance, or, more correctly, lack of resistance, did not measure up to their politically active cousins, the ᶜAlids. It is true that the political adventures of the latter were generally ill-timed, ill-conceived, and destined for spectacular failure, but they confirmed a well-known paradox of history: in certain circumstances, total failure, when properly exploited, can lead to gains that partial victory can never achieve. In death, the lamented martyrs of ᶜAlī's line grew larger than life. Beginning with his son al-Ḥusayn who was killed at Karbalāᵓ their example in having confronted the Umayyads aroused great passion. Forged on the anvil of an authentic history, the saga of al-Ḥusayn and those of ᶜAlī's progeny who followed his path could only have served to strengthen ᶜAlid claims to rule. More significant, it attracted activist elements who seemed forever ready to join their cause in an effort to obtain the fruits of the triumph that had escaped them and gone instead to the undeserving ᶜAbbāsids.

The danger of an ᶜAlid threat was complicated by the internal dynamics of the fledgling ᶜAbbāsid state. By remaining concealed in the background, the ᶜAbbāsid leadership had been forced to delegate inordinate power to others within the revolutionary apparatus. Two agents, Abū Salamah in Iraq and Abū Muslim in Khurāsān, continued to exercise wide authority well into the period marking the transition from Umayyad to ᶜAbbāsid rule. Had these important revolutionaries defected and given military backing to a well-known ᶜAlid contender, the position of the new ruling family would have become precarious, if not untenable.[1] Referring to the ᶜAbbāsid Caliph and the diverse constituencies that brought his family to power, an astute observer was given to quip, "[He] is like the rider of a lion who terrifies those who see him, but who is himself the most terrified of all."[2] The potential for disaster was self-apparent: there were ᶜAlid candidates thought capable of subverting the former revolutionary apparatus. Worse still, there was the concurrent possibility of disaffection in the ranks of an army whose original commitment to the revolution was tied to an unknown leader "from the house of the Prophet," a vague designation that applied to the descendants of ᶜAlī b. Abī Ṭālib as well as the Banū ᶜAbbās.

[1] See J. Lassner, *The Shaping of ᶜAbbāsid Rule*, 57–68 for the historical background of these agents. On a possible defection to the ᶜAlids see Ṭabarī, III/1:58ff.; *FHA*, 212–13; Jahshiyārī, 90.

[2] Ibn al-Muqaffaᶜ, *Risālah fī al-ṣaḥābah*, 347. Appropriately enough when the Caliph later murdered Abū Muslim he recited: "But that lion with which you threatened me has turned upon yourself." See Ibn Khallikān (De Slane), III: 140; *Akhbār*, 256; Khaṭīb, *Taᵓrīkh Baghdād*, X: 208.

With the possibility of an ᶜAlid revolt and the disaffection of former allies or comrades in arms, the ᶜAbbāsids—in particular the Manṣūrid branch of the family—launched an ambitious political program to shore up the shaky foundations of their newly created state and to establish a solid basis for its legitimacy. The pragmatic steps in this program included incarceration, murder, various acts of duplicity, and other devious strategems culled from the traditional repertoire of successful rulers.[3] The focus here is on a second aspect of the program, namely, the attempt to win the hearts and minds of the Faithful. That is, the concern is with the major themes of ᶜAbbāsid propaganda and the various techniques that were utilized in its dissemination.

Propaganda in the post-revolutionary age was directed, first and foremost, against the ᶜAlid pretenders who waited in the wings to capture the revolutionary triumph that had escaped them. This anti-ᶜAlid sentiment has been noted in detailed studies of religious traditions, but it requires further analysis in historical texts, where it is a recurrent and significant theme.[4] The term "anti-ᶜAlid," though it is employed here for lack of a more precise expression, is actually misleading. The ᶜAlid relationship to the ᶜAbbāsid house was extremely complex, as with kinsmen who contend with one another for power. Sharing broad political objectives if not common support during the Umayyad interregnum, the two branches of the Hāshimite clan fully emerged as political rivals following its collapse. Fortunately for the ᶜAbbāsids, the ᶜAlids were more inclined to grand gestures than sustained revolutionary efforts. Generally, their supporters confronted the ᶜAbbāsid regime as they had the Umayyads earlier, with occasional bravado but without any clearly defined strategy for success.[5] Nevertheless, the potential ᶜAlid threat was always taken seriously, for as blood relations of the Prophet they could promote themselves as the heirs to his sacred authority and the leadership of his clan and community.[6]

[3] F. Omar, "Aspects of ᶜAbbāsid Ḥusaynid Relations."

[4] First established by I. Goldziher, *Muslim Studies*, v. 2, esp. 89–125 (= Studien, 88–130); see also J. Wellhausen, *Die religiös-politischen Oppositionsparteien im alten Islam*. On ᶜAbbāsid historiography, important ground has been broken by Nagel's *Untersuchungen*; esp. 9–63.

[5] The issue of opposition touched upon ᶜAbbāsid-ᶜAlid relations as well as the ᶜAlid history of resistance to the Umayyads. Like their ᶜAbbāsid counterparts, the more passive elements among the ᶜAlids had to explain their reluctance to challenge the usurpative Umayyad regime. Such explanations were addressed to the wider community as well as the more militant ᶜAlids who sought leadership within the family. On ᶜAlid-Umayyad relations see the pathbreaking study of E. Kohlberg, "Some Imāmī Shīᶜī Interpretations of Umayyad History," 145–49 (text), 249–54 (notes).

[6] For the revolt of the sons of ᶜAbdallāh al-Maḥḍ, see Lassner, *ᶜAbbāsid Rule*, 69ff.; Omar, *Caliphate*, 223ff.; Nagel, "Ein früher Bericht über den Aufstand von Muḥammad b. ᶜAbdallāh im Jahre 145h," 227–62. A general survey of early ᶜAbbāsid-ᶜAlid relations can be found in Omar, op. cit., 211–58; and his "Abbāsid Ḥusaynid Relations," 170–79. See also Kennedy, *The Early Abbasid Caliphate*, 198–214.

There was, moreover, considerable uncertainty surrounding the claims of the new ruling family. By what rights did the ᶜAbbāsid branch of the Banū Hāshim obtain leadership in the wider community of Islam? The more cynical observer might have argued that the ᶜAbbāsids, who were rather late entries into the struggle against the Umayyads, seemingly began as a family in search of a revolution, or, in any case, as a group of would-be conspirators in need of a revolutionary apparatus. Following the death of their kinsman, the Caliph ᶜAlī b. Abī Ṭālib, the ᶜAbbāsids fully accommodated themselves to the usurpative Umayyad rulers, and when they finally challenged the dynasty that had displaced the Prophet's clan, it was only through a movement and an authority that had been inherited from others some thirty years earlier. Furthermore, this alleged transfer of authority, which formed the basis of ᶜAbbāsid claims, had been deliberately concealed from the community at large until the investiture of the first ᶜAbbāsid Caliph, Abū al-ᶜAbbās. Although it could be argued, and with considerable justification, that the deception was entirely necessary, the early and prolonged silence of the ᶜAbbāsids could only have given rise to serious reservations about the validity of their long suppressed claims.

When examined in detail, the story eventually told by the ᶜAbbāsid apologists taxed the imagination.[7] The sacred authority had been held by Abū Hāshim b. Muḥammad b. al-Ḥanafīyah, a grandson of ᶜAlī b. Abī Ṭālib, but ᶜAlī's grandson had been poisoned by the Umayyads, who feared him and his supporters. On his deathbed, Abū Hāshim, who was without heir, transferred the sacred authority which he claimed to his close friend and kinsman, Muḥammad b. ᶜAlī b. ᶜAbdallāh b. ᶜAbbās. Before death overtook him, the ᶜAlid also handed over his loyal followers and predicted that the ᶜAbbāsid would in turn bequeath these credentials and inherited supporters (subsequently identified as the Hāshimīyah) to his son, Ibrāhīm (al-Imām). The latter was to be followed by two unnamed but identifiable brothers. It thus came to pass that following Ibrāhīm's death, a second of Muḥammad's sons, Abū al-ᶜAbbās, was designated as his brother's successor, albeit under circumstances shrouded with mystery.[8] A third son, Abū Jaᶜfar (al-Manṣūr), then succeeded Abū al-ᶜAbbās with credentials so suspicious that his Caliphate touched off an internecine conflict within the ᶜAbbāsid house.[9] Even if one could have believed that Abū Hāshim's authority was indeed transferred in this highly problematic sequence of events, there would still be those denying that his was the sacred authority originally vested in the Messenger of God. For who was this descendant of ᶜAlī by way of a Ḥanafite concubine to claim the Prophet's legacy? The supporters of Abū Hāshim's half brothers, the descendants of al-Ḥasan and al-Ḥusayn, could argue that their ᶜAlid

[7] See below Chapter II.

[8] The problematic succession of Abū al-ᶜAbbās is discussed by Sharon who skillfully pieces together the particulars. Much of his analysis is conjectural; there is no question, however, that the decision to nominate Abū al-ᶜAbbās as the new imām was made by a very small group within the family and was kept secret from all but a very select group of revolutionaries. See "ᶜAlīyat," 237–61; also Nagel, *Untersuchungen*, 162–66.

[9] See Lassner, *ᶜAbbāsid Rule*, 19–57 esp. 35ff.

patrons were related to the Prophet on both sides of his family: through Muḥammad's first cousin and adopted "brother" ᶜAlī and, more important, by direct blood ties through ᶜAlī's noble wife, the Prophet's daughter Fāṭimah.

Such views are indeed expressed in a series of letters exchanged between the Caliph al-Manṣūr and the ᶜAlid rebel Muḥammad b. ᶜAbdallāh al-Maḥḍ.[10] Responding to the Caliph's call for reconciliation, the rebel produces a carefully phrased argument rich in allusions to the past. "The right to rule is ours," he declares. "You have claimed it through us. To secure rule, you revolted [against the Umayyads] with the aid of our partisans, and [now] you [brazenly] bask in our excellence . . . our ancestor ᶜAlī [b. Abī Ṭālib] was the Prophet's legatee and the imām. How is it that you inherited his authority [*wilāyah*] while his descendants still live . . . you know that no one who has claimed rule can match our genealogical credentials [*mithl nasabinā wa sharafinā wa ahlinā*]. . . . We, and not you, are the sons of the Prophet's daughter Fāṭimah. . . . Indeed God has chosen us and chosen for us. Our progenitor is Muḥammad who is [counted] among the prophets, and our ancestor is ᶜAlī, the first among the Muslims."

Al Manṣūr's rival then goes on to glorify the women who gave birth to the ᶜAlid line from which he descended. There were no non-Arabs or slave girls to besmirch the status of the Ḥasanid offspring by way of Fāṭimah. This was a pointed reference to al-Manṣūr's mother Salāmah, who was a Berber slave, and to various other ᶜAbbāsid family dignitaries who were born to women of humble origin.[11] The intention was also to diminish the status of Abū Hāshim, the grandson of the Ḥanafite concubine from whom the ᶜAbbāsids claimed to have inherited their sacred authority.[12] In contrast, Muḥammad b. ᶜAbdallāh al-Maḥḍ, who was nicknamed the "Righteous" or "Pure Soul" (*al-Nafs al-Zakīyah*), boasted that he represented the very essence of genealogical purity among the clan of Hāshim (*awsaṭ Banī Hāshim nasab wa asraḥuhum ab*). In sum, the ᶜAlid maintained that he was the legitimate successor to the authority originally invested in the Prophet.

Lest one be misled by these assertions, Muḥammad b. ᶜAbdallāh was not vindictive, nor did his boasting betray a lack of political flexibility. He was willing to come to terms with al-Manṣūr provided that the latter recognized the justice of the ᶜAlid claims and submitted to the authority of the Fāṭimid line through the offspring of ᶜAlī's son, al-Ḥasan.

Although Abū Hāshim, ᶜAlī's grandson by way of a Ḥanafite concubine, is not explicitly mentioned in this rather remarkable document, his role in the formation of ᶜAbbāsid doctrine is central to the meaning of the text. When the ᶜAlid complains, "you have claimed it [i.e., the right to rule] from us," he is referring to the ᶜAbbāsid

[10] Ṭabarī, III/1, 209ff.; *FHA*, 240ff.; Azdī, 20. A detailed analysis of these letters is found in Nagel, "Ein früher Bericht." See esp. 247–52. See n. 6 above.

[11] See below Chapter II, Section A.

[12] The argument may also be addressed to the Ḥusaynid branch of the ᶜAlid family. A definitive study of Ḥasanid-Ḥusaynid relations is long overdue.

claim that sacred rule was transferred to them from the heirless (and less prestigious) descendant of the ᶜAlid line. When he asserts, "you have revolted with the aid of our partisans," he draws attention to the cadres of the Hāshimīyah that transferred their allegiance from a dying Abū Hāshim to Muḥammad b. ᶜAlī. The expression "bask in our excellence" is similarly an attempt to indict the ᶜAbbāsids for covering themselves falsely with an ᶜAlid heritage, albeit one which was indirectly acquired. Under any circumstances, the ᶜAbbāsid claim was found entirely lacking; for the crux of the ᶜAlid contention was in denying the sacred authority of Abū Hāshim, rather than in questioning the account of its transfer. Because the ᶜAbbāsids had no claim whatsoever without Abū Hāshim as imām, the rhetorical strategy of the Fāṭimids was to circumvent the offspring of ᶜAlī's concubine and to stress instead the line of direct descent through the Prophet by way of ᶜAlī's noble wife Fāṭimah.

It is not likely that al-Manṣūr was overwhelmed by the logic of this argument; but he understood, no doubt, that he had been put on the defensive. Given the eminence of the Fāṭimid offspring, he could not simply restate the original ᶜAbbāsid claim. Another claim was required, one which would completely undercut the credentials of the ᶜAlid contender. The claims of the Banū ᶜAbbās originally based on the transfer of Abū Hāshim's authority were thus supplemented and eventually replaced by a second notion, indicating that the ᶜAbbāsids obtained their right to rule, not from ᶜAlī's grandson, as originally stated, but from the Prophet's uncle al-ᶜAbbās, the progenitor of the ᶜAbbāsid line. In the absence of male descendants or an appointed successor, authority went, as a rule, to the oldest paternal uncle (*ᶜalā qarābat al-ᶜumūmah*). The corollary to this argument was to deny that the Prophet's authority (or indeed any leader's authority) could have been inherited through a daughter. There was an unquestioned tradition among Muslims that prevented the transfer of authority through female lineage (*sunnah allatī lā ikhtilāf fīhā bayn al-Muslimīn*). No one could deny that Fāṭimah's relationship to the Prophet was meritorious, but, when the legal principles were sorted out, this blood tie should have had no bearing on the political disputes of a later generation. This point, which was the linchpin of the ᶜAbbāsid tradition, was argued by the Caliph with considerable vigor, if not a touch of sarcasm: "The essence of your boasting which rests with claims of inheritance through female lineage [*qarābat al-nisāʾ*] may indeed lead the rabble and the hotheads astray, but God did not elevate women to the same status as paternal uncles and fathers and [other] ancestors of the male line. He made the paternal uncle [and not the female relative] the equivalent of the father [*jaᶜala al-ᶜamm ab*]. . . ."[13]

Scholars who are fond of neatly packaged conceptualizations may be tempted to see ᶜAbbāsid-ᶜAlid contentions in terms of displacing claims and counter-claims.

[13] The Caliph continues his argument by stressing the important role of al-ᶜAbbās in pre-Islamic times and following the advent of Islam. At the same time he denigrates a second of the Prophet's uncles, Abū Ṭālib, the father of ᶜAlī. He points out that the inheritance of the Prophet was with al-ᶜAbbās (*mirāth al-Nabī lahu*) and the Caliphate was with the uncle's descendants (*al-khilāfah fī wuldihi*). I am presently preparing a full study of this document.

There is reason to believe, however, that the contrasting ᶜAbbāsid positions actually overlapped one another. A careful reading of the evidence does not suggest that there was an abrupt shift from a claim based on the transfer of Abū Hāshim's authority to that of a direct inheritance by way of the Prophet's uncle al-ᶜAbbās. Although the latter view displaced the former, it only became official doctrine during the reign of al-Manṣūr's son, the Caliph al-Mahdī, some twenty-three years after the father had been recognized as Commander of the Faithful and fifteen years after the revolt of the ᶜAlids. Indeed, numerous arguments were embroidered into the complex design that represented doctrinal claims and counter-claims. By the turn of the first Islamic century, ᶜAlī had been made the direct recipient of the Prophet's legacy, obviating the need for Fāṭimah. The ᶜAbbāsids, in turn, produced traditions indicating that they too were the direct legatees of the Prophet, and even of ᶜAlī b. Abī Ṭālib. It may seem odd that mutually exclusive doctrinal positions were given wide currency at roughly the same time; however, it should be understood that the diverse constituencies among the Faithful required different strategies of apologetics. The aim of ᶜAbbāsid propaganda was to address the broadest possible following, anticipate the greatest number of objections, and provide the widest range of digestible answers, however contradictory they might seem.

No less dramatic than ᶜAlid-ᶜAbbāsid relations were the internal problems that beset the new ruling family. The dissension within the ᶜAbbāsid house is generally familiar to Islamic historians. Al-Manṣūr, the second Caliph of the line, came to power after defeating his distinguished paternal uncle ᶜAbdallāh b. ᶜAlī in a bitter civil war chronicled by the medieval authors.[14] It is less well known that the conflict was precipitated by the failure of Abū al-ᶜAbbās, the first Caliph of the dynasty, to provide for an orderly succession. For contrary to what was subsequently written by pro-Manṣūrid writers, al-Manṣūr had no binding legal nor moral claims to the Caliphate until shortly before the death of Abū al-ᶜAbbās, when the dying Caliph inexplicably chose his non-descript older brother, the son of Salāmah, a Berber slave-girl, over many more distinguished and certainly better qualified candidates within the ruling family. These included five other paternal uncles, each a hero of the revolution and each a powerful political figure in his own right, and the Caliph's nephew and second heir apparent, ᶜĪsā b. Mūsā.[15]

Given the possibility of a continuing challenge from the remaining paternal uncles, and more significantly, from his nephew, the heir apparent, the Caliph moved boldly and swiftly to solidify his tenuous hold on the regime. He seized control of the Khurāsān army by murdering its creator, the veteran revolutionary Abū Muslim, and then isolated his relatives from critical centers of power that might ultimately threaten his rule.[16] In addition, he formed a line of succession based exclusively on his own progeny by eventually removing ᶜĪsā b. Mūsā in favor of his own son,

[14] See Lassner, *ᶜAbbāsid Rule*, 35–40; Kennedy, *The Early Abbasid Caliphate*, 57ff.; Omar, *Caliphate*, 183ff.

[15] Lassner, *ᶜAbbāsid Rule*, 19–31.

[16] Ibid., 58–90.

Muḥammad (al-Mahdī).[17] In such a fashion, Abū Ja^cfar al-Manṣūr set into motion a series of events that would lead to some five centuries of Manṣūrid rule.

These successes in the political arena were not enough for a ruler who wished to legitimize his accomplishments and preserve them for posterity. There was a compelling need to overcome the limitations of his background by creating a picture of himself that was greater than life; for the Caliph's claims, if honestly presented, would have been incongruous with his lack of distinction during the years of revolutionary activity and the open revolt which followed. Once in power, al-Manṣūr was compelled to rehabilitate his image. The later descriptions of his early career therefore took on certain embellishments which are clearly associated with a historiography, or more correctly hagiography, that had been assembled under official patronage. The achievements of al-Manṣūr's distinguished relatives were thus attributed directly to him. He became the conqueror of Syria and the extirpator of the Umayyad line, titles which more appropriately characterize the activities of his paternal uncle and rival ᶜAbdallāh b. ᶜAlī.[18] The Caliph's humble origins were similarly reversed in order to present him with genealogical credentials befitting his newly acquired position.[19] On ccasion, the polemic against the paternal uncles (*ᶜumūmah*) and ᶜĪsā b. Mūsā was juxtaposed with anti-ᶜAlid arguments making for multi-layered accounts of great complexity.[20] Because the traditions related to internal family concerns have been dealt with elsewhere, there is no need at present for extended discussion.[21] Suffice it to say that the early conflict between the branches of the ruling house was critical to the formation of ᶜAbbāsid government and therefore became a central theme of Manṣūrid apologists.

B. FROM PROPAGANDA TO HISTORY: A HYPOTHESIS

Unlike the substance of the debate between the ruling ᶜAbbāsids and their adversaries, the historical development of ᶜAbbāsid apologetics is hardly known at all.[22] Difficult questions remain to be answered. What was the relationship between strategies of communication and the development of literary forms? And related to that, what was the process by which ᶜAbbāsid propaganda entered Arabic historiography and belles-lettres and thus came to be preserved for future generations? Put somewhat differently, when and how was propaganda transformed into history? What follows is a hypothesis which addresses these questions.

17 Ibid., 50–57; also his *Topography*, 152–54.

18 *ᶜUyūn* (Cairo), I: 206ff. For the complicated problem of the massacre of the Umayyads, see S. Moscati, "Le Massacre des Umayyades dans l'histoire et dans le fragments poétiques," 88–115.

19 See below, Chapter II, Section A.

20 See below, p. 19.

21 Lassner, *ᶜAbbāsid Rule*, 19–90 esp. 19–57.

22 Note also the relationship between political symbolism and ᶜAbbāsid architecture was first broached in Lassner, "Some Speculative Thoughts on the Search for an ᶜAbbāsid

A Hypothesis

Political indoctrination during the clandestine phase of ᶜAbbāsid activity was carefully designed for small gatherings of trusted clients.[23] Even then, many followers did not know the intricate composition of the revolutionary movement, nor could they identify its inner leadership. Given such conditions of secrecy, the language of political discourse was likely to have been highly esoteric so as to conceal its true meaning. In any case, the discussion which it engendered was clearly limited to a handful of initiates screened by ranking agents of the Banū ᶜAbbās. The dissemination of ᶜAbbāsid propaganda was thus deliberately restricted, and its content remained opaque to all but a few select followers. However, beginning with the revolt against the Umayyads, the tightly formed conspiratorial network gave way to a more broadly based polity, and with each military success, the ᶜAbbāsids inherited new adherents that were distributed over an ever-widening geographical landscape. When Umayyad rule finally collapsed, there arose in its stead a nascent regime of truly imperial dimensions. The extensive domains of the state and the diverse composition of its newly-acquired political constituencies, therefore, required an extensive network to inform the public of ᶜAbbāsid views.

The strategy for influencing a broad cross-section of the populace included the use of agitators effective in public gatherings, the posting of announcements, and the distribution of a wide variety of political tracts. Skilled as they were, the designers of this strategy were aware that what proved efficacious with a highly literate audience might not elicit the same response from outlying tribal units, the rural population, or the common people of a burgeoning urban environment. Numerous and indeed different versions of the ᶜAbbāsid line were therefore circulated so as to have the widest possible appeal among intellectually and ideologically diverse groups. Moreover, with increased exposure to audience reaction, the oral presentations were refined, leading to an even more variegated body of material. In this respect, the agitators who brought the ᶜAbbāsid message to the far reaches of the empire could be considered entertainers who told their stories before many different audiences and in distant places. Through a process of trial and error they found the most effective means of communicating with dissimilar groups; the composition and receptiveness of the audience invariably governed the level and type of performance.

The strident apocalyptic tone that occasionally surfaces in ᶜAbbāsid propaganda is reminiscent of a rhetorical style that originated in ancient times. However, unlike the soothsayers of old, who improvised without benefit of a written text, the ᶜAbbāsid agitators may have employed a discourse that was originally based on a

---

Capital," 135–41, 203–10 which essentially equals his *Topography*, 121–37. The ideas set forth there were further developed by C. Wendell, "Baghdad: *Imago Mundi* and Other Foundation Lore," 99–128. For a revision of Lassner's earlier work as well as a critique of Wendell, see Lassner, *ᶜAbbāsid Rule*, 163–241 esp. 163–83.

[23] For an overview of the early movement, see Sharon, "ᶜAlīyat," 84–116.

loosely worded script. Strategies of performance would then have required experimenting with written as well as spoken detail.[24] A political theatre which utilizes scripts, however vaguely worded, may well leave its mark on long range literary developments. In this case, working notes representing the various stages of oral presentation could have been distilled, together with more formal documents, into the elusive written tradition of the second Islamic century, where a version of history promoting ᶜAbbāsid claims was first given broad literary expression.

No single version of events emerges in this literature nor does any uniform view of ᶜAbbāsid claims. The conception of the past which permeates these ᶜAbbāsid historical traditions, reflects instead the diversity of their propaganda in the post-revolutionary age. From the outset of the new regime, apologists for the ruling family had to contend with ᶜAlid counter arguments as well as divergent audiences. As effectively as they presented their claims, dynastic apologists were contested by opponents equally skilled in their craft. Defending the ᶜAbbāsid position required continuous editing to delete material where arguments were no longer appropriate, and to amend and otherwise embellish texts where they were not yet strong enough. Although the debate between rival apologists often shifted ground, paradoxically, there was no decisive break with previously held positions. Instead, revisionist views of history tended to overlap earlier conceptions, and even when a given view was finally displaced by issuing a summary pronouncement, it was not expunged from the written record. The more conservative constituencies presumably held on to their beliefs after prevailing views were officially changed.

Assembled in this eclectic fashion, the ᶜAbbāsid traditions became part of the general historiography of the second century A.H. There are no extant historical works from this period, but fragments of the larger corpus, and the ᶜAbbāsid tradition contained within it, are scattered in later chronicles and in belletristic texts that are based in large measure on historical anecdotes. A later historiography thus preserved ᶜAbbāsid texts that varied widely in detail and meaning, even though they each purportedly described the same event. At times, the seeming contradictions were allowed to stand in stark contrast to one another; on other occasions, subtle attempts were made to harmonize inconsistencies through a variety of well-known literary devices. However, given the sanctity of scripture and its pervasive influence on writing in general, rarely, if ever, did later editors of these accounts tamper directly with a given text or show preference for a particular version to the exclusion of

[24] There is no indication that the performances of the ᶜAbbāsid propagandists ever reached the level of formal theater, either at court or in the street. Once entrenched in power, the new dynasty seems to have drawn upon familiar and time-tested traditions. Privately, they preferred poets and "singers" who articulated political sentiments while entertaining in courtly settings. The general populace was in turn treated to occasional spectacles and public ceremonies heavily laden with political meaning. In later times there was the ghoulish practice of slowly executing rebels and then hanging their dismembered torsos on public monuments. The edifying demonstrations of the authority of the state and its swift justice were self-evident statements that obviously required no further explication.

others. Numerous accounts of a given episode, whether discrete versions or a pastiche of different variants, were catalogued and then spliced together without benefit of formal commentary. Despite the textual incongruities occasioned by this kind of editing, these accounts were casually reported as if they all accurately portrayed the historic past. A medieval reader convinced of his cause found the legendary history of the Banū ᶜAbbās neither true nor false. It was rather a metatruth that transcended the bare particulars of any single account by proclaiming what was more real than the events themselves, namely, the acceptance of the ᶜAbbāsid regime and its claim of an unbroken link to the authority and tradition of the Prophet.

Shaping tradition to serve justifiable ends was not unique to the ᶜAbbāsids, nor did their contemporaries perceive of historiographical license in simplistic terms that might suggest western concepts of fabrication and fiction. Even scholars who examined religious traditions were unsure of how to deal with spurious accounts (*mawḍūᶜāt*) that lent themselves to correct ethical behavior—behavior, which, in reference to the ᶜAbbāsids, would have meant subservience to their rule. The Prophet himself was made to say, "What is . . . related to you as a saying of mine, you will have to compare with the Qurʾān [i.e., my authentic public utterances]. What is in agreement with it [i.e., the Qurʾān] is from me, whether I have, in fact, said it or not [*fahuwa ᶜannī qultuhu aw lam aqulhu*]."[25] This tendency to transgress what modern authorities might consider strict rules of truth and falsehood was apparent by the second Islamic century, and more important, it was recognized for what it was by contemporary Muslims. It is, therefore, evident that the license exercised by ᶜAbbāsid propagandists was well within established literary and intellectual constraints. The historiography of the ᶜAbbāsid rise to power is, in this sense, a literature of profane traditions, albeit one that is justified on religious grounds and permeated by religious themes in accordance with claims that linked the ᶜAbbāsids to the Prophet and the pristine Islam of an earlier age.[26]

C. PROBLEMS OF INTERPRETATION

It is a grievous error for current scholars to accept these sources without question, but we do the ᶜAbbāsid traditions no justice by rejecting them out of hand. Historians who prefer to focus on how and why events were perceived and recorded have come to appreciate the link between apologetics and actual states of the past.[27] Even when an account gives every indication of being fanciful, there may be beneath the story line some allusions to historical circumstances. As a rule, the apologists did

[25] Goldziher, *Muslim Studies*, v. 2: 56(= *Studien*, 49); also 145ff. (= *Studien*, 153ff.). Such views were not intended, however, for traditions dealing with matters of a strictly legal nature.

[26] See Foreword.

[27] Note, however, M. Waldman who warns against the "intentional fallacy" and argues for a wider approach to the reading of historical narratives. See her "Semiotics and Historical Narrative," 167–85 with particular reference to Islamic historiography.

not invent traditions of whole cloth; they preferred instead to weave strands of historical fact into a larger fabric of their own making. In this fashion, they authenticated their creations by drawing on vivid historical memories. Paradigms of ᶜAbbāsid legitimacy which emerge from an informed reading of the text invariably refer, albeit indirectly, to an authentic past and the attitudes it occasioned. Indeed, the coherence of an account may depend entirely on understanding vague references to circumstances and personalities that are embedded in the apologist's argument.

The link between the author's message and the remembrance of things past can be extremely elusive, however, for both the author and medieval reader (or in certain cases the speaker and listener) were originally partners in the act of transmission. Informed contemporaries would have recognized the historical allusions. Some of them were eyewitnesses to the events in question, others might have learned of them from informants who were. In any case, given their detailed knowledge of the past, they were likely to understand the intricate design of the apologist's argument. The partnership has not survived. The author, more or less, remains in the form of the extant text, but the reader of ᶜAbbāsid times has been replaced by a modern counterpart who is, quite naturally, less informed as to the particulars of the discourse. Confronting the ᶜAbbāsid traditions, current readers might not grasp the apologists' message for want of access to the fine detail buried in the sources. Allowing our imagination to wander, we can see a puzzled scholar a thousand years hence attempting to analyze the partially edited script of a political cabaret that has not been performed for a millennium, or we might picture the historian of a future generation trying to contextualize a satiric editorial without access to detailed information. The historian's task will be difficult because satire and propaganda both utilize a language of multiple references and meanings—precisely the kind of discourse whose impact is diluted by fading memories.

Still, one may recover some sense of the apologist's intentions by being particularly sensitive to problems of narrative strategy.[28] A sustained effort to explicate what may seem superfluous detail or stylistic ornamentation can at times reveal the design of the account, that is, the way in which the author combines the various elements of his narrative to form a cohesive text. Because the format of ᶜAbbāsid historiography is often disjointed and anecdotal, determining the design of an account can become rather complicated even when there are numerous variants to compare. Moreover, even when the design seems evident, authorial intention can still prove extremely elusive. One can sense the tension of an author torn between artistic sensibilities and his political assignment. There are occasions when the temptation to turn a phrase, employ titillating imagery, or work within established literary

[28] Historians have, as a rule, shied away from a literary analysis of historical texts. An exception is M. Waldman's *Toward a Theory of Historical Narrative* which utilizes the speech act theory of M. L. Pratt to analyze the *Taʾrīkh-i Bayhaqī* with mixed results at best. See the review of M. Yapp in *TLS*, Sept. 1980:1040; and more recently her use of semiology as expounded by U. Eco. See n. 27. For a more traditional approach to historical texts see the works of A. Noth, "Sammlungen" and *Quellenkritische Studien.*

conventions may simply overwhelm the need to express political ideas clearly and directly. Not every detail in the ᶜAbbāsid traditions can therefore be ascribed to the subtle construction of the apologia. When, at times, the text appears to be overly ornate or marked by extensive digressions, the design may be literary and not tied to political concerns. Often the ability to see through walls is required when analyzing the more opaque ᶜAbbāsid traditions; there is, nevertheless, the danger that some highly imaginative readers will create walls where none exist in order that they might penetrate them in search of a higher truth.

On the other hand, the author who embellished his text for artistic purposes may have exercised restraint in detailing his political message. In conveying his views to the reader, the apologist had to avoid excessive boldness. By invoking the obvious argument in support of his position, he would have immediately revealed his intention, and alerted the audience to his partisan stance. Such a strategy might well have compromised his objective, the certification of the ᶜAbbāsid regime and more specifically the legitimization of the Caliph al-Manṣūr, a problematic figure with suspect credentials. Therefore the author preferred a less direct mode of discourse; he held back explication and merely directed the reader to a given position. Leaving behind traces of a subtle pattern that had been woven into the text, he relied on an inquisitive reader to discover the traces, make the necessary connections, and reconstruct the broader design that explains the central meaning of the account. For the author to have done more would have called the text itself into question and reduced the likelihood of its being accepted. In effect, the argument gave the outward impression of being authentic because it was understated, and as such it encouraged the reader to combine historical memory with powers of observation and reason in order to discover the truth for himself. Upon discovering the truth in this fashion, the reader was likely to defend it with tenacity.

Viewing the same text, less knowledgeable modern scholars may be confused by the author's strategy, for the apologists' use of an indirect mode of discourse is likely to obscure the message which had been implanted in the narrative. Without adequate clues to reconstruct the internal logic of the argument, current readers may regard the account as yet another vague anecdote, a story more valued for its charm than its importance as an historical text.

Example: The Death of Muḥammad

The explication of a specific document may help to illustrate how ᶜAbbāsid apologists utilized indirect modes of discourse in skillfully crafting their arguments. In this instance, the passages which enhance ᶜAbbāsid claims are chosen from the writings of Ibn Isḥāq, an author eminently suited to the present inquiry.[29] A ranking scholar of traditions, Ibn Isḥāq had been compelled to leave al-Madīnah because of personal difficulties. The quality of his scholarship, if not his orthodoxy and public behavior, had been seriously questioned by his learned opponents, principally Mālik

[29] D. ca. 150 A.H./767 A.D. See *EI*[2] s. v. Ibn Isḥāq.

b. Anas and Hishām b. ᶜUrwah.[30] The former accused him of tampering with traditions, the latter of tampering with his wife. The evidence in both instances seems to be inconclusive, and in the case of Ibn ᶜUrwah's wife, it is entirely circumstantial. Nevertheless, Ibn Isḥāq left the holy city in self-imposed exile and traveled about Iraq and Khurāsān before seeking the patronage of the ᶜAbbāsids and settling in their newly established capital, Baghdad.

His greatest contribution to the world of letters, as well as politics, was the work that came to be known as the *Sīrat Rasūl Allāh*, the quintessential biography of the Prophet Muḥammad and his times.[31] A systematic analysis of this work reveals it to be a revisionist history that was most likely written with the encouragement, if not the active support of the ruling house.[32] In any event, the text, which Ibn Isḥāq presented to the Caliph al-Manṣūr,[33] provided the historical evidence necessary to trumpet ᶜAbbāsid claims, and thus insured the author a place of prominence at the court of his new-found patron.

Considering the ideological debate between the ᶜAbbāsids and their ᶜAlid kinsmen, it is not surprising that the *Sīrah* focuses considerable attention on the events surrounding the death and succession of Muḥammad.[34] On the matter of succession, it was critical for the author to suggest that the dying Prophet did not transmit his sacred authority directly to ᶜAlī b. Abī Ṭālib, but that having expired without naming a successor, Muḥammad allowed this authority to go as a matter of course to his oldest surviving paternal uncle, namely, al-ᶜAbbās, the progenitor of the current ruling house. Abū Bakr, the actual successor to the Prophet, was allowed in turn to acquire a certain measure of temporal authority in keeping with the electoral process that brought him to power. In such fashion, the *Sīrah* emphasized that ᶜAlī received neither the Prophet's blessing nor the mandate of the Islamic community he sought to rule. To be sure, the author could have stated this view forthrightly, but

[30] Yāqūt, *Irshād*, VI: 401.

[31] See J. Fück, *Muḥammad ibn Isḥāq*. The introduction to A. Guillaume, *The Life of Muhammad*, xiv–xlvii; also his "A Note on the Sīrah of Ibn Isḥāq," 1–4; J. Horovitz, "The Earliest Biographies of the Prophet and Their Authors," 169–80; J. Jones, "Ibn Isḥāq and al-Wāqidī: The Dream of ᶜAtīka and the Raid to Nakhla in Relation to the Charge of Plagiarism," 41–51; J. Robson, "Ibn Isḥāq's Use of Isnād," 449–65; W. Watt, "The Materials Used by Ibn Isḥāq," 23–24; R. Sellheim, "Prophet, Chalif und Geschichte, Die Muḥammad-Biographie des Ibn Isḥāq."

[32] R. Sellheim, "Prophet, Chalif und Geschichte." Note, however, the reservations of U. Rubin who notes the prominent position of ᶜAlī b. Abī Ṭālib in the text of the *Sīrah*. See his "Prophets and Progenitors in the Early Shīᶜa Tradition," 57. Ibn Isḥāq's treatment of ᶜAlī was compatible, however, with ᶜAbbāsid claims *contra* Fāṭimah's inheritance of her father's authority. The author thus argued for two ᶜAbbāsid lines concurrently, the legacy of Abū Hāshim by way of Alī, and the legacy of al-ᶜAbbās by way of the Prophet himself. If this is correct then the *Sīrah* is vivid proof that both ᶜAbbāsid positions were put forward concurrently.

[33] Ibn Qutaybah, *Maᶜārif*, 247ff.

[34] Ibn Hishām, I/2: 999.

instead, an endorsement of the ᶜAbbāsid position was subtly embedded in the narrative, where particular importance is attached to the activities of the leading Muslims immediately preceding the Prophet's death.[35]

Abū Bakr, who had been chosen by the Prophet to lead prayers during the latter's infirmity, had absented himself from the mosque. The Prophet, who was to die later that day, noticed that his chosen prayer leader had been replaced by ᶜUmar b. al-Khaṭṭāb, and therefore inquired with apparent concern, "Where is Abū Bakr? God and the Muslims forbid this!"[36] The implication was clear enough. The Prophet had considered his father-in-law, Abū Bakr, to be a worthy replacement for him. But having been given this opportunity, Abū Bakr seemingly compromised himself and the community through his unwarranted absence at the time of prayer. And yet, the Faithful did not doubt that Abū Bakr had actually been chosen by the Prophet to be his successor (as he had indeed been named prayer leader). According to the author, they had reason to believe that Muḥammad had nominated his father-in-law to replace him at the head of the community until a deathbed statement attributed to the second Caliph ᶜUmar indicated to them that they were misinformed.

About to die and faced with the problem of his own succession, ᶜUmar reportedly said, "If I choose a successor, someone better than me has done so; and if I leave them [without choosing a successor] someone better than me has left them [without choosing a successor]."[37] As there were only two historic figures to consider, the meaning of the Caliph's political testament would have been self-evident even without Ibn Isḥāq's subsequent explanation. Since it was common knowledge that Abū Bakr had nominated ᶜUmar to succeed him, clearly the Prophet could not have nominated Abū Bakr. The account would thus seem to suggest that the authority assumed by the Prophet's father-in-law after he was elected Caliph was more temporal than spiritual, a notion that was entirely consistent with ᶜAbbāsid views of the early Caliphate. No confusion should exist, however, as to the intention of the author. In essence, his remarks are not directed against Abū Bakr, although the latter was surely absent from prayers on that fateful day—an absence which seemingly earned from him (at least in this account) the Prophet's disapproval.[38] A more subtle

[35] Ibid., 1008.

[36] Ibid., 1009. The author indicates that the Muslims went to the Prophet asking him to lead prayers, but the Prophet, who was ill, suggested that they seek another. The people sought Abū Bakr (who presumably presided over prayers earlier) but he was not present. In turn, they chose ᶜUmar, who found himself compromised as he thought that the Prophet had nominated Abū Bakr to lead prayer. It was subsequently explained to ᶜUmar that in Abū Bakr's absence he was deemed most worthy of leading prayer. The text thus reinforces Abū Bakr's claim as Muḥammad's replacement (and by implication his successor). It also indicates that, after Abū Bakr, ᶜUmar was considered the most worthy of the Muslims, thus explaining why he, like Abū Bakr, was chosen ahead of ᶜAlī for the Caliphate.

[37] Ibid., 1010.

[38] The question of disapproval is actually left nebulous. One could interpret the text as meaning that the Prophet disapproved of those who chose ᶜUmar for not seeking out Abū Bakr. Such a view would have strengthened Abū Bakr's claim. The opponents of the ᶜAbbāsids

argument is embedded here. The question raised by Ibn Isḥāq was not Abū Bakr's standing in relation to the Prophet; that was well known. Discussing Abū Bakr's status was simply a clever ploy to draw the reader's attention. The more significant relationship concerned the Prophet and his first cousin ᶜAlī b. Abī Ṭālib.

If the Prophet had appointed no successor, as ᶜUmar b. al-Khaṭṭāb implied, he could hardly have chosen his closest kin. Without once mentioning ᶜAlī or his adherents by name, the author of the *Sīrah* was able to undercut any claim based on a direct transfer of authority from Muḥammad to ᶜAlī. Moreover, although the aforementioned traditions may seem to be critical of Abū Bakr, there is also a measure of praise for him. The Prophet thought enough of his father-in-law to choose him as his replacement in leading prayer (as it turned out Abū Bakr's absence was explained elsewhere in a very ingenious fashion),[39] and contrary to ᶜĀᵓishah's expectation that "the people would never love a man who occupied the Prophet's place,"[40] the Faithful believed that her father, Abū Bakr, had indeed been worthy of being chosen by Muḥammad as his successor.[41]

It could not be said that the Prophet's cousin ᶜAlī commanded high esteem of this sort. A second tradition which is embedded among the narratives describing the Prophet's final days was presented as evidence that neither Muḥammad nor the community had great expectations of ᶜAlī b. Abī Ṭālib.[42] It is reported that al-ᶜAbbās had encountered ᶜAlī shortly after the latter had visited the Prophet. As a result of his visit, ᶜAlī was convinced that Muḥammad (who had been considered deathly ill) was now on his way to recovery. The uncle shattered this illusion, " ᶜAlī, by God, in three days you will be reduced to someone's lackey. I swear, by God, that I recognize death in the Messenger's face. . . ." The implication of al-ᶜAbbās's comment seems clear. In all likelihood, the authority possessed by the Prophet would pass on after his death, not to ᶜAlī, but to another from among the Faithful (the reader was most likely to have considered Abū Bakr who, in previous accounts, was made prayer leader at the Prophet's insistence).

Rapidly developing circumstances called for an immediate plan of action. Al-ᶜAbbās suggested that he and ᶜAlī visit the Prophet in order to determine the latter's choice of successor. "If the authority is to be with us, we shall know of it and no further action on our part will be required. If it is to be with others, we shall request him to have the people treat us well [meaning, we will preserve for ourselves a measure of political leverage]." ᶜAlī's reply to this modest suggestion was somewhat less than enthusiastic: "By God, I will not do it. If he indeed denies us authority [on this occasion] no successor of his will grant it to us." There is no indication that ᶜAlī had a change of heart before the Prophet died later that day.

---

undoubtedly put a different interpretation on Abū Bakr's absence and it thus had to be dealt with by ᶜAbbāsid apologists.

[39] Ibn Isḥāq's explanation of Abū Bakr's absence is analyzed on pp. 33–36.

[40] Ibn Hishām, I/2: 1008.

[41] In addition to choosing Abū Bakr to lead prayers, the Prophet heaped praise upon him during his illness. See Ibn Hishām, I/2: 1006ff.

[42] Ibid., 1010–11.

Although never explicitly stated, the rationale behind ᶜAlī's action, or more correctly, his lack of action, is clearly suggested. He is pictured as being uncertain of his own worthiness, or worse yet of suspecting that the Prophet was about to name another (presumably Abū Bakr). It was therefore politic to wait out the Prophet's illness. Should he die without naming a successor, there was still the possibility that the Faithful might turn to ᶜAlī. In this case, ᶜAlī's indecision proved to be his undoing; the Prophet died without naming a successor and, as one might have expected from the previous description of events, the community chose Abū Bakr to replace him as Caliph. Once again the author led his reader to a desired conclusion by the use of indirect discourse and the subtle economy with which he argued his case.

D. READER RESPONSE

Retrieving the author's intention, and thus the original design of the text, requires some understanding of the response he expected of his audience. As a rule, modern audiences must read extensively and therefore develop strategies to assimilate massive data for short periods of time. On the other hand, medieval readers were taught to listen and read with considerable care and to ponder the same accounts again and again. Segments of texts, indeed entire works, were committed to memory through constant review in formal classes and private study. This tradition of learning encouraged familiarity with every conceivable nuance; so that when faced with a narrative that seemed to suggest *more* than it said, the audience invariably opted for the more expansive interpretation. In such fashion, the programmed readership satisfied its curiosity by skillful, if at times overly erudite interpretations, and the author proved his point without a belabored explication. That is, once having discovered the encoded message that was difficult to decipher, the audience was not about to admit that the game had forced a change of mind. The reader was not inclined to forfeit the intellectual triumph that was his source of entertainment and the confirmation of the truth he had discovered. In effect, the apologist induced self manipulation on the part of a willing and all too clever audience. The literary devices of the author were deliberately encoded. Words were carefully selected to convey double meanings, apocalyptic visions telescoped future occurrences which were in reality concealed current events, mirror images reflected the careers of rival *dramatis personae*, there were alphabet word games and similar literary puzzles. The reading of the text became an intricate game that succeeded in delighting as well as tantalizing each and every player.

Example: Al-Manṣūr's Dream of Visiting the Kaᶜbah[43]

A representative sample of these literary devices is found in two versions of an apocalyptic vision which occurred to Abū Jaᶜfar al-Manṣūr. In these well-conceived

[43] For political dreams in Islam, see G. von Grunebaum, "Introduction: The Culture Function of the Dream as Illustrated by Classical Islam," 3–22; T. Fahd, "The Dream in Medieval Islamic Society," 351–64, both in von Grunebaum's *The Dream and Human Societies*. See also M. J. Kister, "The Interpretation of Dreams," 67–103.

texts, the Caliph expresses his claims and those of his offspring against the ᶜAlids, against his rebellious uncle ᶜAbdallāh b. ᶜAlī, and against his nephew ᶜĪsā b. Mūsā, the original heir apparent, whom al-Manṣūr later removed in favor of his own son Muḥammad al-Mahdī. When he recalled this dream, Abū Jaᶜfar was reportedly in al-Kūfah following the death of his brother, the Caliph Abū al-ᶜAbbās. He was about to receive the oath of allegiance, an act signifying him to be the titular head of his family, and beyond that, the unquestioned leader of the Faithful. The dream itself allegedly took place, however, before the revolution, when the ᶜAbbāsids still resided in their estate at al-Ḥumaymah.

According to the version of Bayhaqī,[44] the Caliph's paternal uncle ᶜĪsā b. ᶜAlī (a member of the family entourage in al-Kūfah)[45] was asked by al-Manṣūr, "Do you remember my vision at al-Sharāt [i.e., al-Ḥumaymah]?"[46] When queried by his uncle, "Which vision?" al-Mansur quickly responded, "How can the likes of you forget it? You were obliged to write it down on parchment with a pen of gold and then transmit it as your legacy to your sons and grandsons." By having this vision recorded for posterity, and with no less than a gold pen, the ᶜAbbāsid propagandist immediately signaled the reader that this was no innocuous dream. The latter was likely to suspect that, given the sharp tone and the substance of al-Manṣūr's reply, it was directed to potential challengers among the paternal uncles and their offspring. An informed reading of what follows would have confirmed these initial suspicions and set the mood for a "correct" interpretation of the text.

When asked by ᶜĪsā b. ᶜAlī to refresh his memory, the Caliph-to-be recalled the details of the forgotten dream in an elaborate tradition filled with vague references to historical events. The tradition plays on the fact that al-Manṣūr, his half-brother Abū al-ᶜAbbās, and their rebellious uncle ᶜAbdallāh b. ᶜAlī shared the same proper name. The three distinguished ᶜAbbāsids were in Mecca in front of the Kaᶜbah when suddenly, the door to the sacred shrine was opened and a man called out, "ᶜAbdallāh b. Muḥammad." At this, al-Manṣūr rose as did his brother; but the man then added, "Ibn al-Ḥārithīyah," indicating that he meant that Abū al-ᶜAbbās, the son of Rayṭah the noble Ḥārithite woman should come forward. He entered the building, tarried for awhile, and then emerged with a (black) standard. Where he had tarried previously, once outside the Kaᶜbah Abū al-ᶜAbbās strode forward taking five steps; but the standard he was clutching then fell from his grasp. The later unfurling of black flags in Khurāsān signified not only an open declaration against the Umayyad regime, but the anticipated coming of the messianic era. When the revolution was successfully concluded, Abū al-ᶜAbbās, the first ᶜAbbāsid Caliph, forsook Umayyad white and officially adopted black as the color of the new dynasty. The five steps and the dropped standard were emblematic of his short reign which lasted altogether four

[44] Bayhaqī, *Maḥāsin*, 344–45.

[45] The setting of the dream is provided only in the versions of *FHA*, 216; Azdī, 162.

[46] That is, the location of that name between Damascus and the Arabian Peninsula. See Yāqūt, *Muᶜjam*, III: 270–71.

years and nine months. As these facts were common knowledge, the apologist would have had little difficulty in conveying his message. Having been entrusted with the paraphernalia requisite for the coming messianic age, Abū al-ᶜAbbās, was, in effect, ordained to bring about the collapse of the Umayyad Caliphate and the establishment of ᶜAbbāsid rule.[47]

A reader alert to the historical nuances of the text was also likely to understand that Abū al-ᶜAbbās did not tarry because of laziness or indecision. His action before receiving the standard (that is, the mandate to begin the revolution) was emblematic of a political strategy adopted by the ᶜAbbāsids during the long clandestine phase of their struggle. Rashness and bravado were left to ᶜAlī's descendants, perennial failures in their premature attempts to dislodge the Umayyads by force. In this sense, al-Manṣūr's dream is entirely consistent with other accounts showing the ᶜAbbāsids patiently deflecting criticism that they had forsaken black—a criticism which suggested accommodation to Umayyad rule.[48] To be sure, any such suggestion would have been a distortion of the truth. It was clear for the reader to see that once having received the standard, Abū al-ᶜAbbās marched forward to revolution and rule. The ᶜAlids might lay claim to their distinguished history of martyrdom, but the Faithful were better served by those who carried out a destiny that had been ordained in the sacred Kaᶜbah.

Although this didactic message is initially directed toward residual supporters of the ᶜAlid cause, the tradition also focuses on elements that may have questioned the validity of al-Manṣūr's credentials vis-à-vis those of his would-be rivals within the ruling family. The Caliph's rather unpleasant conversation with his paternal uncle suggests that the internal politics of the Banū ᶜAbbās was an important element in shaping his vision. When the banner slipped from Abū al-ᶜAbbās's grasp (the indication of his untimely death), the issue of succession became an immediate concern, so that the herald now called out a second time for ᶜAbdallāh. But since on this occasion he did not specify which ᶜAbdallāh, both al-Manṣūr and ᶜAbdallāh b. ᶜAlī raced forward. The swifter nephew succeeding in blocking his paternal uncle thereby gaining entry into the Kaᶜbah (a not so subtle reference to ᶜAbdallāh b. ᶜAlī's unsuccessful rebellion at the outset of his nephew's reign). Once inside the shrine, the second ᶜAbdallāh to enter its portal found two distinguished figures of the past, both bearing the name Muḥammad: his father Muḥammad b. ᶜAlī and the Prophet

[47] See Chapter III, Section B.

[48] Fahd, "The Dream in Medieval Islamic Society," 352, mentions this specific vision and reads: "Then I [al-Manṣūr] saw him [Abū al-ᶜAbbās] with a flag in his hand, but he had hardly come five steps when the flag fell from his hands." He presumably reads "five" (*khms*) for (*ḥms*). His reading is attested in other editions of Bayhaqī. Note, however, that he relied on Schwally's edition which clearly has *ḥms*. In his reading, the significance of the dropped flag is to allude to the brief reign of the first ᶜAbbāsid Caliph al-Saffāḥ, who actually ruled for four years. His point about the dropped flag is well taken. Indeed a second version of this dream explicitly states that the standard given to Abū al-ᶜAbbās was four cubits in length, that is, one for each year of the Caliph's short reign.

himself.[49] Al-Manṣūr was instructed to begin with the Prophet and so he saluted him. The latter called for a (black) standard, which he tied for the future Caliph, and then said, "This standard is for you *and your offspring. . . .*" The presence of the deceased Muḥammad b. ᶜAlī was to underscore that the family leadership would be transferred through his line and not through his surviving brothers and nephews.[50] So it came to pass that the sacred authority originally vested with the Prophet was inherited by the Manṣūrids and not the paternal uncles and their descendants. Should there have been any doubt of this, ᶜĪsā b. ᶜAlī and his relatives had a text inscribed on parchment to refresh their memories. This had been designated as their legacy; the authority and symbols of rule were destined to be the legacy of others.

Lest one believe that this interpretation suggests more than the text is capable of yielding, there is a second version of the account which is more detailed and, indeed, more revealing of the apologists' craft.[51] According to the second author, the Prophet was in the Kaᶜbah and the door was open but no one came forward. A herald called out, "Where is ᶜAbdallāh?" as if to indicate the Prophet was granting an audience. Abū al-ᶜAbbās went to the first step and was led by the hand to return shortly thereafter with a (black) standard four cubits in length. The gift of the revolutionary standard thus acquired additional meaning. By having the Prophet himself give Abū al-ᶜAbbās the black flag for safekeeping, the author signified the symbolic transfer of authority directly through God's appointed messenger to a chosen successor, thus bridging the hiatus between "primitive Islam" and contemporary times. The last notion is entirely consistent with ᶜAbbāsid propaganda, which stressed a return to the ethos of an earlier age, when moral authority was vested in true believers, whose interests were now quite properly represented by the newly established dynasty. As was true in the tradition mentioned earlier, the standard given to Abū al-ᶜAbbās also denoted his untimely death. It symbolized that the future Caliph was destined to lead the family for four years after the overthrow of the Umayyad regime, one year for each cubit in the standard.

[49] The presence of the Prophet signifies the direct transfer of his authority to the ᶜAbbāsids. Moreover, dreams in which the Prophet appeared were considered good and sound. See Kister, "The Interpretation of Dreams," 73, n. 2. Seeing the Prophet in a dream is like seeing him in reality. Note the story of a Baghdādī woman who dreamt that she saw the Prophet leaning against the qiblah wall of a mosque. The Prophet told her she would die the following day at the time of the ᶜAṣr prayer. She went to that mosque the following day. Seeing the imprint of a palm (the Prophet's) on the qiblah wall, she then fell dead at the designated time. See Khaṭīb, *Taʾrīkh Baghdād* (Cairo), I:100 = (Paris): 63–64.

[50] Other political dreams portending al-Manṣūr's supremacy over his brothers are found in *Akhbār*, 138; also 139–40; Masᶜūdī, *Murūj* (Beirut), III: 282. The former account indicates that the Caliph's grandfather ᶜAlī b. ᶜAbdallāh foresaw al-Manṣūr's conquest of his uncle in a contest of snakes. The latter story indicates that while pregnant, al-Manṣūr's mother Salāmah al-Barbarīyah saw her son emerge as a young lion cub from her loins; whereupon all the other lions bowed to him.

[51] *FHA*, 216; Azdī, 162.

In this variant, the case for the Manṣūrid line is presented in a complex passage filled with many subtle references to historical events. Indeed, readers of this tradition were likely to be delighted by an ornate argumentation that challenged their interpretive skills. Awaiting the oath of allegiance that would signify his election to the Caliphate, al-Manṣūr revealed what had happened to him in the Kaᶜbah, after he had outraced his uncle to appear before the Prophet. As with Abū al-ᶜAbbās, the Prophet tied a standard for al-Manṣūr. The latter was, however, the recipient of additional gifts. The Prophet also willed (*awṣā*) him his community (*ummah*), and placing a turban with twenty-three folds on his head, he said, "Take it for yourself, Father of Caliphs, until the Day of Resurrection." This last reference signifies the onset of the end of days when the messianic age is to be ushered in. Just as his brother received the symbolic tools required to overthrow the Umayyads in anticipation of a new era, al-Manṣūr was now granted the symbols of his Caliphate to do the same.

There are, however, still more subtle nuances to be recognized in this multi-layered tradition. Al-Manṣūr did not consider ᶜAbdallāh b. ᶜAlī the only threat to himself and the political hopes that he held for his offspring. There remained his nephew, the heir apparent ᶜĪsā b. Mūsā who stood directly before the Caliph's son Muḥammad al-Mahdī. A conspiratorial figure by nature, al-Manṣūr could not be sure that once in power, ᶜĪsā b. Mūsā would honor his commitment to respect the rights of the Caliph's eldest son (a projection, no doubt, of what the Caliph would have done in comparable circumstances). He therefore forced ᶜĪsā b. Mūsā to relinquish his position as heir apparent and made him take second place in the line of succession. Later, he succeeded in eliminating ᶜĪsā altogether, thus guaranteeing the continuous rule of the Caliph's progeny. These events are also clearly reflected in the tradition. For, in one well-chosen vision, the Caliph not only turned aside the claims of ᶜAbdallāh b. ᶜAlī, but with the gift of the turban, the appelation "Father of Caliphs," and the reference to the Day of Resurrection, he undercut the legitimate aspirations of his nephew, the heir apparent.

The reference to "Father of Caliphs" clearly indicates that the Prophet revealed, even before the revolution had been formally declared, that the future line of succession would eventually be through al-Manṣūr's son Muḥammad, thereby eliminating the paternal relatives and the descendants of ᶜĪsā b. Mūsā. This is in itself not unusual, for Muḥammad followed the designated heir apparent in the line of succession. However, the reference to the turban, which was held until the Day of Resurrection, provides an additional meaning. It not only refers to the eternal existence of al-Manṣūr's line (that is, the turban will be held until the end of days), but also represents a double entendre, for it identifies his successor. The rather subtle reference here is not to ᶜĪsā b. Mūsā, the designated heir apparent, but to the man who was to displace him.

It is no coincidence that the elaborate headdress that was to be held by al-Manṣūr contained twenty-three folds. Although the text offers no explanation for this curious fact, it would have been abundantly clear to all capable of simple arithmetic that the folds specifically represented the twenty-three years of al-Manṣūr's Caliphate. It is therefore implied that the Prophet gave this turban to al-Manṣūr for safekeeping until the latter's death, just as earlier he had presented Abū al-ᶜAbbās with a standard signifying the length of this tenure. The Caliph's passing was then to be followed by the Day of Resurrection, an event which clearly denotes the beginning of the messianic age; however, in this context the allusions of death, resurrection, and the advent of messianic times are intended to be symbolic. The messianic era about to come is but a thinly disguised reference to the reign of the Caliph's son Muḥammad, whose acquired regnal title al-Mahdī is loosely translated "Messiah." Therefore, according to this vision al-Manṣūr was destined to pass the Caliphate directly on to his son, and not the original heir apparent, ᶜĪsā b. Mūsā. When the various literary devices were sorted out, the secondary meaning was all too clear. The Prophet legitimized not only al-Manṣūr, but also his sons and grandsons after him. Once acquired, the Caliphate would be held in perpetuity for the Manṣūrid branch of the ruling family. The very presence of the Prophet in the dream was evidence that al-Manṣūr's vision was clear, and that the expectations that it gave rise to would therefore be realized by events yet to come.

Reader Response and the Modern Historian

The craft of the author in this literary game eventually overcame the interpretive skills of his audiences. For while knowledgeable contemporaries could fit the pieces of these puzzles into a coherent whole, the modern historian often strains to decipher the encoded passages. Even when sensing the author's strategy, the latter may simply lack the information to deal with the medieval text.[52] Indeed, the detailed understanding of many accounts was already beyond the later generation of medieval readers. Simply put, the lack of a critical mechanism to preserve contemporary interpretations left no foundation for a subsequent understanding of the text. Historical writing never gave rise to the type of detailed commentary which accompanied and then became part of the religious canon. Elements of major texts might be paraphrased or even slavishly copied in later generations, but there was no systematic effort at reviewing the older material by subjecting it to extensive literary or historical analysis.

Nevertheless, some chronicles employ a system of criticism which is not based on formal explication. Following a convention of the religious sciences, frequent use is made of technical terms to describe the reception of authoritative statements. These terms, marked by different shades of nuance, are then read as keys to the acceptability of the transmitted account. In such fashion, the historian is able to form an opinion about the soundness of a given tradition without having to analyze the text itself. It has been suggested, largely in the absence of evidence, that various chronicles also utilize an internal system of criticism, one that is based on the subtle positioning of sources.[53] In such a system, the sequential arrangement of contradictory stories may indicate the author's preference for the historicity of a particular account without his being openly judgmental of the text before him.

[52] See p. 14

[53] See for example the remarks of Guillaume on the *Sīrah* of Ibn Isḥāq, *The Life of Muhammad*, xixff.; S. Jafri, *The Origins and Early Development of Shiʾa Islam* (on Ṭabarī).

One might be able to cite specific examples of this internal criticism, but more generally, the rationale to the arrangement of the individual reports seems to be innocuous. Like the tesserae of a patternless mosaic, the discrete reports that made up the more extensive accounts were interchangeable within the borders of the larger whole. To claim more is to argue for a design so subtle that it remains incomprehensible to even the most sensitive reader. Furthermore, the greatest chronicles describing early ᶜAbbāsid history are composite works that do not bear the clear stamp of an acknowledged author. Compiled from accounts drawn from earlier treatises, these impressive texts give the impression of having been assembled by an editor supported by numerous assistants. Even with frequent references to chains of transmission, where several accounts appear in sequence, it is often difficult to determine whether the order of presentation should be credited to the original author or to a later editor.[54] In any case, this process of collating and editing accounts is no substitute for a systematic exegesis.

Without an adequate mechanism to store contemporary readings of historical texts, the retrieval of earlier interpretations became increasingly difficult. Fading historical and even philological memories led, in effect, to the creation of new historical texts, for even when the transmitted account remained exactly the same, its basic meaning could be altered by interpretations rooted in the experiences of a later generation. In this sense, the images of the past were filtered through contemporary lenses and became distortions of their original meaning.[55]

Example: The Changing Interpretation of "Glad Tidings Will Accompany the Hāshimite dawlah"

A piquant example of this kind of distortion is preserved in the fourteenth century belletristic work of Ibn Ṭabāṭabā.[56] Utilizing a style and format reminiscent of the *Fürstenspiegel* genre, the author has written a didactic essay in which broad political themes are woven into a lengthy and highly schematized historical survey. The basic organizing principle is the sequential treatment of Islamic dynasties and the leading figures who shaped the course of historical events. Although Ibn Ṭabāṭabā is almost unrestrained in his zeal for the ᶜAlids, the nature of his discourse also required

[54] The reference here is to Ṭabarī and Balādhurī's *Ansāb*; that is, works of enormous scope that often preserve multiple versions of the same events. R. S. Humphreys is currently preparing a major study of these historiographical issues.

[55] The process reminds one of a game played by school children in varied cultural settings. An anecdote is written down and then whispered into the ear of a student who is obliged to relate it in the same fashion to a second child. The chain of transmission continues until all who are assembled have finished relating the story. The last recipient is finally called upon to write down his anecdote. Despite various controls which may be built into the game, two very dissimilar stories always seem to emerge; and where there is a likeness between the versions, it is invariably marked by confusion of detail. Such a system of communication has built into it the seeds of its own destruction, for if the class were to reach a certain theoretical limit, the retelling of the anecdote would ultimately result in a discrete tale and perhaps the beginning of an entirely new tradition.

[56] Ibn Ṭabāṭabā, 143.

the explication of ᶜAbbāsid views. The text which is of interest here focuses on the claims of the Banū ᶜAbbās and appears under the rubric: "The Beginnings of the ᶜAbbāsid Dynasty [*dawlah*]."

More narrowly defined, the account under review is a lengthy exegetical comment on the meaning of a statement attributed to the Prophet. The precise wording of the Prophet's dictum is not preserved, but he is said to have revealed that glad tidings will accompany the (emergence of) the Hāshimite dynasty (*kāna yajrī ᶜalā lafẓihi al-sharīf mā maᶜnāhu al-bishārah bidawlah Hāshimīyah*). From the ensuing commentary it is clear that this rendering of the Prophet's original statement is framed within a discussion linking the right to rule and the sacred authority of the imām, and that the expression "glad tidings will accompany the Hāshimite dynasty [*al-bishārah bidawlah Hāshimīyah*]" took on the efficacy of a proof text, as if it had been the actual pronouncement of the Prophet, and not merely a paraphrase of his words. That is to say, based on this "authoritative" text, the Hāshimīyah, bearing authentic credentials to rule, were considered destined to assume the leadership of the Islamic community. As the statement included the eschatological code words "glad tidings" it would have been clear to the informed reader that the emergence of the Hāshimīyah was not a mere happenstance, but an event that would usher in the long anticipated messianic age.

Critical to understanding this passage is, of course, the identity of the Hāshimīyah. Ibn Ṭabāṭabā preserves two divergent views, each based on an alleged comment of the Prophet. Although it is not explicitly stated, both statements link the Hāshimīyah to Hāshim b. ᶜAbd Manāf, the progenitor of Muḥammad's clan. The author thus notes, "Some maintain that the Prophet said: The dynasty will descend from one of my offspring [a not so veiled reference to the ᶜAlids descended from Muḥammad's daughter Fāṭimah]. Others report that the Prophet told his paternal uncle al-ᶜAbbās: It will descend from your offspring [a statement reflecting ᶜAbbāsid claims of legitimacy]." Given these divergent opinions, *al-bishārah bidawlah Hāshimīyah* could have been used as a proof text to support the legitimacy of either the ᶜAbbāsids or their ᶜAlid rivals. In this instance, the inclusion of vague statements to support conflicting traditions is probably deliberate. It enables the author to discuss ᶜAbbāsid claims without compromising his privately held views, for Ibn Ṭabāṭabā was himself the descendant of a martyred namesake of Fāṭimah's line.[57]

Among the Prophet's daughters (his one son did not survive) only Fāṭimah bore children. There was no need, therefore, to clarify the ᶜAlid claim; it was abundantly clear that the Hāshimīyah of the proof text referred to her descendants. "Glad tidings will accompany the Hāshimite *dawlah*" was, according to this view, the prediction of an eschatological event yet to take place, namely, the emergence of an ᶜAlid dynasty of Fāṭimid origins. The ᶜAbbāsid claim is, on the other hand, ambiguous, as there were two doctrinal positions involving the offspring of the Prophet's paternal uncle. One view held that al-ᶜAbbās inherited his authority directly from the Prophet when the latter, who died without any surviving male offspring, failed to designate a

[57] See *EI*² s.v. Ibn al-Ṭiḳṭaḳā.

successor. According to this view, the authority was then transmitted through al-ᶜAbbās's progeny beginning with his son ᶜAbdallāh and continuing through the dynasts of the ᶜAbbāsid line. Faced with this contention, the ᶜAlids countered that Muḥammad had indeed designated his cousin ᶜAlī b. Abī Ṭālib to be Caliph.[58] Despite attempts by dynastic propagandists to undercut the ᶜAlid position, the belief that Muḥammad had actually chosen someone to replace him continued to appeal to various elements of the larger community. ᶜAbbāsid apologists therefore found it expedient to preempt the underlying basis of the ᶜAlid argument rather than to deny it completely. Later pro-ᶜAbbāsid accounts indicate that Muḥammad personally transferred the sacred authority and esoteric knowledge required for rule not to ᶜAlī b. Abī Ṭālib but to another cousin, ᶜAbdallāh, the oldest son of the Prophet's uncle al-ᶜAbbās.

Which of these ᶜAbbāsid doctrines is reflected in the Prophet's comment to his uncle? According to Ibn Ṭabāṭabā, those favoring the ᶜAbbāsid interpretation maintained that al-ᶜAbbās had brought his son ᶜAbdallāh to the Prophet, whereupon the latter welcomed the infant into the community of believers. That is, the Prophet conducted the brief ceremony which later was to accompany the birth of each Muslim male. From the birth of ᶜAbdallāh b. al-Zubayr—the first of the community born at al-Madīnah—it was customary to recite the call to prayer in the infant's ear and then spit into his mouth.[59] But in this instance, some elements were added to what became a well-known practice. Having finished with ᶜAbdallāh, the Prophet declared, "Instruct him [ᶜAbdallāh] in religious law [*faqqihhu fī al-dīn*] and in the [esoteric] interpretation of sacred writing (*ᶜallimhu al-taʾwīl*]. Then returning to the proud parent, he said, "Take the Father of [future] Rulers [*khudh ilayka abā al-amlāk*]."[60]

It is almost certain that ᶜAbbāsid writers embellished this account of the naming ceremony because of an ideological debate between the rival factions of the Banū Hāshim. Since the time the ᶜAlid Jaᶜfar al-Ṣādiq articulated Shīᶜite doctrine in the eighth century, the link between sacred learning and the authority to rule became a recurrent theme of political disputes.[61] Needless to say, the apologists for the ᶜAbbāsid house could not sit idly while their counterparts preempted sacred knowledge on behalf of ᶜAlid patrons. The description of Muḥammad's actions and words while holding the child in his arms was intended to counter these ᶜAlid contentions and establish a direct claim for his kinsmen, the Banū ᶜAbbās.

By spitting in ᶜAbdallāh's mouth, the Prophet is seen investing the young ᶜAbbāsid with authority over the community of believers. For the act of spitting in

[58] A general survey of ᶜAlid views written from the perspective of a strong supporter can be found in Jafri, *Shiʾa Islam*.

[59] Ibn Quataybah, *Maᶜārif*, 116; also E. Amar's tr. of Ibn Ṭabāṭabā, 227, n. 2.

[60] See also *Akhbār*, 25ff.; also p. 40 in reference to ᶜAlī b. ᶜAbdallāh b. ᶜAbbās receiving the blessing of ᶜAlī b. Abī Ṭālib.

[61] See W. Madelung, "Das Imāmat in der frühen ismailitischen Lehre," 43–135; and more generally Jafri, *Shiʾa Islam*, 285–316.

the mouth of a child was a residual fiction reflecting an old bedouin custom known as *taḥnīq*, wherein a tribal shaykh consumed the flesh of a date and then rubbed the pit in the cheek or on the palate of his chosen successor. Reciting the *ādhān* in the boy's ear, the Prophet transferred in symbolic fashion the esoteric knowledge required of a sacred ruler. Having received this knowledge, it would be young ᶜAbdallāh's function to interpret it to his constituency when he later assumed the position of imām. Therein lay the need for his instruction in *dīn* and *taʾwīl*, disciplines that required mastering before one could lay claim to the imāmate, and more generally, to religious authority. ᶜAbdallāh b. ᶜAbbās was, in fact, among the greatest traditions scholars of his age. In this regard, he presented no problem for subsequent ᶜAbbāsid writers who portrayed him as having been a true imām. The same verdict could not be so easily rendered, however, for his descendants, all of whom were, despite accounts to the contrary, without substantive learning.[62] Nevertheless, the story told by Ibn Ṭabāṭabā provided as well for their legitimacy. For the Prophet made it clear that the passing of ᶜAbdallāh b. ᶜAbbās would not signal an end to ᶜAbbāsid rights; the sacred authority (*imamāh*) would indeed be transferred to others within the ᶜAbbāsid family, and that family alone. With the expression *khudh ilayka abā al-amlāk*, the Prophet himself explicitly designated ᶜAbdallāh b. ᶜAbbās as the "Father of [future] Rulers." The debate concerning al-ᶜAbbās's right to inherit and transmit his nephew's authority was therefore rendered superfluous, for the Prophet had made a personal choice in favor of ᶜAbdallāh b. ᶜAbbās and his descendants.

The story of ᶜAbdallāh's encounter with the Prophet thus defined the ᶜAbbāsid claim articulated in this text—or to be more precise, it defined that claim as Ibn Ṭabāṭabā understood it in the fourteenth century. A closer examination of the account suggests still another, and indeed earlier ᶜAbbāsid interpretation of "Glad tidings will accompany the Hāshimite *dawlah*." One may argue that when properly understood, the Prophet revealed that the sacred authority would be inherited, not by al-ᶜAbbās nor his son ᶜAbdallāh, but by a great grandson, Muḥammad b. ᶜAlī b. ᶜAbdallāh b. ᶜAbbās, the progenitor of the ᶜAbbāsid revolution. The fourth reading of the text, to which the author makes no direct reference, reflects the earliest ᶜAbbāsid doctrine, namely, the claim that Muḥammad b. ᶜAlī inherited Abū Hāshim's authority and revolutionary cadres when the childless ᶜAlid died, the victim of a subtle Umayyad plot.

Interpreting the Prophet's dictum in accordance with this view requires reassessing another critical term. The ambiguity of the paraphrased statement which resulted in conflicting interpretations of Hāshimīyah extends also to the meaning of *dawlah*. In this passage Ibn Ṭabāṭabā understood *dawlah* to mean "dynasty" or "turn at rule." This reading is demonstrated by his reference to an oppressive and corrupt Umayyad *dawlah*, whose destruction was eagerly awaited by the populace of the regional centers. But *dawlah* may also signify a turning point occasioned by a great

[62] Note, for example, the glowing description of Muḥammad b. ᶜAlī's learning in the *Akhbār*, 161–62. He is compared favorably with his grandfather ᶜAbdallāh b. ᶜAlī while expounding in the mosque at Mecca.

victory, in which case, the passage in question might originally have meant: "Glad tidings will accompany the victorious revolution of the Hāshimīyah."[63] Seen in this light, the linking of Hāshimīyah to the descendants of Hāshim b. ᶜAbd Manāf was most likely a later exegetical effort. The original reference would have been to the earliest ᶜAbbāsid revolutionaries who, having first been supporters of ᶜAlī's grandson, Abū Hāshim, were named after him. Understood this way, the proof text would have been the apocalyptic prediction of an event later fulfilled by the overthrow of the Umayyad regime. Since only the ᶜAbbāsids and their followers could lay claim to this momentous triumph, the earliest understanding of the Prophet's words would have excluded reference to Fāṭimah's descendants or, for that matter, any other ᶜAlid claimants.

In the apocalyptic literature, the recycling of a proof text was a common rhetorical strategy. Faced with an ᶜAbbāsid polemic rooted in a vague text which had been attributed, albeit indirectly, to the Prophet, the ᶜAlids reinterpreted Muḥammad to suit their own doctrinal purposes. Given their reading of the text, *dawlah* became "dynasty" or "turn at rule" and the Hāshimīyah became the descendants of Hāshim b. ᶜAbd Manāf, more particularly, the ᶜAlids descended by way of the Prophet's daughter Fāṭimah. But the recycled text could also give rise to a new interpretation, one that favored a shifting ᶜAbbāsid doctrine. Originally invoked to legitimize ᶜAbbāsid claims based on the transfer of Abū Hāshim's authority, the preserved version of Muḥammad's dictum was later restated by the regime's apologists to oppose the counterclaim of Fāṭimah's descendants. In this instance, it was probably read as a proof text to herald a new ᶜAbbāsid position, one which claimed authority directly through the line of the Prophet's paternal uncle and, following that, through the ᶜAbbāsid ᶜAbdallāh b. ᶜAlī who inherited directly from the Prophet. Moreover, the relationship of the Hāshimīyah to the Banū Hāshim would not have been inimical to any claims which the ᶜAbbāsids derived from their revolutionary triumph. On the contrary, it underscored the intense rivalry between the clans of Hāshim and Umayyah. This rivalry, which could allegedly be traced back to the era of Muḥammad's grandfather, was also represented by the struggle between the Prophet and the oligarchy of Quraysh, and later by the conflict between the revolutionary movement and the Umayyad dynasty that had displaced the Banū Hāshim from power. The ᶜAbbāsid victory was thus seen as avenging grievances that were nursed over several generations in a recurring struggle for power among these two branches of Quraysh.[64]

At least four interpretations of *al-bishārah bidawlah Hāshimīyah* could have existed, each reflecting a different ᶜAbbāsid claim or ᶜAlid counterclaim. Only two of these versions are found, however, in Ibn Ṭabāṭabā's explication of the text, the legitimacy of Fāṭimah's offspring and the direct transfer of the Prophet's authority to ᶜAbdallāh b. ᶜAbbās. The author was certainly aware of the doctrinal position which underlay the omitted versions of ᶜAbbāsid claims. He mentions unnamed

[63] See *EI*[2] s.v. Dawla; also Foreword, n. 1.

[64] For mirror images and back projections see Foreword.

authorities who assert that the sacred authority was inherited by ᶜAlī's son Muḥammad and that before his death, the latter, who was the offspring of a Ḥanafite concubine, had bequeathed it to his son Abū Hāshim, who then transferred his rights and revolutionary following to an ᶜAbbāsid kinsman, Muḥammad b. ᶜAlī b. ᶜAbdallāh b. ᶜAbbās.

The circumstances of his alleged acquisition, and what it implied for the course of future events, is discussed by Ibn Ṭabāṭabā in considerable detail. He describes Abū Hāshim's ill-fated visit to the Umayyad court, the decision of the Caliph to poison the ᶜAlid, and the death-bed scene in which Abū Hāshim purportedly set the ᶜAbbāsid family on the road to revolution and power. Given knowledge of this tradition, it shouldn't have been difficult for Ibn Ṭabāṭabā to reconstruct the original meaning of "Glad tidings will accompany the Hāshimite *dawlah*," and then counter this view with a proper argument favoring the ᶜAlid cause he espoused. And yet, there is no trace of the earlier ᶜAbbāsid doctrine in explicating the proof text. One may suppose that the original ᶜAbbāsid interpretation of this text was more dimly heard with each successive generation until no trace of it could be detected. The text thus remained the same but its original meaning was distorted by fading historical memories.

E. THE STRATIGRAPHY OF HISTORICAL TRADITIONS

For modern historians, recovering traces of the ᶜAbbāsid past requires differentiating parallel, divergent, and often conflicting versions of complex stories. Borrowing a term from archaeology, one may refer to this task as establishing the stratigraphy of a text. To this end there is a compelling need to impose a semblance of chronological order on multi-layered traditions. However, as text-critical scholars have discovered in related disciplines—most notably biblical studies—the search for a documentary hypothesis that can explain all textual sequences is bound to be elusive. All the more so in this case because the Arabic chroniclers lacked an effective hermeneutic system with which to differentiate literary strata and the sources themselves seem incapable of yielding such a system even to the most imaginative modern readers. And yet, the literature detailing the rise of the ᶜAbbāsids does suggest some general guidelines for obtaining a broad profile of its textual stratigraphy. Regardless of how sketchily it is drawn, such a profile allows for a more coherent picture of ᶜAbbāsid attitudes, as well as a better understanding of the men and events who brought the Banū ᶜAbbās to power.

One may begin a discussion of these guidelines with an observation that seems at first to require little commentary. In any tradition preserving different versions of a given episode, historical context is the most likely guide for establishing the sequential order of variants. Like the sherds of an archaeological dig that has been carefully planned and meticulously executed, the allusions to datable historic moments become the chronological markers of the versions studied. However vague, identifiable references to later occurrences, when found in a text describing an earlier event, are clear signs that in its present form, at least, the variant is the literary creation of a period subsequent to the event described.

But context, like archaeological trenching, can be a tricky business. Accurate readings are often elusive for those not prepared to gloss over difficulties. The cautious scholar soon learns that various texts are without neatly positioned chronological markers. There may be no convenient reference to historical developments, or even when such references are evident, the allusion to specific events may be so vague as to be beyond recognition. In addition, the accounts of the chronicles can and often do combine several versions within a single text. Therefore, when the testimony of an eyewitness echoes historical occurrences beyond his experiential range, it does not necessarily follow that the entire account is a fictive construction. The embellishment may be grafted onto or conflated with a version which, in all other regards, is authentic in portraying historical detail. In such fashion even the most tendentious reports may contain the kernel of an historical truth. A text which appears highly embellished invites broad skepticism as a matter of course, but later accretions are not, in and of themselves, sufficient reason to deny the basic historicity of any account. As with archaeologists trained to distinguish between intrusive deposits and the genuine artifacts of earlier levels, learned and discerning readers can often spot the added material and sort out the original elements from the larger whole. When, however, several variants have been fused into a unique version which defies separation, the recovery of the individual levels is largely, if not entirely, a matter of conjecture. Prudence may ultimately dictate that such difficult sources be set aside until the component parts can be sorted out, however restrictive and even punishing this may at times seem to a scholar with bold inclinations. As a rule, historians in search of data would be wise to recall what archaeologists have long known, namely, there are circumstances when rubbish is actually rubbish and not a guide for establishing stratigraphy.

Are there other ways of establishing discrete textual sequences? Although less specific than unambiguous references to historical events, doctrinal thrust may also serve as a chronological marker. That is, when later doctrinal formulations give coherence to an "early" text that cannot otherwise be explicated, one may surmise that this version is the product of a later age. But here as well context can be misleading; for doctrinal positions were not always aired in discrete sequences of claims and counterclaims. To the contrary, they often overlapped and were addressed concurrently to divergent audiences. The intrusion of a later formulation, in what otherwise appears to be an early setting, is frequently but not always indicative of a later authorial voice. Moreover, as with institutions, ideas have precursors, and it is sometimes difficult to ascertain which referent commands attention, the concept which originated in the past or the more recent formulation in which it is mirrored. In sum, isolating doctrinal arguments to date historical sources remains highly problematic, a technique which may be utilized to great advantage, but one which also invites much caution.

More generally, scholars should be wary of any method which uses context to explain text while choosing text to define context. This circular approach to a corpus of dimly understood traditions, while perhaps inevitable, conjures up visions of an epistemological minefield. Obviously, certain dates may be taken at face value, and particular events may be clearly linked to a well established chronology, but the need for invented history has a way of creating a conventional wisdom that overwhelms reality. Time and again, we have noted that that which appears factual, and hence a convenient starting point for historical investigation, may simply be another disguised element in an elaborately embellished discourse. The propensity of ᶜAbbāsid (and indeed all Islamic) apologists to mirror historical events regardless of their setting in time and place, and for partisan reasons besides, obviously adds to the substantial burden of isolating authentic chronological markers.

When references to historical events are unavailable or inappropriate as chronological markers and when doctrinal thrust is too ambiguous to establish the layers of a given tradition, the modern historian is advised to abandon a hasty search for states of the past and begin his analysis instead with the rhetorical strategies employed by ᶜAbbāsid writers. We have already noted that as a rule medieval apologists masked their intentions in heavily encoded texts that were, as such texts are wont to be, extremely vague. To understand the text, the contemporary reader was obliged to pick up various clues that had been delicately woven into the pattern of the narrative and to determine thereby the greater design that gave meaning to what may have seemed, at first, an elusive if not incongruous story. In such fashion clever authors engaged clever readers in an intricate game of textual interpretation. Quite obviously, the author depended on his reader being able to recognize subtle nuances and thus draw logical conclusions where none seemed possible. But in time philological and historical memories grew dim and still dimmer, so that logical connections were indeed lost.

Often when the meaning of the text became obscure, later authors began extensive editing to make it more comprehensible. At the more advanced stages of tradition-building, earlier formulations, pregnant with a nuance that was no longer fathomable, were displaced by simpler exposition. Important information previously conveyed through subtle expression was jettisoned, a sacrifice to the desire for a more felicitous style and to the need for a structural conciseness that made for easier understanding.

One would assume that in the heavily encoded literature of ᶜAbbāsid apologetics, the earliest versions of complex traditions are likely to be somewhat disjointed stories in which the author most subtly presents his biases. Had the apologist expressed his views forthrightly, his reader would have been inclined to reject them at the outset, in effect dismissing the presentation as a rather clumsy attempt at political indoctrination. Intricate arguments which challenge the interpretive skills of the audience would therefore represent the first stages of the discourse when there are gaps separating text from context, but none so wide as to cause the reader to lose touch with the basic design of the account. And yet, there is a received wisdom that the more detailed and coherent a text, the more likely it is that it is an early formulation. According to this second view, the terse and seemingly disjointed account is the later version, a version which could not preserve over an extended period of time the full meaning of the original narrative. Which of these conceptions is more appropriate to analyzing ᶜAbbāsid historiography?

The well worn notion that more detailed versions reflect older variants might hold true if the detail merely embroiders a text in accordance with well established literary tastes or conventions. But detail would not indicate an early stage of development if it directly and unambiguously supplies the means of interpretation. Quite the reverse, a variant which explains textual difficulties would have to be considered a secondary formation. Only if detail subverts information placed before an inquisitive reader, thus encouraging him to engage in greater interpretive efforts, is the account likely to represent an early stratum. For only by mastering a seemingly incongruous text was the confident reader likely to accept its inner truth in a triumph of self deception.

Example: Abū Bakr's Absence from the Mosque

This reversal of conventional wisdom is best illustrated by a full translation and brief explication of two closely linked texts. The accounts, chosen from the *Sīrah* of Ibn Isḥāq, once again reflect events alleged to have taken place on the last day of the Prophet's life.[65]

1) Ibn Isḥāq and al-Zuhrī . . . . Anas b. Mālik: On that Monday on which God gathered His messenger to Himself, the latter went out to the people while they were at prayer. The curtain lifted and the door opened, whereupon the Messenger of God stood at ᶜĀʾishah's door.[66] The Muslims were almost seduced into not saying their prayers for the joy of seeing him. They were distracted and he motioned for them to continue. The Messenger of God smiled with joy when he saw them at prayer. I never saw him better disposed than he was at that moment. Then he returned [to ᶜĀʾishah's apartment] and the people left, thinking that the Messenger had recovered from his illness. At that time, Abū Bakr returned to his family in al-Sunḥ.[67]
2) Ibn Isḥāq . . . . Abū Bakr b. ᶜAbdallāh b. Abī Mulaykah: On Monday the Messenger of God came out to the morning prayer with his head bandaged[68]—Abū Bakr was leading prayer. When the Messenger of God emerged, the people became distracted. Abū Bakr understood that the people would not have acted thus unless the Messenger of God had come [to the mosque], so he withdrew from his place [that of the prayer-leader]. But the Messenger of God patted him on the back saying, "Lead the people in prayer," and then sat down at Abū Bakr's side. The Messenger of God then prayed while seated to the right of Abū Bakr. When he finished praying, the Messenger of God turned to the people and addressed them, raising his voice so it could be heard beyond the portal of the mosque: "O people, the fire is kindled and rebellions [*fitan*] come like the segments of a dark night. By God, you can charge me with nothing. I allow only what the Qurʾān allows and forbid only what the Qurʾān forbids." When the Messenger of God finished speaking, Abū Bakr said to him, "O Prophet of God, I see that this

[65] Ibn Hishām, I/2: 1009, 1010.

[66] That is, ᶜĀʾishah's apartment was situated adjacent to the Prophet's mosque at al-Madīnah.

[67] One of the neighborhoods (*maḥallah*) of al-Madīnah. The reference here is presumably to the residence at the outskirts of the town which was the domicile of Abū Bakr and Ḥabībah bt. Khārijah. It is not to be confused with a place of that name in the Najd. See Yāqūt, *Muᶜjam*, III: 163 s.v. Sunḥ.

[68] The treatment administered to the Prophet is discussed earlier in the text. See Ibn Hishām, I/2: 1005ff.

> morning you enjoy the favor of God and his grace as we desire. Today is the day for Bint Khārijah.[69] May I go to her?" The Prophet answered, "Yes." Then the Messenger of God went into [ᶜĀᵓishah's apartment] and Abū Bakr went to his family at al-Sunḥ.

The extensive tradition of the Prophet's last day, in which these two segments are found, is marked by a serious problem, namely, Abū Bakr's absence from the later assemblies of prayer. The significance of this absence has been mentioned previously;[70] it is enough to recall that Abū Bakr had taken Muḥammad's place in the mosque during the latter's fatal illness—to some, a sign that he was to be designated successor. However, for neglecting his duty, Abū Bakr allegedly earned the Prophet's admonition, an indication that Muḥammad might have grown less inclined to hand over authority to him.[71] Because doubts concerning Abū Bakr were sure to enhance claims on behalf of ᶜAlī b. Abī Ṭālib, it served ᶜAbbāsid interests to promote the former as having been a proper choice for temporal authority (spiritual authority would have been reserved for them) thus denying, albeit indirectly, that ᶜAlī had any authentic claims.

A suitable reason had to be found which would explain Abū Bakr's failure to attend the mosque later that day. According to both accounts cited here, his absence could be explained by two separate but related circumstances. The Prophet gave the appearance of having recovered from his illness, hence obviating any need for Abū Bakr to continue as prayer leader, and the latter was obligated to move to his domicile at al-Sunḥ away from town (al-Madīnah) in order to spend time with Bint Khārijah, his wife of the occasion. Freed from one obligation, he simply fulfilled the other. Were this made clear, only the malicious could have found fault with his behavior.

It is the nature of the apologia that draws attention here. A careful analysis of the rhetorical strategies employed in both accounts suggests that, based on the economy of the argument, the first variant is the earlier version. In the account attributed to Anas b. Mālik, we cannot be sure, at first, of the Prophet's seeming recovery. Needless to say, his very appearance was an encouraging sign, but Muhammad did not enter the interior of the mosque, nor is there any indication of how long he remained before the congregation. He merely stood at the door separating the mosque from ᶜĀᵓishah's apartment (where he had lain ill). His gesturing (*ashāra*) to those present to continue prayer was apparently no more than a wave of the hand.[72] Yet, the Muslims rejoiced, as well they should, for the Prophet (judging from the previous account in the *Sīrah*) had been deathly ill, giving rise to fears that he would not survive. It is only at the end of the narrative that the eyewitness states, "I never saw the Prophet better disposed than he was at that moment."

[69] See n. 67.
[70] See pp. 15ff.
[71] See n. 38.
[72] Ṭabarī, I/4: 1009.

To be sure, this is hardly conclusive evidence that the Prophet seemed well, but given his presence at the mosque and Anas b. Mālik's testimony as to his condition, an alert reader would no doubt have drawn that conclusion. Indeed, the text goes on to state, "the people left thinking that the Messenger had recovered from his illness." At this point, and without explanation, we are informed that Abū Bakr (who is not previously mentioned) left al-Madīnah and went to his family in al-Sunḥ. The careful reader was left to ferret out the reason for Abū Bakr's decision to leave in accordance with information hitherto conveyed. As did all the other congregants, Abū Bakr believed that the Prophet had passed his crisis and was therefore ready to resume his duties as the head of the Faithful. The Prophet's replacement to lead prayer could now realign his priorities and return to his family. It happened that the Prophet died later that day, but this was an unexpected occurrence that no one present at the morning prayer could have foreseen.

Because some readers might not have caught the subtle argument here, the reasons for Abū Bakr's absence are presented more directly and with greater persuasive force in the version of Abū Bakr b. ᶜAbdallāh b. Abī Mulaykah. There, the seriousness of Muḥammad's illness and the extent of his recovery are more dramatically illustrated. He appears at prayers with his head bandaged and the Muslims are quite naturally distracted. The Prophet does not stand at ᶜĀʾishah's door while gesturing to the assembled congregation with a wave of the hand; he is much more vigorous in his response. First he pats Abū Bakr on the back, ordering him to continue (a not so veiled endorsement of Abū Bakr's performance at leading the prayer). Following that, the Prophet goes to his side, and although seated (a sign of recent illness), he actively participates in the service. Then at the conclusion of his prayers, Muḥammad turns to the assembled group and delivers a sermon in a strong voice that carries beyond the building.

With this description of the Prophet's activities, no eyewitness would have been needed to speculate about his health; there should have been no doubt that a man so active was well on his way to total recovery, in which case Abū Bakr would not have been required to lead prayers later that day. But for those readers who were still slow to make the connections between the Prophet's new found energy and Abū Bakr's absence from the mosque, the account goes on. When the Prophet finishes speaking, Abū Bakr turns to him and expresses his opinion that the Prophet awoke that morning in better health. Continuing, Abū Bakr explains that this is the day to begin the visit with Bint Khārijah, and he is requesting the Prophet's permission to go to her. Given the nature of the request (to fulfill an obligation) and the Prophet's seeming recovery from his grave illness, the answer is an unequivocal "yes." Muḥammad then entered (ᶜĀʾishah's apartment) and Abū Bakr went to his family in al-Sunḥ. The latter's absence from prayer later that day was not simply occasioned by a perception he shared with other congregants at the mosque, namely, that the Prophet had recovered. Abū Bakr left al-Madīnah with the full knowledge and explicit permission of his companion and spiritual leader.

The underlying issue of political succession, which is deeply buried in the shorter account, is brought closer to the surface by the Prophet's timely sermon. For most readers, the vague allusions to fires kindled and rebellions coming like segments of the dark night might have conjured up images of the earliest opposition to a recently born Islamic state. According to received wisdom, this opposition, which had already manifested itself during the last year of the Prophet's life, grew rapidly immediately following his death and was finally put down by his successor, Abū Bakr.[73] A more reflective audience might have gone several steps further, however, in understanding this parting address. The aforementioned rebellions might have been viewed as oblique references to the chronic civil strife that was to plague the Islamic community. In successive generations following the death of its founder, numerous claimants to rule sought to wrap themselves in the symbols of his authority. The most egregious of these were the descendants of ᶜAlī b. Abī Ṭālib. Skilled readers of the first version would have understood all of this without the benefit of extended commentary.

Which of these versions represents the earliest stage in the formation of a tradition, the terse and seemingly disjointed narrative of Anas b. Mālik, or the more detailed and more easily understood account attributed to Abū Bakr b. ᶜAbdallāh b. Abī Mulaykah? As it is presented here, Anas b. Mālik's recollection is not the faded memory of a distant past. Skillfully crafted in every respect, it challenges the reader to supply the context that will enable him to leap over intentional gaps in the argumentation. He had to be both clever and informed to piece together the various clues which explained Abū Bakr's absence from prayer on that fateful day. Readers of the second and more expansive account required less imagination to reconstruct the circumstances which permitted the Prophet's stand-in to leave for his residence at the edge of town. The additional detail probably made for a more interesting story, but the author did not provide it for that purpose alone. His intention was to make it clear to all that Abū Bakr was beyond reproach for his actions.

Cautious scholars are well aware of the limits to this kind of inquiry. An analysis of rhetorical strategies may provide for more narrowly defined sequences within traditions, but the question of precise dates for each layer can still remain elusive in the absence of specific chronological markers. Furthermore, if one assumes that audiences of diverse background required different versions of the same text, it is almost certain that subtle and more accessible variants alike developed contemporaneously. Indeed, the time-line separating certain versions may be so indistinct that it cannot be retraced using conventional tools of analysis. Attempts to distinguish the layers of a tradition from one another often require a leap of faith; and, if nothing else, faith is highly personal and difficult to evaluate. Because every typology is by definition a contrivance, any literary–historical study based on these projected guidelines will be highly subjective and given to judgments that may engender spirited discussion, if not profound disagreement.

[73] See E. Shoufani, *Al-Riddah and the Muslim Conquest of Arabia*; F. Donner, *The Early Islamic Conquests*, 82–90.

PART TWO: CASE STUDIES

Revolutionaries and the Path to Revolution that Should Have Been

I

ᶜALĪ B. ᶜABDALLĀH B. ᶜABBĀS AND THE BEGINNINGS OF ᶜABBĀSID RESISTANCE: HAGIOGRAPHY OR HISTORY

> There is no virtue in exhortation to action, if it is not tempered by forebearing.
>
> ᶜAlī b. ᶜAbdallāh

One might have accused Muḥammad b. ᶜAlī and the later ᶜAbbāsid patriarchs of being overly cautious, but there was never any doubt that they recognized the usurpative character of the Umayyad regime and actively plotted its downfall. Unfortunately, the same could not be claimed for Muḥammad b. ᶜAlī's grandfather, ᶜAbdallāh, nor his father, ᶜAlī. To the contrary, the two actively supported the Umayyads against the counter-Caliphate of ᶜAbdallāh b. al-Zubayr, and they were generally held in high regard by the reigning authorities. The later decision to trace ᶜAbbāsid claims directly through the Prophet's uncle al-ᶜAbbās therefore presented apologists of the ruling house with a vexing problem. Given that the two early patriarchs were now direct links in the chain of authority that led to ᶜAbbāsid rule, some reworking of their life stories was necessary in order to imbue them with proper revolutionary credentials. The past, as it actually occurred, thus gave way to a legendary history that was the creation of a subsequent age. The revisionist version of ᶜAbdallāh b. ᶜAbbās's career has long been recognized and is, in any event, reserved for another occasion;[1] the concern here is with the hagiography of his son ᶜAlī, the first ᶜAbbāsid raised entirely under the Umayyads.

Although the youngest of his father's sons, ᶜAlī b. ᶜAbdallāh was destined from the outset to assume the leadership of the Banū ᶜAbbās.[2] More important still according to later ᶜAbbāsid tradition, he was empowered to transfer the sacred authority vested in him to his descendants. These rights were predicated on the unusual circumstances of his birth, an event which coincided with the assassination of his namesake and uncle, the Caliph ᶜAlī b. Abī Ṭālib.[3] On that fateful day, the

[1] See *EI*² s.v. ᶜAbdallāh b. ᶜAbbās.

[2] *Akhbār*, 134.

[3] *Akhbār*, 134–35; Zubayrī, *Nasab*, 29; also Balādhurī, *Ansāb*, III: 70; Ibn Khallikān (De Slane), III: 264.

Davidson College Library

Caliph had noted that the pious ᶜAbdallāh b. ᶜAbbās was missing from the morning prayers. A subsequent inquiry revealed that a son had just been born to the ᶜAbbāsid thereby explaining his unusual absence from the mosque. Once apprised of this happy development, ᶜAlī led a delegation of worshipers to rejoice with his first cousin on the birth of his child. Offering congratulations, the Caliph asked what name had been chosen. ᶜAbdallāh replied that the boy was yet to be named, because that honor had been reserved for the Caliph himself. The infant was then given to ᶜAlī who rubbed (a date pit on) his palate (*ḥannaqahu*) and wished him well (*daᶜā lahu*).[4] Then returning him to the proud father, he proclaimed, "Take the Father of [future] Rulers. I have named him ᶜAlī and nicknamed him Abū al-Ḥasan."

The tragic death that was to befall ᶜAlī b. Abī Ṭālib later that day only served to underscore the significance of his actions after the morning prayers. At first glance, the concurrence of young ᶜAlī's birth and old ᶜAlī's death may seem a mere coincidence, but the ᶜAbbāsid tradition implies that contemporaries actually witnessed converging events that were part of a great cosmic design. The Caliph's subsequent assassination would inevitably lead to the usurpative Umayyad regime; nevertheless the community and more particularly the Banū Hāshim would not be left without a future champion to take up the cause of the true faith. In this instance, the ancient bedouin practice of rubbing a would-be successor's palate (*taḥnīq*) and the formulaic recitation before returning the newly-named child to his father carried an unmistakable message. That is, bearing the *ism* and *kunyah* of his famous uncle, the newest addition to the Prophet's clan inherited not only the Caliph's proper name and teknonym, but with the expression "Father of [future] Rulers," he inherited his authority and the right to transfer that authority within the ᶜAbbāsid line.[5]

There was, however, one glaring flaw that threatened the symmetry of this artistic construction. In real life ᶜAlī b. ᶜAbdallāh b. ᶜAbbās bore the teknonym "Abū Muḥammad" and not "Abū al-Ḥasan." Not to be dismayed, the ᶜAbbāsid apologists explained this seeming incongruity and turned it into a political asset. ᶜAlī b. ᶜAbdallāh had indeed been named Abū al-Ḥasan, but following ᶜAlī b. Abi Ṭālib's assassination, the Umayyad authorities forced the change to Abū Muḥammad. The unusual intervention of the first Umayyad Caliph in a matter as innocuous as the naming of a son served to emphasize the significance of the ceremony and what it implied about the eventual struggle against Umayyad rule. Having fought ᶜAlī b. Abī Ṭālib to a standstill after a long and arduous struggle, the Umayyads were not about to face his ᶜAbbāsid namesake in some future confrontation.[6] Later ᶜAbbāsid writers

[4] There is a play on words here. The word *daᶜā* is also meant to suggest that the Caliph issued a call for support of the new-born ᶜAbbāsid, and that this support was to be linked to the eventual ᶜAbbāsid cause (*daᶜwah*).

[5] Note the similar tradition of how ᶜAbdallāh b. ᶜAbbās received the authority of the Prophet when he was brought to the latter by his father, al-ᶜAbbās. In both instances there was the practice of *taḥnīq* and the expression "Father of [future] Rulers." See Prolegomena, pp. 27ff.; see also p. 23 describing al-Manṣūr's vision in which the Prophet gives him (i.e., al-Manṣūr) the requisite paraphernalis to rule and says, "Take it, Father of [future] Caliphs."

[6] *Akhbār*, 134–35; Anonymous, 243b; Balādhurī, *Ansāb*, III: 70; Ibn Khallikān (De Slane), III: 264.

thus created the impression that the Umayyads feared the intentions of the Banū ᶜAbbās from the very outset of their ill-fated dynasty. Other accounts depict sovereigns of the Banū Umayyah fatalistically contemplating ᶜAbbāsid hegemony, as if to indicate that the ᶜAbbāsid revolution had been predestined, and therefore could not be contravened.[7] Seen from this perspective, the ᶜAlid resistance to the Umayyad dynasty was not without its glory, but it was to have been clear that the greater destiny—that is, the assumption of universally recognized rule—was reserved for their ᶜAbbāsid kinsmen among the Banū Hāshim.

A. THE DISGRACE OF ᶜALĪ B. ᶜABDALLĀH AND THE FIRST STEPS TOWARD REBELLION

Imbuing the ᶜAbbāsid patriarch with a propitious birth was only the first step in rehabilitating his image. The history of ᶜAlī b. ᶜAbdallāh's later career was accordingly rewritten to portray him as a committed revolutionary who had suffered disgraceful indignities under the yoke of Umayyad rule. This left the ᶜAbbāsid somewhat short of being a real martyr but, all things considered, it was a modest step forward in strengthening his credentials. Alī's alienation, such as it was, reportedly began when he received two whippings and was then banished from court by the Umayyad Caliph, al-Walīd b. ᶜAbd al-Malik. The first beating, curiously enough, was because the ᶜAbbāsid had married Lubābah, the grandniece of ᶜAlī b. Abī Ṭalib.[8] Since marriage, although at times punishment, was not a punishable offense, a word of explanation is perhaps in order. It appears that the noble Lubābah had been the wife of al-Walīd's father, the Caliph ᶜAbd al-Malik, before a rather bizarre social indiscretion on her part caused him to seek a divorce. The story has it that ᶜAbd al-Malik tossed her an apple after having bitten into it. Lubābah then took a knife, and before eating the fruit, sliced off the "damaged" part, a precaution that was necessary because the Caliph suffered from bad breath. Another account[9] describes Lubābah as acting more discreetly; she simply suggested to her husband that he might wish to consider cleansing his teeth. In either case, her reaction to the Caliph's halitosis was more than he was prepared to endure, and her presumption in offering unsolicited advice led to divorce.

[7] See for example Balādhurī, *Ansāb*, III: 85–86. The author indicates that the Umayyad Caliph Hishām b. ᶜAbd al-Malik wanted to imprison Muḥammad b. ᶜAlī and his offspring saying, "They are of the opinion that the Caliphate will go to them." An advisor points out: "If it is destined [*maqdūr*] for them to get it, by God, there is nothing that can be done [to alter this]." The Caliph then desisted. Balādhurī then cites a second account in which ᶜAbd al-Malik was admiring Muḥammad b. ᶜAlī when the latter was but a youth (i.e., before he received the authority from Abū Hāshim). One of the Umayyad family then points out that Muḥammad's (future) offspring will be destined to rule until the coming of the Messiah. There are numerous traditions of this sort. Directly or indirectly they are intended to denigrate ᶜAlid claims.

[8] *Akhbār*, 138–39; Balādhurī, *Ansāb*, III: 82; Ibn Qutaybah, *Maᶜārif*, 207; Ibn Khallikān (DeSlane), III: 265; also Mubarrad, *Kāmil*, II: 217–18.

[9] Ibn Khallikān (De Slane), III: 265.

The scientific principles which guided Lubābah regarding the damaged fruit are left for others to discover; it is the aftermath of her sudden fall from grace that is the concern here. In ordinary circumstances, divorce would have carried a stigma difficult to overcome, but in this case the divorcee bore genealogical credentials that merited special consideration. She was, after all, a distinguished lady of the Banū Hāshim. Undaunted by Lubābah's shame (and, no doubt, sufficiently confident of his own oral hygiene) ᶜAlī b. ᶜAbdallāh married her and thus redeemed her honor. But having done so, he earned for himself al-Walīd's wrath and a lesson in history. Unmoved by ᶜAlī's explanation that he was compelled to marry his kinswoman in order to protect her, and by implication the honor of his clan, the Caliph countered, "One marries the [former] consorts of Caliphs in order to humble their offspring. So it was with Marwān b. al-Ḥakam. He only married the mother of Khālid b. Yazīd b. Muᶜāwiyah in order to humble Khālid."[10] With these words the Caliph recalled how his own grandfather (Marwān) arranged for an "appropriate" union in order to discredit Yazīd's son and thereby serve the needs of the Marwānid line at the expense of their Sufyānid relatives. Once in power, the Marwānid progeny of the Banū Umayyah ruled uninterrupted for some sixty years. The comic anecdote concerning Lubābah and the apple therefore became deadly serious when political meaning was injected into a story probably intended for social commentary. The focus of the narrative, which explains how ᶜAlī lost favor at the Umayyad court, was thus shifted from Lubābah's faulty behavior to anti-Umayyad designs on the part of the ᶜAbbāsids.

One could surely argue that the Caliph's interpretation of events was based on a personal and highly biased perception that grossly exaggerated the original circumstances. Accepting this tradition at face value, the marriage does not necessarily reflect seditious intentions on behalf of the ᶜAbbāsid family, which had previously enjoyed the respect and honor of the ruling house.[11] ᶜAlī b. ᶜAbdallāh's explanation for having married Lubābah seems plausible enough; what kinsman would not marry his cousin in order to protect her honor and well being? A variant of this account indeed contains a less revealing condemnation of ᶜAli's actions. When informed that the ᶜAbbāsid had married his former wife, an angry ᶜAbd al-Malik (he, and not his son, was after all the aggrieved party) is said to have remarked, "His praying is but hypocrisy and a sham," an illusion to the thousand *rakᶜah*s a day that ᶜAlī allegedly performed, thus recalling his nickname, "the Prostrator [*al-Sajjād*]."[12] However angry he might have been, the Caliph appears to have taken no action against the

[10] *Akhbār*, 139; Ibn Khallikān (DeSlane), III: 265; also Mubarrad, *Kāmil*, II: 217.

[11] These relations too required an explanation; for it would not have been acceptable for the Umayyads to have favored the ᶜAbbāsids over the militant ᶜAlids. See for example *Akhbār*, 154, which indicates that the ᶜAbbāsids accepted Umayyad favors in order to dissimulate their revolutionary activities. The less militant ᶜAlids were similarly stained by their good standing with the Umayyads. See Kohlberg, "Shīᶜī Interpretations."

[12] Balādhurī, *Ansāb*, III: 82; also Mubarrad, *Kāmil*, II: 218; Ibn Khallikān (DeSlane), III: 265–66 quoting Mubarrad.

ᶜAbbāsid. It is only when al-Walīd b. ᶜAbd al-Malik succeeded to the Caliphate that he accused ᶜAlī of shameful behavior toward his father and exiled him from court, a punishment which seems most appropriate given the nature of ᶜAlī's indiscretion and the extent of the Umayyad grievance.[13] There is no indication of any beating in this rendering of events, nor that politics may have been the root of the Caliph's concern. Seen in this light, ᶜAlī's offense was a serious breach of social convention, but nothing more.

For the apologist seeking some traces of revolutionary spirit among the early ᶜAbbāsids, this last interpretation of events would hardly suffice. A more dramatic explanation rich in political nuance would have to be discovered. The repressive Umayyad response to ᶜAlī's actions would have been credible only if it were occasioned by some implied, if not direct, threat of seditious behavior by the ᶜAbbāsid patriarch. A second beating allegedly administered by al-Walīd was therefore recorded to prove that ᶜAlī's marriage to Lubābah had been politically motivated as the Caliph had first surmised.[14] After being whipped a second time, the ᶜAbbāsid was placed upon a camel with his face pointed to the animal's rump. Were this indignity not enough, he was paraded about the markets by a herald who cried out, "This is ᶜAlī b. ᶜAbdallāh, the imposter [*al-kadhdhāb*]"[15] a seeming reference to Muḥammad's rival, the false prophet, Musaylimah al-Kadhdhāb. This shabby treatment meted out to a scion of one of the most distinguished houses of the Islamic community begged for an explanation. When asked by a passerby to explain his newly acquired title, ᶜAlī replied that a (damaging) statement of his had come to the attention of the Umayyad authorities. He had said: "Surely the authority to rule shall come to rest with my offspring [*inna hādhā al-amr sayakūnu fī wuldī*]. By God it will surely remain with them until they are in turn ruled over by slaves of theirs possessing small eyes, round visages, and faces like hammered shields [given the identifiable racial characteristics of the times, this last comment was an unmistakable reference to the Turks]."[16]

This remark of ᶜAlī b. ᶜAbdallāh could hardly be characterized as an impolite quip at the expense of the ruling authority. As reported here, it was nothing less than a direct statement of the ᶜAbbāsid's political pretensions (if not his actual intentions). The informed reading audience of early ᶜAbbāsid times, for whom all these traditions were intended, understood only too well the full implications of ᶜAlī's remarks in this account. They were familiar with various traditions (needless to say, all favorable to the ᶜAbbāsid line) in which ᶜAlī's grandfather (al-ᶜAbbās) had been informed by the Prophet that the Faithful would someday be ruled by the ᶜAbbāsid offspring.[17] They had read that as a child, ᶜAlī's father (ᶜAbdallāh) had been taken to the Prophet, who

[13] Ibid.

[14] *Akhbār*, 139; also Mubarrad, *Kāmil*, 218; Ibn Khallikān (DeSlane), III: 265–66 quoting Mubarrad.

[15] Ibid.

[16] Ibid.

[17] See n. 5.

personally invested the infant with sacred authority, and that on the day of his birth, ᶜAlī himself had similarly received the recognition of his famous namesake ᶜAlī b. Abī Ṭālib while cradled in the Caliph's arms. In both cases, following the ceremony of *taḥnīq*, that is, the oral investiture of authority from one figure to another, the child is returned to the proud parent with the words "Take the Father of [future] Rulers."[18] Having digested all of this information, the reader was sure to conclude that ᶜAlī's indiscreet revelation must have served as a direct warning to the Umayyads. Studying this account of ᶜAlī's second beating, he would have understood only too well why the ruling authorities responded so severely to the ᶜAbbāsid's unfortunate slip of the tongue.

It is of course unlikely that the scene in the market took place as it is described—if indeed it took place at all. If nothing else, the veiled reference to the physiognomy and ascendancy of the Turks is an indication that in its present form, the tradition cannot be dated earlier than the ninth century when the Turkic units of the ᶜAbbāsid army dominated their former patrons. One need not conclude, however, that the story of ᶜAlī's thrashing was a total fabrication. A variant of this account speaks of yet another beating. In this case, the reference is to the "long and famous story" of Salīṭ.

An explication of this last remarkable episode will be undertaken in an entirely different context.[19] It is sufficient to point out here that ᶜAlī's right to inherit his father's authority and wealth had been challenged by a certian Salīṭ, who claimed direct descent from ᶜAbdallāh b. ᶜAbbās. Because of its significance, the case was brought before the Caliph al-Walīd for adjudication. According to the *Akhbār al-dawlah*,[20] the Umayyad was about to rule in Salīṭ's favor and against the new ᶜAbbāsid patriarch; but before the matter could be settled, Salīṭ disappeared. Given the inheritance at stake, there was the obvious possibility that he had met with foul play. A subsequent investigation indeed revealed that the *corpus delecti* was buried under a waterwheel at ᶜAlī's estate. The ᶜAbbāsid notable was then brought before the enraged Caliph who had him beaten and hung in the sun while the ᶜAbbāsid kinsmen stood by in disgrace unable to intervene. When ᶜAlī was fully recovered from his ordeal, al-Walīd had him exiled, and although he eventually returned to the ᶜAbbāsid estate at al-Ḥumaymah,[21] ᶜAlī was never allowed by al-Walīd to grace the court that had honored his family in the past.

A more detailed version of these events provides a defense of the ᶜAbbāsid and sharpens the enmity between him and the Umayyad Caliph. According to Balādhurī,[22] it was al-Walīd himself who had instigated Salīṭ to seek the family inheritance. Bearing a grudge against ᶜAlī b. ᶜAbdallāh (presumably because he had the temerity to marry Lubābah), the Umayyad Caliph became embroiled in an evil

[18] Ibid.
[19] See Chapter IV regarding the alleged claim of Abū Muslim that he was the son of Salīṭ.
[20] *Akhbār*, 149–50.
[21] See Prolegomena, n. 56.
[22] *Ansāb*, III: 762ff.

plot against the ᶜAbbāsid. Although he was terribly distressed over this turn of events, ᶜAlī was nevertheless appalled when one of his clients volunteered to murder Salīṭ. Rather than pursue violence, the ᶜAbbāsid befriended the man who sought his inheritance, and invited him to visit in an effort to defuse the dispute between them. However, unbeknownst to the patriarch, his impetuous client and the burdensome pretender to the family name became involved in a heated argument. The quarrel, which began over a trivial matter, ended with Salīṭ dead and his body buried in a large garden on ᶜAlī's estate.

Throughout this last episode ᶜAlī was elsewhere busy at prayers. Those who are themselves without spiritual inclination may be tempted to view his absence with a measure of suspicion, but the medieval reader would not have found it unusual. It was not that ᶜAlī had intentionally absented himself from a murder that he had planned; one would not even surmise that he had been a bad host. A man of unusual piety, ᶜAlī "al-Sajjād" spent so much time at prayer that he missed the tragedy taking place. Given his recently expressed feelings towards Salīṭ, and his negative reaction to the possible use of violence, there is no doubt that he would have prevented the unfortunate incident had he been present instead of bowing 500 times, as was his custom.[23]

One of Salīṭ's companion's became concerned when he failed to return to the garden entrance. He searched the premises but found no one because Salīṭ had already been entombed in a hidden grave and the murderer had fled. Riding off on the dead man's mount, he began an extensive investigation, but his inquiry led nowhere. As a result, Salīṭ's mother personally brought the matter of her missing son before the Caliph al-Walīd.[24] The Umayyad jumped at the opportunity to vent his feelings against ᶜAlī b. ᶜAbdallāh. He sent for the ᶜAbbāsid, and as might be expected, the latter claimed total ignorance of what had happened. When an official investigation later revealed the site of the hidden grave, al-Walīd was given sufficient cause to have ᶜAlī beaten and tortured. The Caliph thus hoped that the ᶜAbbāsid might reveal the whereabouts of the murderer (and by implication, admit his complicity in this appalling crime).

The detailed description of the punishment graphically illustrates the brutality meted out against ᶜAlī, a leading member of the Banū Hāshim. Like the early martyrs of Islam, he was made to stand in the sun with oil on his head (a terrible punishment

[23] On his piety, see for example Balādhurī, *Ansāb*, III: 75; *Akhbār*, 135, 144–45; Mubarrad, *Kāmil*, II: 217; also Ibn Khallikān (DeSlane), III: 263. It was said that ᶜAlī had 500 olive trees and performed two *rakaᶜhs* at each, every day. He was thus known as Dhū al-Thafināt, that is, the "Possessor of the Callouses," having acquired the mark (on his forehead) from having bowed down so many times. This designation was applied, however, to others and the ᶜAbbāsids who followed ᶜAlī were similarly credited with spending much time at prayer. See Balādhurī, op. cit., 87 (Muḥammad b. ᶜAlī) and 123 (Ibrāhīm al-Imām). Note the title "al-Sajjād" also applied to his namesake the ᶜAlid, ᶜAlī b. al-Ḥasan b. al-Ḥusayn b. Alī b. Abī Ṭālib.

[24] Balādhurī, *Ansāb*, III: 77–78.

made even more severe because unfortunately ᶜAli was completely bald).[25] Following this he was administered 60 or 61 lashes and only then did he return to his cell for further interrogation.[26] This process was repeated day after day until friendly intervention put a halt to the beatings. The punishment did not end with this, however. ᶜAlī was subsequently exiled and remained *persona non grata* at the Umayyad court until the reign of al-Walīd's successor, Sulaymān b. ᶜAbd al-Malik. Clearly, ᶜAlī had been made the innocent victim of al-Walīd's smoldering resentment.[27]

On the other hand, still another source reports that ᶜAlī actually boasted of having had his rival killed. According to Yaᶜqūbī, who is mildly inclined to the ᶜAlids, the ᶜAbbāsid patriarch confessed to his role in Salīṭ's murder. When asked by al-Walīd, "Did you kill your brother," he proclaimed defiantly, "He's no brother of mine; he's my slave. I killed him."[28] In this case, the Caliph's punishment would seem to have been rather mild. One might even argue that had it not been for the prestige of the ᶜAbbāsid family and the high esteem in which they were held by the ruling house, the response to ᶜAlī's high-handed action might have been more severe.[29] Regardless of the ᶜAbbāsid's role in these events, the incident was sufficiently noteworthy to create strained, if not irreparably damaged relations between his family and the ruling house of Umayyah.[30]

As told in these accounts, the story of ᶜAlī's beatings contains no political overtones. ᶜAlī was abused and exiled on a matter of personal honor. The ᶜAbbāsid apologists, however, were not prepared to let the story end there. Disgraced by the

[25] On his baldness, see Ibn Khallikān (DeSlane), III: 265. The author reports an anecdote in which ᶜAbd al-Malik sent a girl to pull the skull cap off ᶜAlī's head thus exposing his bald pate to Lubābah who sat next to him. The story reflects ᶜAbd al-Malik's anger at the ᶜAbbāsid for having married the Caliph's former wife. Lubābah rose to the occasion, however, and pointed out that she preferred the bald pate of a Hāshimite to the foul breath of an Umayyad.

[26] Al-Haytham b. ᶜAdī reports that ᶜAlī received 500 lashes (the total?). See Balādhurī, *Ansāb*, III: 78.

[27] The impression is created in various accounts that ᶜAlī was immediately exiled to his estate at al-Ḥumaymah. See *Akhbār*, 150; Balādhurī, *Ansāb* III: 78 quoting al-Haytham b. ᶜAdī. However, a more detailed account attributed to ᶜAbbās b. Hishām indicates that the punishment was more severe than that. Following many beatings, ᶜAlī was imprisoned on the distant island of Dahlak which was situated in the Red Sea. See Balādhurī, ibid. For Dahlak, see Yāqūt, *Muᶜjam*, II: 634. Only later was he released and allowed to settle at al-Ḥijr (al-Ḥumaymah?) in the Wādī al-Qurā between Damascus and the Ḥijāz. See Yāqūt, op. cit., 208.

[28] *Historiae*, II: 348.

[29] See, however, n. 27.

[30] Balādhurī, *Ansāb*, III: 78–79, contains a story that al-Walīd who had reviled ᶜAlī b. ᶜAbdallāh saw his father in a dream. ᶜAbd al-Malik asked his son what he wanted from the ᶜAbbāsid, for he had treated him unjustly. As a result the latter's offspring would now relieve the Umayyads of their rule. The dream only increased the Caliph's anger, so that when he had ᶜAlī beaten, he also had dispatches sent to all the provinces reviling ᶜAlī and saying that the latter had (actually) killed his brother.

Umayyad Caliph and sent off into exile, ᶜAlī b. ᶜAbdallāh is pictured as turning his estate at al-Ḥumaymah into a recruiting center for revolutionaries.[31] An eyewitness describes an extremely hospitable ᶜAlī gathering information from a steady stream of visitors. There is no explicit indication that these dealings had any political ramifications; indeed the rubric to this anecdote and those which follow is "The Generosity of ᶜAlī b. ᶜAbdallāh." Since the generosity and caring for guests were time honored virtues in Arab society, these accounts were, at face value, intended to call attention to ᶜAlī's noble qualities. But the contemporary reader who remembered al-Ḥumaymah as a center of revolutionary intrigue in the time of ᶜAlī's successors would have been inclined to look beyond the obvious didactic message. A careful and learned reading would have revealed a more dramatic theme subtly imbedded within the narrative.

The text speaks of a visitor to al-Ḥumaymah, a certain ᶜAbd al-Malik al-ᶜUdhrī, who had previously been upbraided and denied a personal request by the ᶜAbbāsid's tormentor, al-Walīd.[32] Spurned by the Caliph, he turned to ᶜAlī b. ᶜAbdallāh who satisfied his request and honored him profusely. The grateful visitor, a member of the Umayyad house with a political grievance against the current ruling family, returned the favor with some stirring verses. The surface meaning of the poem was to draw attention once again to ᶜAlī's generosity. He is given the teknonym "Father of Guests [*Abū al-Aḍyāf*]," and is described as the "ally of generosity [*ḥalīf al-jūd*]." The real intent of the poem is, however, reserved for the first three and last three lines:[33]

I testify that you are the best of
Your kinsmen (*qawm*), and that
You are from the family of the Prophet Muḥammad.

....

Indeed those who hope for leadership
Outside of yours, while you are the
Legatees of the righteous heir, are truly misguided.

Indeed I hope that you will become imāms, ruling
Over whomever you wish, with
Rule that is duly supported

Indeed I shall be faithful to those
Who would serve you, as
Indeed I shall be black poison to those opposing you.

All references to generosity aside, this poem is a political statement clearly directed against the partisans of ᶜAlī b. Abī Ṭālib, "those who hope for leadership outside of yours." The reference to the "righteous heir [*al-wārith al-zakī*]" would

[31] *Akhbār*, 142–44, 45; Balādhurī, *Ansāb*, III: 75.
[32] *Akhbār*, 143–44; Balādhurī, *Ansāb*, III: 72–73.
[33] *Akhbār*, 144; Balādhurī, *Ansāb*, III: 73.

seem to be a play on words directed against the claims of the ᶜAlid rebel, Muḥammad b. ᶜAbdallāh, who was known among his followers as *al-Nafs al-Zakīyah*, "the Righteous [or Pure] Soul."[34] It is the ᶜAbbāsids and not the ᶜAlids who are "the best" of the Prophet's kinsmen, a sharp retort to ᶜAlid claims based on their direct family connection to Muḥammad through his daughter Fāṭimah.[35] And if the ᶜAlid faithful were to complain of ᶜAbbāsid passivity to Umayyad rule, let them heed the words of the Umayyad poet, who was himself a volunteer to the revolutionary cause against his own kinsmen. For when al-ᶜUdhrī proclaims, "indeed I shall be black poison to those who oppose you," he is referring in not so subtle fashion to the later unfurling of the black banners which signified the beginning of the ᶜAbbāsid revolt.[36] Generosity is often its own reward, but in this case ᶜAlī b. ᶜAbdallāh would seem to have calculated a much higher dividend. The political message that the poet wished to convey may have been disguised, but it was not hidden. The ᶜAbbāsids, and not their ᶜAlid kinsmen, were destined to overthrow the Umayyads and restore the rule of the Islamic community to the Prophet's rightful heirs.

The propagandists of the post-revolutionary age were not always so circumspect in reporting ᶜAlī's intentions. Another eyewitness to the activities at al-Ḥumaymah mentions that he went riding with ᶜAlī one day in the vicinity of the estate.[37] Returning from their ride, the two horsemen came upon ᶜAlī's sons who were taking carefully supervised target practice with bow and arrow. The ᶜAbbāsid notable turned to this companion and asked, "O brother of Quṣayy, do you see them worthy of exacting revenge?" His guest promptly responded, "Such was my thought," and then in order to emphasize the intensity of the ᶜAbbāsid's feelings and expectations, he recalled an appropriate verse recited earlier by Zufar b. Ḥārith al-Kilābī at the Battle of Marj Rāhiṭ when rival Umayyad armies were pitted against one another:[38]

> The pasture has become verdant from the dung of revenge
> But the wounds of the soul remain as they are.

The original sentiments embodied within these verses seem rooted in ancient love poetry. The allusion is to the heartache caused by the parting of a lover, whose abandoned campsite rubbish has turned the pasture green. For the Umayyads the parting of lovers took on a political meaning occasioned by the civil strife that gave rise to Marj Rāhiṭ, the bloody battle that brought al-Walīd's grandfather to power. ᶜAli's companion in turn drew attention to the rift between al-Walīd and the ᶜAbbāsid family which had formerly been honored by the Umayyad house. In this last case, the pasture had not yet become verdant from the dung of revenge, but the inevitable change of landscape was eagerly anticipated.

[34] See Prolegomena, pp. 7ff.

[35] Ibid.

[36] For the black banners see Chapter III, p. 92.

[37] *Akhbār*, 147.

[38] For a summary of events, see Wellhausen, *Arab Kingdom*, 171–73, 175–77, 180–82, 184.

Still another account has the ᶜAbbāsid brazenly flaunting his passions before a kinsman of the Umayyad house.[39] On this occasion the "guest" at al-Ḥumaymah was a man of the Banū Makhzūm who had recently visited at court. The two met by chance at the ᶜAbbāsid's mosque when ᶜAlī was surrounded by his sons and clients. ᶜAlī rejoiced at having a guest; he inquired as to his health and the circumstances of his travels, and then pressed him for information about the Umayyads in Syria and the Ḥijāz. When he finished with these inquiries, ᶜAlī turned to his sons. He ordered them to display their considerable prowess in religious learning—which they did—and afterward, he bade them review the material among themselves. Learning, like generosity, is its own reward; but in this instance, one has the feeling the author wishes to indicate that the ᶜAbbāsids took instruction in *dīn* and *taʾwīl* in order to emulate their scholarly grandfather and strengthen their future claims to sacred authority.[40] Returning to his guest the ᶜAbbāsid asked, "O brother of the Makhzūm, what is your opinion of the youth of the Banū Hāshim?" The impressed visitor answered, "I see them filled with virtue and dislike of the enemy." ᶜAlī b. ᶜAbdallāh slapped his thigh and proclaimed, "O brother of the Makhzūm, by God, they will not sleep until they find the revenge they are seeking."

B. THE MOTIVATION UNDERLYING ᶜALĪ'S REVENGE

Assuming that traditions of this sort accurately project ᶜAlī's sentiments and intentions, what is it that ᶜAlī was seeking to avenge? When al-Ḥusayn, the son of ᶜAlī b. Abī Ṭālib, was killed by the Umayyads at Karbalāʾ, the issues seemed clearly defined. He was en route to al-Kūfah to be acknowledged by his supporters. A successful rebellion in Iraq was to herald the overthrow of the Umayyad regime and the restoration of the Banū Hāshim to primacy, for the community of the Faithful had been in the hands of usurpers, descended not from the Prophet's family, but from the ancestors of his enemies. Moreover, by establishing Yazīd b. Muᶜāwiyah as his father's successor while the latter still lived, the house of Umayyah had set a precedent for succession that would have institutionalized their current hold on power and preserved it for them in perpetuity. Al-Ḥusayn, therefore, acted as the champion of political sentiments that were fervently held by a significant cross-section of public opinion. To avenge the death of al-Ḥusayn and subsequent ᶜAlid martyrs was to strike a blow for political principles as well as to exact blood revenge.

The apologists for the new dynasty were hardly prepared to accept less from ᶜAlī b. ᶜAbdallāh. As a result, the personal grievances nursed by the disgraced patriarch had to be framed in a much wider context that invoked the political sympathies of numerous elements among the Faithful. There is a tradition preserved in the "official history" of the ᶜAbbāsid house that seemingly suggests this wider context.[41] The setting of the account is a conversation which took place in the great mosque of

[39] *Akhbār*, 150–51.

[40] See Prolegomena, p. 28.

[41] *Akhbār*, 146–47.

Damascus between the ᶜAbbāsid patriarch and the grandfather of a certain Muḥammad b. ᶜAbd al-Raḥmān al-Jumaḥī. Upon entering the building, al-Jumaḥī saw ᶜAlī b. ᶜAbdallāh seated and sat down next to him. ᶜAlī opened the conversation, "Listen to what these Shaykhs are saying."[42] His companion turned around and observed that the Syrian shaykhs were extolling the Banū Umayyah and defaming the Banū Hāshim. Apparently offended, al-Jumaḥī started to counter their remarks, but ᶜAlī b. ᶜAbdallāh grabbed him by the hand (as if ordering him to desist). Both men then stood up and left the mosque. Upon leaving, ᶜAlī explained his response—or more appropriately, his lack of response—by reciting some suitable verses of the poet ᶜAbdallāh b. Qays:[43]

> There is no virtue in exhortation to action (*jahl*), if it is not
> Tempered by forebearing (*ḥalīm*); what compells events insures their conclusion.
> But there is no virtue in reasoned response (*ḥilm*), if there is no passion[43a] to protect what is pure from being sullied.

The ᶜAbbāsid, in effect, maintained that no good comes from impetuosity if it is not tempered by forebearance; similarly no good comes of forebearance which is all too compromising. Lest there was any doubt concerning the ᶜAbbāsid's failure to confront the Syrians, ᶜAlī let it be known in his own rather subtle fashion that he was waiting for a more propitious moment. Only then would he exact the revenge he so eagerly sought.[44]

When examined closely, the tradition may suggest a good deal more than it actually says. The deprecating remarks of the Syrians towards the Banū Hāshim may reflect the so-called "cursing of ᶜAlī [b. Abī Ṭālib]" which became part of the Friday prayers under the first Umayyad Caliph, Muᶜāwiyah b. Abī Sufyān. Similarly al-Jumaḥī's desire to play the role of pre-Islamic *jāhil* and exhort his people to conflict, recalls the celebrated case of Ḥujr b. ᶜAdī al-Kindī.[45] A native of al-Kūfah, Ḥujr b. ᶜAdī reacted to the cursing of ᶜAlī by taunting the Umayyad authorities in the Friday mosque. This practice continued until he finally abused his unofficial license to

[42] Ibid., 146.

[43] Ibid., 147.

[43a] Text: *mawārid*; read *bawādir* as in the *Rasāʾil al-Bulaqhāʾ*, 305 (ed. M. ᶜAlī) and other collections. Note the lines in the *Rasāʾil* are also reversed. These references were called to my attention by J. Bellamy.

[44] This view would seem to sum up ᶜAbbāsid sentiments all through the clandestine period of revolutionary activity, even when they were provoked. This was true during the years of Muḥammad b. ᶜAlī, the progenitor of the revolution. See the numerous sayings attributed to him in Balādhurī, *Ansāb*, III: 83ff.; *Akhbār*, 163ff. One can, of course, say this was all recorded after the fact to give the ᶜAbbāsids wisdom when cowardice would more appropriately describe their behavior. There is, however, no compelling reason to doubt that their fears of provoking the authorities with a premature response were real, and that the ᶜAbbāsid policy of forebearance was an historical truth and intelligently conceived, if embarrassing to them.

[45] See *EI*^{2} s.v. Hudjr b ᶜAdī al-Kindī.

complain by displaying militant behavior. For this reckless undertaking and the senseless bravado which followed, Ḥujr b. ᶜAdī was shackled and then executed. It is perhaps a fitting touch of irony that he was put to death by the much insulted Caliph, Muᶜāwiyah, a sovereign who was nevertheless reknowned for his practice of forebearance.

Did the author intend to draw a connection between Ḥujr b. ᶜAdī's response to the cursing of ᶜAlī, and ᶜAlī b. ᶜAbdallāh's seeming forebearance at the deprecation of his brethren? Such a question cannot be answered with certainty, but it is a safe assumption that the reader would have been familiar with the facts of the Kūfan's behavior and the consequences of his actions. The episode of Ḥujr b. ᶜAdī should have been a lesson to all future revolutionaries. There is a vast difference between posture and action, and between impetuous behavior and revolutionary planning. The partisans of ᶜAlī b. Abī Ṭālib may have shown great courage in resisting the Umayyads, but such pyrrhic victories do not make for successful revolutions. The true political activist knew better than to betray his cause by acting prematurely. By holding back his companion, ᶜAlī b. ᶜAbdallāh was opting for a pragmatic policy that was geared to restraint and designed for the long run. Although such a controversial policy had to be defended before and after the revolution, later events proved the ᶜAbbāsids correct in delaying their confrontation with the Umayyad regime.

Since the conversation reportedly took place in the mosque of Damascus during the reign of al-Walīd, the reader of this tradition was likely to connect it with events taking place before ᶜAlī was disgraced and exiled from the city. The account therefore suggests that ᶜAlī's opposition to the Umayyads was rooted in the long political struggle between Hāshim and Umayyah, and not simply based on personal grievances derived from his public humiliation. This impression is reinforced by a description of ᶜAlī's actions following the Battle of al-Ḥarrah, an infamous event which took place in 63 A.H., that is, some years before the Caliphate of al-Walīd.[46]

The broad details of the battle and its aftermath are well known. When certain elements in al-Madīnah withdrew their recognition of the second Umayyad Caliph, Yazīd b. Muᶜāwiyah, a Syrian army was sent to subdue them under the command of Muslim b. ᶜUqbah al-Murrī.[47] The command had previously been refused by two notables of Quraysh. One of them, ᶜUbaydallāh b. Ziyād was wary of attacking the holy city, particularly after he had killed al-Ḥusayn at Karbalāᶜ. This judgment

[46] See *EI*^{2} s.v. al-Ḥarra.

[47] By emphasizing the failure of the local populace to recognize Yazīd, the chroniclers leave the impression that the Medinese were making a dramatic statement against his unprecedented succession. That is to say, he received the oath of allegiance while his father ruled in good health. If continued, this practice would have insured the continuous rule of the Umayyads at the expense of the Prophet's family. A close reading of the sources reveals, however, that the issues underlying the Medinese response were based on broader considerations and were determined in large part by conflicting economic interests. In this case both the ᶜAlids and the ᶜAbbāsids seized the opportunity to reinterpret this major event to suit their purposes. See M. J. Kister, "The Battle of Ḥarra."

proved sound; for following their success in battle, the Syrians murdered, raped, looted and pillaged for three consecutive days. The depravity of Muslim's troops in the holy city became a *cause célèbre* that was invoked by future generations, and he was henceforth called "Musrif," a play on names designed to indicate a person who exceeds all bounds of propriety. The living testimony to his excesses were a thousand illegitimate children who had allegedly been sired by Muslim's rapacious warriors, and a generation of anxious fathers who could not guarantee their daughter's virginity when attempting to arrange suitable marriages. Allowing for a certain measure of exaggeration among the chroniclers, the severity of the Umayyad response to what was really a tempest in a teapot gave rise to deep passions. Coming as they did after the martyrdom of the Prophet's grandson, al-Ḥusayn, and the unprecedented manner in which Yazīd was chosen to succeed his father (Muᶜāwiyah) as Caliph, the events of al-Ḥarrah created a rift between the clans of Hāshim and Umayyah that could never be properly healed.

ᶜAlī b. ᶜAbdallāh's role at al-Ḥarrah, or more correctly the role ascribed to him by ᶜAbbāsid apologists, was meant to reveal a certain measure of political independence, and thereby project for him the image of a future rebel. At the conclusion of the carnage, Muslim b. ᶜUqbah reportedly compelled the defeated Medinese to renew their loyalty to the Umayyad Caliph. Then, exceeding what was called for, he allegedly demanded that those taking the oath to Yazīd declare themselves to be servants of the Caliph. Those Medinese refusing to comply with this extraordinary and certainly illegal demand were summarily executed. When it was ᶜAlī b. ᶜAbdallāh's turn to declare his servitude or face death, one of his maternal kinsmen among the Syrian troops (a certain Ḥaṣīn b. Numayr) intervened. Against his commander's protestations he insisted that ᶜAlī would take the usual oath "according to the Book of God and the precedent (*sunnah*) of Muḥammad his Prophet."[48] Moreover, when ᶜAlī finally extended his hand to the Umayyad in order to pledge his fealty to Yazīd according to the old formula, Ḥaṣīn held him back. By this act, he prevented the ᶜAbbāsid from pledging his allegiance directly through Muslim b. ᶜUqbah al-Murrī. Instead ᶜAlī took Ḥaṣīn's hand, and the latter in turn took the hand of the Umayyad commander. ᶜAlī b. ᶜAbdallāh then boasted:

> My ancestor al-ᶜAbbās was chief of the Banū Luwayy,[49]
> My maternal relatives, rulers from the Banū Walīᶜah
> They protected my sacred honor that day, when
> Musrif's troops arrived with the Banū Lakīᶜah[50]
> He (Musrif) wished of me that which would have been disgraceful
> But a redoubtable hand prevented me from doing what was hateful.

[48] Masᶜūdī, *Murūj* (Beirut), III: 69ff.; *Akhbār*, 136–37; Balādhurī, *Ansāb*, III: 79; Mubarrad, *Kāmil*, I: 260ff.

[49] Mubarrad, *Kāmil*, I: 260: *Quṣayy*.

[50] There is no such family group as the Banū Lakīᶜah. The expression means "evil men," but it is retained here as is for the sake of the rhyme.

Whoever read this account understood only too well that ᶜAlī b. ᶜAbdallāh did not give full recognition to Umayyad authority. His actions, his words, and the rather peculiar fashion in which he pledged his fealty indicate that his allegiance to the ruling house was tainted.

There is, moreover, a postscript to this story preserved in the work of the ᶜAbbāsid apologist. The only other inhabitant defying Musrif's order was ᶜAlī, the son of the recently martyred al-Ḥusayn who reportedly came forth and pledged his fealty "according to the formula used by my kinsman [*ᶜalā mā bāyaᶜa ᶜalayhi ibn ᶜammī*]."[51] It thus came to pass that ᶜAlī b. Abī Ṭālib's grandson emulated the courage of his ᶜAbbāsid relative. One should not believe, however, that ᶜAlī b. al-Ḥusayn expressed defiance while in danger of his life. The author hastens to add that Musrif was under strict orders from the Caliph to deal gently with the ᶜAlid. It was assumed that a second ᶜAlid martyr so quickly on the heels of the first (and in this case a surviving son) was hardly a desideratum of state policy. The real glory, if indeed there was any on this occasion, belonged to the ᶜAbbāsid ᶜAlī, that is ᶜAlī b. ᶜAbdallāh, and his maternal kinsman Ḥaṣīn b. Numayr.[52] However defiant, the ᶜAbbāsid's gesture at al-Ḥarrah was far from a call to open rebellion. Even if the accounts suggesting a passionate desire for revenge truly reflect the patriarch's sentiments, the expression of these sentiments was hardly the same as coordinating a revolutionary movement. Considering the tendentious nature of all these traditions, one is obliged to ask if ᶜAlī b. ᶜAbdallāh was actually involved in a revolutionary effort, or if he even articulated a position based on political principle. To state the question somewhat differently, were ᶜAli's revolutionary credentials authentic or, dictated by later ideological developments, were they an invention designed to mirror the reported exploits of his son and grandsons?

There is no doubt that ᶜAlī's son Muḥammad was the progenitor of the ᶜAbbāsid revolution. The task fell to him because of an unusual combination of circumstances culminating in the transfer of authority from Abū Hāshim b. Muḥammad b. al-Ḥanafīyah shortly before the turn of the first Islamic century.[53] Had it not been for the legacy of the heirless Abū Hāshim, the ᶜAbbāsids would have had neither the ideological basis nor the initial organization to challenge the Umayyad regime. The transfer of authority to Muḥammad b. ᶜAlī did not preclude, however, a role for his father in the revolutionary apparatus. ᶜAlī b. ᶜAbdallāh was hardly old and infirm when his son began the business of revolution. The ᶜAbbāsid patriarch was the youngest of ᶜAbdallāh's children and had fathered Muḥammad by the time he was fourten years of age. Given Muḥammad's propensity to dye his beard (a mature) red and ᶜAlī to dye his black (to appear more youthful), the two reportedly were confused for one another. Another source indicates that it was only through the

[51] *Akhbār*, 137.

[52] Ibid. This is attested in several sources.

[53] See Chapter II.

color of the dye that one could actually tell them apart.[54] Furthermore, the ᶜAbbāsid patriarch was apparently in good health when his son began to direct the revolutionary cadres. It was only some twenty years later that ᶜAlī died in 118 A.H.[55]

For an individual given to passionate feelings of revenge against the Umayyads, ᶜAlī b. ᶜAbdallāh displayed a remarkably low profile during these twenty years of political activity. There is, in fact, no direct evidence of his involvement with the revolutionary apparatus during the clandestine struggle against Umayyad rule. Forebearance may have been a noble quality, and it was surely the most judicious response to the exigencies of the moment; nevertheless twenty years of inactivity cannot be dismissed so lightly. The conclusion to be drawn is inescapable. Contrary to the accounts cited earlier, ᶜAlī b. ᶜAbdallāh had little impact, if any, on the revolutionary movement. His alleged contributions to the cause are the result of a later historiographical effort designed to rehabilitate his image.

[54] See Balādhurī, *Ansāb*, III: 71–72, 80; *Akhbār*, 161; Anonymous, 235a; Ibn Qutaybah; *Maᶜārif*, 123.

[55] The tradition hints at a certain uneasiness in the relationship between ᶜAlī and his eldest son Muḥammad. One can, of course, imagine how difficult it must have been for ᶜAlī to raise a son while he himself was so young. Note that the leadership of the family was given by ᶜAlī, not to Muḥammad, his eldest son, but to Sulaymān. There is, moreover, evidence that Muḥammad wished to have his father's blessing. See *Akhbār*, 160; Ibn ᶜAbd Rabbihi, *ᶜIqd*, V: 105; also Mubarrad, *Kāmil*, II: 220–21. The explanations offered by ᶜAbbāsid traditions for ᶜAlīs strange choice, i.e., he did not wish to disgrace Muḥammad (by burdening him with family affairs, suggesting he would be busy at creating a revolution?) seems forced. Note that another tradition indicates ᶜAlī actually offered Muḥammad his blessing, but the latter refused saying, "Father, shall I take on two burdens, your debts and your family?" See *Akhbār*, 160. The ᶜAbbāsid family may, indeed, have been heavily in debt. Note the account of ᶜAlī's attendance at the court of Sulaymān b. ᶜAbd al-Malik where he informs the latter of his need for 30,000 dirhams to liquidate a debt. See *Akhbār*, 139–40; also Mubarrad, *Kāmil*, 218–19; Ibn Khallikān (DeSlane), III: 266. There is also the possibility that ᶜAlī feared that the discovery of his son's revolutionary involvement would harm family interests and thus he did not give Muḥammad his blessing. ᶜAlī certainly disapproved of Abū Hāshim who transferred his authority and revolutionary cadres to Muḥammad. See ᶜAkhbār, 173.

II

HISTORY *CUM* PROPHECY: ABŪ HĀSHIM, MUḤAMMAD B. ᶜALĪ AND THE ROAD TO REVOLUTION

> Indeed the first (believers) followed the path of tradition (*sunnah*), and the later believers similarly invoke it . . . Surely your *sunnah* is the *sunnah* of the Banū Isrāᵓīl and the *sunnah* of the Prophet.
>
> Bukayr b. Māhān

Among the more intriguing accounts of Abū Hāshim's last will and testament is a report preserved by the Andalusian litterateur Ibn ᶜAbd Rabbihi (d. 328 A.H.).[1] Writing in a time and place far removed from the events under consideration, Ibn ᶜAbd Rabbihi is, nevertheless, an important source for early ᶜAbbāsid times, for he is generally careful in identifying the provenance of his material. In this instance his account is related on the authority of the historian al-Haytham b. ᶜAdī (d. 206, 207, or 208 A.H.), a scholar with strong credentials as an apologist for the ᶜAbbāsid house and a frequent visitor to the court of the Caliph al-Manṣūr.[2] It has indeed been claimed that this report of Abū Hāshim's death is a fragment of al-Haytham b. ᶜAdī's lost *Kitāb al-dawlah*, a work which allegedly reflects the earliest effort of an officially sanctioned ᶜAbbāsid historiography.[3] Considering Ibn ᶜAdī's special relationship to Manṣūrid circles, any account based on his authority is to be treated with considerable interest and, needless to say, a certain measure of skepticism.

A. THE FUTURE ᶜABBĀSID LINE ACCORDING TO AL-HAYTHAM B. ᶜADĪ

Under the rubric "History of the ᶜAbbāsid Triumph [*dawlah*]," al-Haytham b. ᶜAdī sets out to authenticate the claims of the ᶜAbbāsid house, and in particular those of the Manṣūrid line, by reworking a well-known story concerning the alleged murder of Abū Hāshim b. Muḥammad b. al-Ḥanafīyah (d. ca. 98 A.H.).[4] Fearful that ᶜAlī b. Abī Ṭālib's grandson would utilize his considerable talents and followers to

[1] ᶜ*Iqd*, IV: 475ff.; see also Yaᶜqūbī, *Historiae*, II: 356–58 (essentially same account but no *isnād* given. See, however, n. 21 for a major difference).

[2] See *EI*[2] s.v. al-Haytham b. ᶜAdī.

[3] Nagel, *Untersuchungen*, 13–63; esp. 26–37.

[4] See Sharon, "ᶜAlīyat," 58–75; S. Moscati, "Il testamento di Abū Hāshim"; Omar, *Caliphate*, 59–67; Nagel, *Untersuchungen*, 45–55.

promote an insurrection against them, the Umayyad authorities were reportedly determined to pursue a bold plan of action. They decided to eliminate the heirless inheritor of ᶜAlī b. Abī Ṭālib's mantle by doing away with him on his return from the caliphal court where, ironically, he previously had enjoyed their hospitality. The assassins, armed with a subtle but deadly potion, adopted the devious strategem of hastily setting up concession stands in advance of Abū Hāshim's party. Their presumed objective was to slowly poison the ᶜAlid leader without drawing attention to their designs or to the complicity of their patrons. On that fateful hot day, at various points along the road, the thirsty leader found himself imbibing tainted milk or yogurt that had been generously offered to him by persons situated nearby.

Only after consuming a bellyfull did Abū Hāshim realize that something was wrong. "I'm dying!" he exclaimed to his followers. "Find out who those people are."[5] His retainers came back empty-handed, however, for the clever assassins had literally folded their tents and stolen away. The sudden disappearance of the ubiquitous concessionaires probably confirmed the ᶜAlid's worst suspicions. He was indeed dying, the victim of a subtle plot, and with no recognized successor to carry out his mission against the Umayyads. Time was now of the essence. He gave instructions that he should be brought to the residence of his ᶜAbbāsid kinsman, Muḥammad b. ᶜAlī in al-Ḥumaymah.[6] In these circumstances, the slow acting potion administered to Abū Hāshim actually worked to the advantage of ᶜAbbāsid interests, because the ᶜAlid lingered long enough to reach Muḥammad b. ᶜAlī's estate. There, at death's door, he managed to transfer his authority to the ᶜAbbāsid notable. Even then he still had sufficient time to deliver the support of his cadres to Muḥammad b. ᶜAlī, to offer his legatee some gratuitous political advice on tribal organization, to predict various political patterns that would develop in Khurāsān, to indicate the year and the circumstances that would mark the beginning of the end for the Umayyad regime, and last, but certainly not least, to prophesy the future reigns of the ᶜAbbāsid Caliphs Abū al-ᶜAbbās and Abū Jaᶜfar al-Manṣūr. If nothing else, Abū Hāshim b. Muḥammad b. al-Ḥanafīyah was portrayed as a tidy man putting his house in order before vacating it for a better world yet to come.

There is a popular wisdom that men are capable of extraordinary vision when facing certain death. The ᶜAlid's ability to foresee the broad outlines and even small details of future developments in his final hour might be regarded as demonstrable proof of this proposition. For despite the almost interminable nature of his parting, no death was more certain, and no vision more accurate, than that of Abū Hāshim. The more cynically inclined may note, however, a certain sense of familiarity in his final declaration.[7] A careful analysis of the last will and testament suggests that the future supposedly predicted by the ᶜAlid leader was already part of the historical record, and that these words were first attributed to him only several decades later by a propagandist serving the ᶜAbbāsid house. By this deception, the author intended to

[5] ᶜ*Iqd*, Iv: 476; Yaᶜqūbī, *Historiae*, II: 356.

[6] See Prolegomena, n. 56.

[7] See Lassner, ᶜ*Abbāsid Rule*, 24–31.

support the claims of his patrons, and more particularly to promote the legitimacy of the Caliph al-Manṣūr, a figure whose credentials were found lacking even within the ᶜAbbāsid family.

Proof of this assertion can already be seen in the ᶜAlid's opening comments.[8] Upon reaching Muḥammad b. ᶜAlī, Abū Hāshim allegedly called out, "O my kinsman, I am dying. I have therefore turned to you. You shall be the possessor of this [sacred] authority [*anta ṣāḥib hadhā al-amr*], and your son will administer it [*wa waladuka al-qāᵓim bihi*] as will his brother after him [*thumma akhūhu min baᶜdihi*]." At first glance, this statement has all the ear-marks of an anti-ᶜAlid polemic. The terms *ṣāḥib al-amr* and *al-qāᵓim* were derived from Shīᶜite political vocabulary and, in time, came to signify titles that were to be held by a messianic figure who would restore the Prophet's family to its rightful place at the head of the Faithful.[9] By choosing his words carefully, the ᶜAbbāsid apologist speaking through Abū Hāshim preempted both the language and claims of his patron's adversaries. But there is more to be gleaned here; for embedded within this terse statement is a subtle defense of al-Manṣūr's right to rule vis-à-vis rivals and potential rivals within his own family, the house of al-ᶜAbbās.

Since there is no explicit statement identifying the two offspring, the casual reader might have assumed that the anonymous sons were Muḥammad's immediate successors, the patriarch Ibrāhīm al-Imām, who died before the advent of the ᶜAbbāsid regime, and the latter's brother, Abū al-ᶜAbbās, the first dynast of the family line. But in this context, a literal reading of *al-qāᵓim bihi* (that is, he who not only possesses authority, but wields it) suggests that the first son is to be associated with the onset of ᶜAbbāsid rule. The expression (*al-qāᵓim bihi*) could also have been understood as a regnal title, calling attention to the long expected dynasts of the ᶜAbbāsid house,[10] and concurrent with that, a universally recognized authority. This clearly eliminated Ibrāhīm al-Imām who died mysteriously on the eve of the ᶜAbbāsid triumph while incarcerated at Ḥarrān. The two anonymous sons were therefore to be identified as the first ᶜAbbāsid Caliph, Abū al-ᶜAbbās (ᶜAbdallāh) al-Saffāḥ and his brother successor Abū Jaᶜfar (ᶜAbdallāh) al-Manṣūr. The widespread suspicions concerning al-Manṣūr's eleventh hour claims to rule would thus be set aside. In this instance, the propagandist cleverly suggested that the second brother's ascendance to the Caliphate was nothing less than the fulfillment of a prophecy that had already been revealed by the dying ᶜAlid when he transferred his authority to the ᶜAbbāsid line.

For those who might not have understood the subtle nuances, Abū Hāshim would later issue a more explicit statement specifying the various links in the ᶜAbbāsid chain of authority. After describing the virtues of Khurāsān and the broad outlines of the successful revolution yet to come, he returned to the theme of his

[8] ᶜ*Iqd*, IV: 476.

[9] For a thumbnail sketch of these titles see A. Sachedina, *Islamic Messianism*, 60–64; see also *EI*² s.v. Ḳāᵓim Āl Muḥammad.

[10] On the regnal titles of the ᶜAbbāsids, see Lewis, "Regnal Titles."

opening remarks. Speaking once again through his ᶜAlid interlocutor, the ᶜAbbāsid propagandist now identified the anonymous links in the dynastic line of succession. Abū Hāshim let it be known that the authority inherited by Muḥammad b. ᶜAlī would be transferred to two of his sons: ᶜAbdallāh, the offspring of the Ḥārithite woman, and following him, a second son also named ᶜAbdallāh: "And know ye, that the holder of this authority shall be from your offspring, ᶜAbdallāh b. al-Ḥārithīyah and then ᶜAbdallāh his brother [*waiᶜlam anna ṣāḥib hadhā al-amr min wuldika ᶜAbdallāh b. al-Ḥārithīyah thumma ᶜAbdallāh akhūhu*]."[11]

If there is any truth to this version of events, these final words of Abū Hāshim are likely to have startled Muḥammad b. ᶜAlī, who was not yet blessed with a son, let alone two sons named ᶜAbdallāh. The matter was, however, soon corrected (as is easily done when the past is portrayed as the future). By way of explication, al-Haytham b. ᶜAdī notes that when two sons were later born to the Ḥārithite woman, first Abū al-ᶜAbbās (al-Saffāḥ), and then Abū Jaᶜfar (al-Manṣūr), they were not only called ᶜAbdallāh, but each in turn became Caliph of the realm as Abū Hāshim had predicted in his final testament: "And two sons were born [to Muḥammad b. ᶜAlī] by the Ḥārithite woman. Both of them were named ᶜAbdallāh. Abū al-ᶜAbbās was the older and Abū Jaᶜfar, the younger. Both of them went on to become Caliphs [*fa wulida lahu min al-Ḥārithīyah waladān summiya kull wāḥid minhum ᶜAbdallāh wakāna al-akbar Abā al-ᶜAbbās wa al-aṣghar Abā Jaᶜfar fa waliyā jamīᶜan al-khilāfah*]."[12]

The theme of the Ḥārithite siblings destined for future rule is also found in the *Kitāb al-buldān* of Ibn Aᶜtham al-Kūfī[13] where Abū Hāshim's final declaration provides the framework for describing a subsequent historic moment, the legacy of Muḥammad b. ᶜAlī. Given the changed time frame, there are, to be sure, variations in the plot and in the context, but the images from which the second tradition is fashioned are abundantly clear. In al-Kūfī, the words are attributed to an aging Muḥammad b. ᶜAlī, not quite on his deathbed as the ᶜAlid was, but feeble and doubtful about his future. Having recalled (albeit in reworked fashion) Abū Hāshim's prophecy of the coming revolution in Khurāsān, he now alludes to his kinsman's vision of the future ᶜAbbāsid leadership. Turning to some Khurāsānī adherents who had come to visit him during the season of the pilgrimage, Muḥammad b. ᶜAlī proclaims, "I have passed the right to rule to my son Ibrāhīm [al-Imām] who is staying in Ḥarrān. Should anything happen to him, then [it should go] to my son ᶜAbdallāh b. al-Ḥārithīyah. Should anything happen to him, then [it should go] to my [other son] ᶜAbdallāh b. al-Ḥārithīyah, that is, Abū Jaᶜfar al-Manṣūr." There is no explicit mention here that Abū Jaᶜfar was the younger son,

[11] ᶜ*Iqd*, IV: 476–77. See also Yaᶜqūbī, *Historiae*, II: 357 and text above for an important variant.

[12] ᶜ*Iqd*, IV: 477. Note Balādhurī, *Ansāb*, III: 81–82 indicating the significance of Abū al-ᶜAbbās's birth and giving the year as 100 or 101.

[13] Kūfī, *Futūḥ*, VIII: 155.

although this may be inferred from the order of succession and the assertion that he was also born of the Ḥārithite woman.

It was not uncommon to grant several sons the same proper name. The practice was determined by two interlocking considerations, the desire to retain certain names, thereby preserving family memories in successive generations, and the great mortality rate among infants and young children. It would appear that the ᶜAbdallāhs of the ᶜAbbāsid line were particularly vulnerable. Muḥammad b. ᶜAlī is credited with four brothers of that name, of whom only one survived long enough to produce his own offspring.[14] The circumstances in the accounts of Ibn ᶜAdī and al-Kūfī are, however, quite different in that two living sons of the same woman were given identical names. This most unusual occurrence is rooted in the significance of this particular mother and in the literary history of this particular tradition.

The Ḥārithite woman was the noble Rayṭah b. ᶜUbaydallāh who traced her ancestry to Ziyād b. al-Ḥārith.[15] Since her kinsmen, the Banū Muslīyah were particularly active in the ᶜAbbāsid cause, the political advantages of being linked with Rayṭah and, hence, the Banū Muslīyah were significant. Indeed several of Muḥammad b. ᶜAlī's most prominent supporters were recruited from among the clients of Rayṭah's relations. The earliest document pertaining to the organizational structure of the ᶜAbbāsid movement was allegedly a scroll on which Muḥammad b. ᶜAlī himself recorded the names of his newly-acquired following.[16] Dictated by the veteran revolutionary Salamah b. Bujayr, the list drew upon the Kūfan supporters of the recently deceased Abū Hāshim. It was headed by Sālim al-Aᶜmā, and included several other clients of the Banū Muslīyah, among them Bukayr b. Māhān and Abū Salamah al-Khallāl.[17] Following the lead of Sālim, the latter two eventually assumed command of the revolutionary apparatus in al-Kūfah, and as an extension of their duties in Iraq, they also played a critical role in expanding the ᶜAbbāsid mission to Khurāsān. According to Sālim's son, Muḥammad, his father was given to boasting that the ᶜAbbāsid cause was first taken up by the Banū Muslīyah (in al-Kūfah). Muḥammad then added, with evident pride, that his kinsmen had been responsible for disseminating the ᶜAbbāsid propaganda (in other regions). In any event, the early clandestine gatherings of the ᶜAbbāsid conspirators were held in the residential

[14] *Akhbār*, 147–48. For a shorter list of ᶜAlī's offspring, see Ibn Ḥazm, *Jamharah*, 20; Ibn Qutaybah, *Maᶜārif*, 163.

[15] Ibn Ḥazm, *Jamharah*, 20; *Akhbār*, 234. Note there are also traditions that the ᶜAlid, ᶜAbdallāh b. Muᶜāwiyah, was the son of the Ḥārithite woman and the recipient of Abū Hāshim's authority. See Nagel, *Untersuchungen*, 52–53. For ᶜAbdallāh b. Muᶜāwiyah, see Chapter III, Section C.

[16] *Akhbār*, 191–92.

[17] For the activities of Salamah b. Bujayr and Sālim al-Aᶜmā, see *Akhbār*, 180, 182–93; 196 (Ibn Bujayr), 183, 186, 191–92, 194–97, 201, 205 (al-Aᶜmā). Also belonging to the Banū Muslīyah was Ḥafṣ al-Asīr, who was reportedly imprisoned in al-Kūfah at the time of Abū Muslim's conversion to the ᶜAbbāsid cause. See p. 130.

quarter of the Banū Muslīyah, either at the place of Sālim al-Aᶜmā, or at the house of one of his associates.[18]

Such devotion to the ᶜAbbāsid cause was not lost on Muḥammad b. ᶜAlī. Romantic love has always had its place, but in this case, there is reason to suspect that the patriarch's marriage to Rayṭah might have been rooted in the politics of the times. The importance of the political relationship seemingly carried to the next generation. That is, where no link existed between Rayṭah and an ᶜAbbāsid aspiring to universal recognition, it was useful to have one invented. This would have been especially true of the Caliph al-Manṣūr, for whatever his virtues, the real facts of al-Manṣūr's origins seemingly worked against him. His mother, a manumitted concubine, was no Arab, let alone the noble Ḥārithite of the apocalyptic traditions.[19] The account of his birth to Rayṭah subsequent to the birth of his brother Abū al-ᶜAbbās can thus be seen as a carefully worked out fiction designed to enhance al-Manṣūr's weak claims to the Caliphate.

In its present form, al-Haytham b. ᶜAdī's passage dealing with the birth of siblings represents the reworking of an earlier tradition by attacking a point of disturbance that was vexing to apologists of the Manṣūrid line; namely, Abū Jaᶜfar had no claims to pure Arab lineage since he was, in fact, the son of Salāmah, a Berber slave, and more significant still, he was not the younger, but the older of the two ᶜAbdallāhs.[20] Indeed, if we were to ignore al-Haytham b. ᶜAdī's postscript and rely only on the text of Abū Hāshim's testament, one would not necessarily conclude that the two future Caliphs were born of the same mother. Where the Ḥārithite woman is mentioned by Abū Hāshim, the text simply indicates that authority will come to "ᶜAbdallāh b. al-Ḥārithīyah and then ᶜAbdallāh, his brother." A close variant of the ᶜAlid's last testament goes a step further by adding several significant words to this formulation. An account in Yaᶜqūbī reads: "And know ye, that the holder of this authority shall be from your offspring: ᶜAbdallāh b. al-Ḥārithīyah and then ᶜAbdallāh, his brother *who is older than he is* [*waiᶜlam anna ṣāḥib hādhā al-amr min wuldika ᶜAbdallāh b. al-Ḥārithīyah thumma ᶜAbdallāh akhūhu* alladhī huwa akbaru minhu]."[21] The later version of al-Haytham b. ᶜAdī which spoke of two Ḥārithite offspring not only eliminated the embarrassment of al-Manṣūr's humble

[18] Ibid., 192. Note Ṭabarī, III/1:50–51 reports *sub anno* 132 that one of Banū Muslīyah was destined to kill Marwān al-Ḥimār thus putting an end to the Umayyad dynasty. The prophecy is put into the mouths of Bukayr b. Māhān, himself a Muslī, and other unidentified figures in al-Kūfah, a city where the revolutionaries of the Banū Muslīyah resided. See also *Akhbār*, 182, for a similar prophecy. Note also the special homage paid to the Banū Muslīyah by Muḥammad b. ᶜAlī when the latter was on his deathbed. See *Akhbār*, 238–39.

[19] See for example *Akhbār*, 168–69. The death of the Umayyads is predicted along with Abū al-ᶜAbbās's destiny to rule as the son of the Ḥārithite woman.

[20] For al-Manṣūr, the son of Salāmah, see Lassner, *ᶜAbbāsid Rule*, 26–27. See also Ibn Ḥazm, *Jamharah*, 20–21, and *Akhbār*, 234, which mention the offspring of Muḥammad b. ᶜAlī. The pro-Manṣūrid thrust of this tradition is briefly noted by Nagel, *Untersuchungen*, 48–49.

[21] *Historiae*, II: 357.

origins, but in reversing the order of birth, it gave satisfactory explanation as to why al-Manṣūr was initially passed over in favor of a younger Abū al^cAbbas.

Al-Kūfī's account of the Ḥārithite siblings is marked by another distortion.[22] The order of succession designated by the aging Muḥammad b. ᶜAlī is Ibrāhīm al-Imām, who was reportedly in Ḥarrān, Abū al-ᶜAbbās, and then Abu Jaᶜfar al-Manṣūr. In this case, a problem arises from the specific reference to the city of Ḥarrān, where Muḥammad's successor Ibrāhīm was suddenly incarcerated by the Umayyad authorities. His imprisonment, apparently without warning, must have sent shock waves throughout the ᶜAbbāsid family. There was the danger that the imprisonment of the hidden imām might lead to the exposure of the ᶜAbbāsid apparatus. With that setback, the long campaign which was about to culminate in the messianic era would have been in serious jeopardy. In addition, many of the revolutionary constituencies were tied exclusively to the imām, so that a break in the chain of authority at this juncture would have completely undercut ᶜAbbāsid claims to rule. That the family should have taken measures at the time of Ibrāhīm's incarceration to provide for a future succession and insure the safety of its key notables is understandable. But Muḥammad b. ᶜAlī, who was inserted here by the author to legitimize these efforts, actually had no role to play in this matter; for he had, in fact, expired several years before Ibrāhīm was removed from public view in 129 A.H.[23]

Still another account (*sub anno* 125 A.H.) has Muḥammad b. ᶜAlī expressing grave doubts that he would meet his supporters during the pilgrimage of the following season.[24] He had entered his seventh decade and was, no doubt, feeling the effects of a long and active life. To insure the future success of the ᶜAbbāsid cause, he appointed his son Ibrāhīm to be his successor. However, in this rendering of the patriarch's final address, there is absolutely no indication of a more extensive line. There is no mention of offspring born to a Ḥārithite woman.[25]

Historical facts are invariably subordinate to the major ideological thrust of these texts, which was to establish a legitimate rationale for ᶜAbbāsid rule and for the line of Muḥammad b. ᶜAlī in particular. Among the ᶜAbbāsid faithful there was no doubt of Ibrāhīm al-Imām; and despite a possible uneasiness in the ranks, the legitimacy of Abū al-ᶜAbbās also came to be accepted—certainly after his ascendance to the Caliphate and the strengthening of the nascent regime. It was rather the claim of Abū al-ᶜAbbās's older brother ᶜAbdallāh that was the most vulnerable to public

[22] Kūfī, *Futūḥ*, VIII: 155.

[23] For the problematic episode of Ibrāhīm's death, see Sharon, "ᶜAlīyat," 237–60. Various dates are given for the death of Muḥammad b. ᶜAlī (see text p. 83ff.) but none fits this chronology. That is, in all accounts Muḥammad b. ᶜAlī was dead by the time Ibrāhīm was incarcerated in Ḥarrān. Azdī, 107, 118, 120 indicates that the latter was immprisoned in 129; *Akhbār*, 388ff. (he was imprisoned after the pilgrimage of 129).

[24] Ṭabarī, II/3: 176; *Akhbār*, 238 (no date); also Azdī, 53.

[25] Note also Balādhurī, *Ansāb*, III: 114. The author indicates that Ibrāhīm was chosen by Muḥammad b. ᶜAlī to be his successor at the time the latter received the sacred authority from Abū Hāshim, that is, before the births of al-Manṣūr and Abū al-ᶜAbbās.

scrutiny. The rehabilitation of al-Manṣūr's image therefore became the desideratum of an ᶜAbbāsid historiography assembled under official patronage. Its main purpose, in addition to countering ᶜAlid claims, was to search and, if necessary, to invent the historic past in order to establish the legitimacy of al-Manṣūr's Caliphate and that of his offspring. In such fashion, the dynastic apologists denied future pretenders from other branches within the ruling family and those external to it.

B. PROPHECY AND THE GEOPOLITICS OF THE ᶜABBĀSID REVOLT

Sandwiched between Abū Hāshim's two predictions of the future ᶜAbbāsid line is a lengthy statement on the role of Khurāsān in the impending struggle against the Umayyads.[26] Although this segment of the text is less specifically tied to Manṣūrid interests, Abū Hāshim's comments on the political geography of the revolt consistently reveal the skillful hand of the propagandist. Speaking through the martyred ᶜAlid, the author again threads his way through the historical record in order to arm the ᶜAbbāsids with a prophecy waiting to be fulfilled.

A common destiny may have brought the two Hāshimite notables together in Palestine, but Khurāsān, the vast province of the east, was the geographical epicenter of Abū Hāshim's thinking. The ᶜAlid pointed out that the authority (vested in the ᶜAbbāsid family) would only become fully effective when the black banners were brought forth from Khurāsān. From there they would be carried victoriously to the outer reaches of a growing empire encompassing all the domains from Ḥaḍramawt to North Africa, and from al-Hind to Farghānah. He then bequeathed the ᶜAbbāsid his loyal cadres (*fa ᶜalayka bihāʾulāʾi al-shīᶜah*) while enjoining him to receive them kindly, "for they are your propagandists [*duᶜātuka*] and your supporters [*anṣāruka*]."[27] Having thus supplied his kinsman the tools as well as the vision necessary to incite a revolt, Abū Hāshim unveiled the blueprint for a future victory. Khurāsān, and more specifically (the area of) Marw, was to be the target of the ᶜAbbāsid mission and the location from which the revolt would be proclaimed. With these words he anticipated, indeed he accurately predicted the digging of the trenches and the unfurling of the black banners in the villages and hamlets that surrounded Marw. These initial acts of defiance, which took place only three decades later, might have led to a successful local insurrection, but they could hardly have portended the end of Umayyad rule. The old Arab settlers of the area who represented the hard core of the ᶜAbbāsid following could not be expected to sustain an effort against the veteran Umayyad armies of ᶜĀmir b. Ḍubārah and Nubātah b. Hanẓalah. Divine intervention was, of course, anticipated, but the ᶜAbbāsids were sufficiently cynical to appreciate that God is often on the side of the big battalions.

The overthrow of the Umayyads eventually called for an intricate strategy that balanced political and military considerations in Khurāsān. According to Ibn ᶜAdī, this future development was also foreseen by Abū Hāshim.[28] The dying ᶜAlid thus left

26 *ᶜIqd*, IV: 476; see also Yaᶜqūbī, *Historiae*, II: 357.

27 Ibid.

28 Ibid.

instructions for revolutionary agents to infiltrate the tribal associations of the Yaman, and then link them to the Rabīᶜah, for it is through the Yaman (and their southern allies) that the current regime would be overturned. Conversely, Abū Hāshim let it be known that those who disobey God, the Qays and Tamīm (northern tribes, hence possible allies of the Banū Umayyah) should be kept at arms' length. Once again the ᶜAlid was made to predict, and with great perspicacity, the turn of events that would lead to the long-expected revolution. Awaiting the end of the first Islamic century, the revolutionaries lacked the military capability to challenge the professional armies of the Umayyad regime, but some thirty years later an intertribal conflict in Khurāsān produced large numbers of disaffected fighting men from among the southern tribes.[29] These units were coopted by the ᶜAbbāsids in a series of brilliant diplomatic coups, and they then came to serve as the military foundation of the new regime.[30]

To be sure, prophecies generally seem more accurate when seen from a vantage point in the future. In retrospect, the world to come as outlined by Abū Hāshim indicated great things for the Banū ᶜAbbās and their allies; however, even with hindsight, the ᶜAbbāsid victory was no small achievement. An effective and loyal revolutionary infrastructure was required to control the diverse supporters of the ᶜAbbāsid cause. Muḥammad b. ᶜAlī was made to understand this need well in advance of any military action by his successors. Abū Hāshim suggested that he utilize two groups of operatives in order to secure the revolutionary apparatus. One group would consist of twelve agents (*naqīb*, pl. *nuqabāʾ*) and a second of seventy, thus following an earlier pattern first observed in the time of the Banū Isrāʾīl, and then again during the time of the Prophet.[31] Through agents of this sort God had set the affairs of the ancient Israelites in proper order; the Prophet, in turn, made use of chosen representatives from among the recently converted Medinese to enforce and validate his authority at the most critical moment of his career.

The words attributed to Abū Hāshim therefore alluded to historic memories deeply rooted among the revolutionaries gathered at al-Ḥumaymah and also among the later generation of ᶜAbbāsid supporters. Properly explicated, his testament left little room for ambiguity. The reference to the Banū Isrāʾīl drew upon two verses in the Qurʾān:[32] "And Moses chose his people, seventy men to meet with us," and, "We raised up from among them (from the Banū Isrāʾīl) twelve leaders."[33] Analogous to these developments, some seventy men from among the Aws and Khazraj swore allegiance to the Prophet Muḥammad during the secret conclave at al-ᶜAqabah, and following this clandestine meeting twelve individuals were chosen from among them to represent the Prophet's interests among the new adherents to his cause.[34] Their

[29] Sharon, "ᶜAlīyat," 138–54.

[30] See Lassner, *ᶜAbbāsid Rule*, 98–136.

[31] See Chapter III, Section B. See also Rubin, "Prophets and Progenitors."

[32] Qurʾān, VII: 155.

[33] Qurʾān, V: 16. The most likely allusion is to the twelve spies in Num., XIII, that is, those secret operatives who paved the way for the Israelite conquest of Canaan.

[34] Ibn Hishām, I/1, 295 (73 men), 297 (names of the *nuqabāʾ*).

mission was to return to al-Madīnah and pave the way for the emigration of the frustrated Muslims in Mecca, thereby setting into motion the hijrah, the single most important event in the history of the proto-Islamic community.

Although Abū Hāshim spoke of the historic past, once again, he is portrayed as clearly foreseeing future developments. His instructions concerning the *nuqabāʾ* were reportedly implemented by an emissary sent to the region about the turn of the century and then again by the ʿAbbāsid agent Bukayr b. Māhān during a clandestine visit to Khurāsān about 120 A.H.[35] It was, in fact, during Bukayr's secret mission, an analogue to the meeting at al-ʿAqabah, that the operative plans leading to the open revolt were first agreed upon.[36] One aspect of the deliberations is particularly noteworthy. A document was drawn up, presumably to serve as a charter for the newly formed revolutionary units. It was dictated by Bukayr b. Māhān, and according to the *Akhbār al-dawlah*, it reportedly read as follows:[37]

> In the name of God, the Most Compassionate and Merciful. Indeed the first (believers) followed the path of tradition (*sunnah*) and later believers similarly invoke it. God says, "And Moses chose his people, seventy men to meet with us." And in another verse He said, "And we raised up [*baʿathnā*] from among them [the Banū Isrāʾīl] twelve leaders." Indeed, seventy men of the Aws and Khazraj met with the Prophet the night of al-ʿAqabah and pledged allegiance to him; whereupon he appointed twelve leaders [*naqīb*] from among them. Surely your *sunnah* is the *sunnah* of the Banū Isrāʾīl and the *sunnah* of the Prophet.

Abū Hāshim's effort to link the Banū Isrāʾīl and Muḥammad, the Prophet, to the ʿAbbāsid revolutionaries and Muḥammad b. ʿAlī is hardly accidental; nor is it mere coincidence that Bukayr b. Māhān should have attempted to draw the same

[35] Ṭabarī, II/3: 1358 *sub anno* 100 indicates that Muḥammad b. ʿAlī sent several emissaries to Khurāsān. These included Muḥammad b. Khunays, Abū ʿIkrimah al-Sarrāj, and Ḥayyān al-ʿAṭṭār. Among those answering the ʿAbbāsid call twelve were chosen as *nuqabāʾ* (from among 70). These are essentially the same figures who were present at Bukayr's visit in 120 A.H. Hence, if this tradition is accurate and does not confuse two historic moments, the hard core of the ʿAbbāsid movement had been in place for some two decades before it became more fully active. See also op. cit., 1988, *sub anno* 130 but describing events that reportedly took place in 103 or 104; Azdī, 26, *sub anno* 107 indicates that Bukayr sent Abū ʿIkrimah to Khurāsān to recruit the *nuqabāʾ*. According to the *Akhbār*, 203, it was Muḥammad b. ʿAlī who sent Abū ʿIkrimah to Khurāsān. Note, however, *Akhbār*, 201–2 which reports in detail that Bukayr b. Māhān and Saʿīd al-Khursī (al-Ḥarrashī?) went to Khurāsān on behalf of Muḥammad b. ʿAlī and set the *daʿwah* into motion there. The former then continued to al-Sind. The author indicates that it was at this point that the principal *nuqabāʾ* were brought into the movement. The process was slow and secretive, each figure bringing in carefully chosen recruits. This would seem to indicate that Abū ʿIkrimah was sent at a later time. Needless to say, the chronology is confused. The traditions probably confuse several missions. For Bukayr's mission in 120 A.H., see Chapter III. See also Nagel, *Untersuchungen*, 63ff.

[36] See pp. 77ff.

[37] *Akhbār*, 215.

analogy. By establishing their revolutionary apparatus according to a time-tested model, the ᶜAbbāsids invoked the authority that had previously accrued to God's chosen agents and those of his Messenger. The historic past relived was the proof of Muḥammad b. ᶜAlī's legitimacy as well as the legitimacy of those who followed him in the family line. The ᶜAbbasid future predicted by Abū Hāshim, but actually seen in retrospect, mirrored the triumphs of their celebrated predecessors and portended the successes of Bukayr b. Māhān's revolutionaries on their behalf.

The propagandist had only to indicate through Abū Hāshim the precise moment when all these "future" events would be set into motion. Those present at the deathbed vigil were not left disappointed because the ᶜAlid instructed his legatees to await the Year of the Donkey (*sanat al-ḥimār*).[38] The onset of that year would serve as the signal for Muḥammad b. ᶜAlī to send his messengers to Khurāsān and begin the process of ending Umayyad rule. Some agents would not survive the dangerous mission, but the revolutionaries were implored to remain active until their patrons left the obscure anonymity (they had deliberately chosen for themselves) and emerged into full view and then triumph.

Although the cryptic reference to a *sanat al-ḥimār* was intended to reassure the ᶜAbbāsid supporters insofar as it predicted glad tidings for their cause, it could not have been very informative for someone who would have to plan the dates and details of a revolt. The ᶜAbbāsid patriarch was therefore compelled to make inquiries of his benefactor. When Muḥammad b. ᶜAlī asked him about the meaning of this so-called year, Abū Hāshim indicated rather obliquely that the collapse of Umayyad rule was to start a century after the beginnings of the prophetic age; for no era introduced by prophecy is destined to survive a hundred years without a cataclysmic breakdown in order (*lam tamḍi miʾah sanah min nubuwwah qaṭṭu illā intaqaḍa amruhā*).[39] This disarray was, however, only *preparatio* to a new era that would resurrect the time-honored values of the past. Abū Hāshim then reminded his listeners that such a year would begin with the Year of the Donkey, and that this event was already heralded in an apocalyptic verse of the Qurʾān:[40]

> Or like him who passed by a city
> Which had fallen completely in ruins.
> He said: How will God bring this to life after death?
> So God caused him to die for a hundred years
> And then raised him up again.
> He said: How long have you remained thus?
> He said: I have remained thus for a day or part of a day.
> He said: No you have remained for a hundred years.
> But look at your food and drink which have not become stale
> And look at your donkey in order that we may make
> You a sign unto your people.

[38] ᶜ*Iqd*, IV: 476; also Kūfī, *Futūḥ*, VIII: 154–55. See also Nagel, *Untersuchungen*, 55–63.
[39] ᶜ*Iqd*, IV: 476.
[40] Qurʾān, II: 261.

The prophetic vision based on the Qurʾānic proof text did not call for delayed gratification in some distant eschatological era. Although relying on a Qurʾānic verse dealing with resurrection and generally infused with messianic allusions,[41] Abū Hāshim's prophecy concerning the Year of the Donkey clearly refers to the impending turn of the first Islamic century and, not coincidentally, to the beginning of ᶜAbbāsid operations in Khurāsān. A century earlier, the Prophet, his path prepared by the aforementioned *nuqabāʾ*, migrated from the city of his origins to the place that would become the administrative center of his realm, thereby introducing a new era. The Prophet's activities at Mecca were met with opposition, his message was essentially rejected, and given the complex nature of blood relations, his room for political maneuver was narrowly restricted. But at al-Madīnah, the Prophet became lawgiver, statesman, warrior, and if one can be granted license for descriptive language, a revolutionary. The hijrah could therefore be considered a watershed in the political history of the Faithful. It led to the formation of a visible Islamic community and provided the setting from which to launch the activist phase in the mission to spread Islam. The hijrah was, indeed, of such significance that it marked a convenient point from which to begin reckoning time according to a newly established Muslim calendar, a calendar tailored, so to speak, for the prophetic age.[42]

If Abū Hāshim's dictum is properly understood, the second Islamic century would mark a similar turning point in the fortunes of the righteous. The preliminary indications were there to be seen. Like their kinsman, Muḥammad, the ᶜAbbāsids had left their ancestral home. From their new residence in al-Ḥumaymah, and from their new base of revolutionary activites in Khurāsān, they would weave a web of intrigue that would ensnare those opposing them. For Muḥammad the Prophet, the opposition had been the oligarchy of Quraysh that ruled Mecca. For Muḥammad the revolutionary, the enemy was the Banū Umayyah, that is the descendants of the antagonistic Quraysh. The present dynasty had usurped the authority of the Banū

[41] The figure of the Qurʾānic passage cannot be identified. According to later Muslim tradition, God ordered Jeremiah to return to Jerusalem (it had been conquered and destroyed by Nebuchadnezzar). But, upon returning to the holy city, the Prophet found it in ruins. He thus wondered when God would restore it as he had indeed promised. Jeremiah then went to sleep; his donkey and provision basket were with him. He slept for 70 years during which time a new ruler ordered the city to be rebuilt. When Jeremiah awoke he was 100 years old. He thought that he had slept but for an hour. See Ṭabarī, I/2: 647–48. A variant of this story is even more to the point. Jeremiah came to Jerusalem on his donkey, carrying with him a vessel of grape juice and a basket of figs. Upon reaching Jerusalem he began to have doubts that God would revive it. God then caused him and his provision laden donkey to lie dead for 100 years. When the Prophet awoke, God recited the aforementioned verse in the Qurʾān, and Jeremiah saw how the animal had come to life and the produce became fresh. See Ṭabarī, ibid., 666. The story may echo Jerem., XXXIX: 1–7 or XL: 7–10. The prototype would seem, however, to be the rabbinic legends of Honi the Circlemaker and Jeremiah's disciple Baruch ben Neriah. See L. Ginzberg, *Legends of the Jews*, VI: 409ff.; Speyer, *Erzählungen*, 425.

[42] For a summary of discussions on dating in Islam, see Suyūtī, *al-Shāmarīkh fī ᶜilm al-taʾrīkh*.

Hāshim and had cultivated rule to suit their own ends, but they would not prevail. Their destiny was written in God's book and was hence unalterable. The prophetic era which had begun in pristine fashion with the hijrah had been sullied by the politics of the Umayyads, but the Qurʾān made it clear that the past would be born again in its former image. Speaking through Abū Hāshim, the ʿAbbāsid propagandist let it be known that Muḥammad b. ʿAlī and his followers had been chosen to play the critical role in this process.

The authors who skillfully crafted these didactic accounts could also speak through Abū Hāshim's successor. After receiving the sacred authority from his lamented ʿAlid kinsman, Muḥammad b. ʿAlī was made to explain the significance of the year 100 A.H. to his newly acquired adherents. The *Akhbār al-dawlah* thus relates[43] that shortly after the death of Abū Hāshim, the ʿAbbāsid leader enjoined his followers "to restrain your revolutionary zeal until the finest of the Banū Umayyah perishes [*wa amsikū ʿan al-jadd fī amrikum*[44] *ḥattā yahliku ashajj Banī Umayyah*]." For the death of this unnamed Umayyad would mark the passing of the (first Islamic) century, "that is, the Years of the Donkey's Master [*wa hiya sinū ṣāḥib al-ḥimār*]." The allusions to an unknown ruler and a cryptic sequence of time puzzled those gathered around the ʿAbbāsid. They felt the need to inquire about the mysterious *sinū ṣāḥib al-ḥimār*. The patriarch, having already been the recipient of Abū Hāshim's wisdom, was able to answer the very question that he himself had raised but a short time earlier. He fielded the query, as did his precedessor, by quoting the aforementioned apocalyptic verse of the Qurʾān. The text, which spoke of a man and his donkey who had been resurrected after a hundred years' sleep, should have been a clear sign to those who understood that (after a self-imposed delay) the ʿAbbāsid resistance would soon begin.

While these verses presumably explained the gist of the patriarch's message, the revolutionaries still had to identify the anonymous figure—the "finest" among the Banū Umayyah. This knowledge would have enabled them to determine with certainty the mysterious turn of the century, and thus would have allowed them to establish a timetable for (the full resumption of) revolutionary activities. For those who viewed history in retrospect, the identification of the so-called "finest" would not have been particularly difficult. Among the Umayyads, ʿUmar b. ʿAbd al-ʿAzīz was *sui generis*. Given to the influence of theologians and ascetics, he was, in contrast to his hated relatives, a man of great personal and public piety. Moreover, he championed the cause of the *mawālī* by instituting complex, if unsuccessful, fiscal reforms. He also discontinued the practice of "cursing" ʿAlī from the pulpit during the Friday prayers, and he returned to the ʿAlids their confiscated properties, thereby earning the respect of those who generally opposed the incumbent regime.[45]

[43] *Akhbār*, 193.

[44] Anonymous, 250a: "Restrain yourselves and *conceal your revolutionary activities*." This variant emphasizes even more strongly the need to delay gratification in promoting a successful revolution.

[45] For a brief view of his activities, see Wellhausen, *Arab Kingdom*, 267–311; *EI* s.v. ʿUmar b. ʿAbd al-ʿAzīz.

These aspects of his career were not lost to posterity. Even among the ᶜAbbāsids ᶜUmar II was highly thought of. When the ᶜAbbāsids desecrated the tombs of their predecessors in Damascus, an act which signified the obliteration of the Umayyad house, the grave of ᶜUmar II was the single burial site left undisturbed. Not all of the Umayyad's actions were, however, given universal approval. While adjudicating a property case in the *maẓālim* courts, the ᶜAbbāsid Caliph al-Mahdī enthusiastically expressed his admiration for ᶜUmar's sense of justice. It was left for a litigant to remind him that (despite his reputation) the Umayyad still favored his own family over the Caliph's kinsmen, the Banū Hāshim.[46] Such a limitation notwithstanding, ᶜUmar b. ᶜAbd al-ᶜAzīz was indeed the "finest" of his kin, even if this description only marked him as the very best of the very worst.

Since the revolutionaries gathered about their new leader had no claims to prophetic insight, they could hardly have foreseen the future role that was to be played by ᶜUmar II. When they met with Muḥammad b. ᶜAlī, ca. 98 A.H., the Umayyad Caliph was Sulaymān b. ᶜAbd al-Malik. Like his brother (al-Walīd I) and his father before him, Sulaymān was an energetic and forceful ruler. There was therefore every expectation that he would follow the established precedent and validate a successor from the progeny of his father. ᶜAbd al-Malik had indeed nominated a third son (the future Caliph Yazīd II) to succeed Sulaymān, but the latter was anxious to transfer authority to his own offspring. Sulaymān thus nominated a son, Ayyūb, to replace his brother Yazīd in the line of succession. The premature demise of the new heir apparent somewhat later was to have led to the nomination of still another of Sulaymān's sons, Dāwūd, but the Caliph, who was himself near death, hastily chose outside his immediate blood line and selected instead his pious cousin ᶜUmar b. ᶜAbd al-ᶜAzīz.[47] This fortuitous turn of events, which closed out the first Islamic century, may have been entirely unexpected among the revolutionaries, but the later ᶜAbbāsid propagandist made sure that it was foreseen by Muḥammad b. ᶜAlī. The patriarch's followers were made to understand that his ability to predict ᶜUmar's succession and subsequent reputation was derived from the sacred knowledge (*ᶜilm*) that had been transmitted to him by his ᶜAlid predecessor (*qālū: qāla dhālika min faḍl ᶜilmihi*). When the ᶜAbbāsid's vision was borne out by subsequent events, it came to be regarded as proof of his legitimacy (*wa kānat hādhihi min al-umūr allatī zādat al-shīᶜah basīrah fī Muḥammad b. ᶜAlī*).[48]

[46] Ṭabarī, III/1: 543. Note Wellhausen, op. cit., 310 cites this tradition but incorrectly attributes this estimate of ᶜUmar's virtue to al-Manṣūr. He also errs giving the pagination of Ṭabarī.

[47] See Wellhausen, *Arab Kingdom*, 263–66. See *Akhbār*, 168–69 for an apocalyptic tradition in which Muḥammad b. ᶜAlī is told by a mysterious figure in a mosque of ᶜUmar II's unscheduled rise to power. Sometime after all this comes to pass, Muḥammad b. ᶜAlī encounters the man who had predicted ᶜUmar's Caliphate and asks: "Who shall rule after Yazīd b. ᶜAbd al-Malik [the current Caliph]?" The mysterious figure then accurately predicts the fall of Banū Umayyah and the ascendancy of the ᶜAbbāsids through the son of the Ḥārithite woman.

[48] *Akhbār*, 193.

History itself has a way of embellishing the elaborate efforts of those who record it for their own purposes. The visions of the future, which were tied to the year 100 of the Islamic calendar, came in time to be regarded as problematic. The turning point of the first Islamic century may have given rise to millenarian (or more precisely centenarian)[49] expectations, but it failed to produce the messianic era. The beginning of the ᶜAbbāsid missions in Khurāsān was, no doubt, eagerly anticipated, but some twenty-five years later the Umayyads were still entrenched in power. To be sure, the dying Abū Hāshim did not predict that the Year of the Donkey would lead directly to revolution; his language, if anything, was rather guarded.[50] Muḥammad b. ᶜAlī was even more circumspect in addressing his new-found followers, as he cautiously sought to restrain their activities lest they disclose their intentions prematurely. A quarter of a century is, nevertheless, a rather long period of time, given the activist sentiments than prevalent.

It often happens that, when prophetic slogans and historical realities seem at variance, it is the exegesis and not the text which is initially found lacking. The intentional vagueness of prophetic traditions can thus give rise to multiple meanings. The account of al-Kūfī, previously cited,[51] focuses on a later historic moment and offers yet another interpretation of what was meant by the Year of the Donkey. As reported by the author, this second scene takes place some three decades after Abū Hāshim had transferred his authority and cadres to his ᶜAbbāsid kinsmen, and twenty-five years after the turn of the first Islamic century. An enfeebled Muḥammad b. ᶜAlī, about to issue *his* last will and testament, is addressing his revolutionary supporters during the clandestine stage of the struggle against the Umayyads. When he expresses his hopes that the regime will soon be overthrown, his companions ask, "O Imām, when will this come to pass? The rule of the Banū Umayyah has grown [too] long."[52] It may well be that the question had a rhetorical edge, as if to indicate that the agents in the field were anxious to promote greater activity in their campaign to oust the present rulers. Other texts indeed suggest that the impatience of the Khurāsānīs had become a major issue facing the ᶜAbbāsid leadership in the waning years of Umayyad rule.[53] The question put to the ᶜAbbāsid patriarch might therefore be regarded as a muted criticism of his restrained policy.

Invoking the authority of his forefathers (either spiritual or actual), Muḥammad b. ᶜAlī answers forcefully, "This, by God, is our era [*zamān*] and this is our turn, the time of our revolution [*waqt dawlatina*]."[54] By way of explanation, he then recalled what his predecessors (*abāʾ*) had mentioned concerning the Year of the Donkey, and

[49] For centenarian expectations in Islam, see Nagel, *Untersuchungen*, 58; Azizi, *Domination Arabe*, 107ff., argues for an Iranian origin to centenarian expectations. See also n. 57.

[50] Note the references to losses among the agents. See ᶜ*Iqd*, IV: 476.

[51] *Futūḥ*, VIII: 154ff.

[52] Ibid., 154.

[53] See Chapter III; esp. pp. 91ff.

[54] Kūfī, *Futūḥ*, VIII: 154. The term *zamān* is often used to indicate the inception of the messianic era.

in that connection, he spoke of the dramatic times about to befall the community. In this context, the reference to the fated Year of the Donkey was not to 100 A.H. (for Abū Hāshim's prediction had already come and passed, as had his own vision based on the reign of ᶜUmar II), but to an impending moment in the history of the ᶜAbbāsid struggle. The allusion is not to the secretive movement which Muḥammad b. ᶜAlī had built in Khurāsān around the turn of the first Islamic century, but to the long awaited rebellion and the cataclysmic military campaigns which would follow the creation of a revolutionary army. "The coming of the Year of the Donkey will be marked by a rebellion [*yaẓharu amrunā*] in which our call [*daᶜwah*] will be heeded, bringing death to the rule of the Banū Umayyah. The [black] banners and standards will appear in the districts of Marw in Khurāsān, and the Umayyads will lay slain under every rock and clod of earth."[55]

When the gathered revolutionaries ask for proof of the Year of the Donkey, the ᶜAbbāsid patriarch recalls a prophetic slogan which was, in effect, a variant of the utterance previously attributed to the dying Abū Hāshim. The original statement read: "A hundred years will not pass from the beginning of a prophetic age before there is a breakdown in order." Here the prophecy reads: "A hundred years will not pass [in the history] of a group before its rule is overturned [*lan tamḍiya miʾah sanah min amr qawm* . . .]."[56] Although at first glance the change in wording may seem innocuous, it is nevertheless instructive. The use of the word *qawm* (which probably signifies association according to kinship) as opposed to the possible use of *ummah*, which signifies religious ties, and hence the community of the Faithful, is an indication that the Umayyad dynasty was intended. The reference is not to the community at large in the prophetic age, but to the reign of the Umayyad family which altogether lasted almost one hundred years (41–132 A.H.).[57]

The year of the Donkey originally explained by Abū Hāshim to Muḥammad b. ᶜAlī, and shortly thereafter by the ᶜAbbāsid to his followers, represented the start of ᶜAbbāsid activities against the ruling dynasty at the close of the first century. This original understanding of the text probably began some time after the year one hundred during the lengthy clandestine stage of revolutionary activity. As explained by an aged Muḥammad b. ᶜAlī to his cohort in 124 A.H., the Year of the Donkey marked the tenth and last decade of the Umayyad regime. In this last instance, the dynastic apologist had the patriarch reinterpret the proof text to make it consonant with later political developments, namely, the disintegration of Umayyad rule and the expected emergence of the revolutionary armies. In the latter version, the expression *sanat al-ḥimār* represents a double entendre, for taken in the context of

[55] Ibid., 154–55.

[56] Ibid., 155.

[57] For Azizi, the origins of these Messianic expectations are to be found in Iranian legends that were strongly believed by the native population of Khurāsān. The original tabulation was thus 100 years from the death of Yazdegard III. The tradition was later Islamized to deal with Marwān II and the ᶜAbbāsid revolution. His view should be treated with great caution. See *Domination Arabe*, 107ff.

Muḥammad b. ᶜAlī's remarks concerning the death knell of the old dynasty, it alludes to the coming reign of the very last Umayyad sovereign, Marwān II (127–32 A.H.),[58] a ruler otherwise known by his appellative, Marwān "the Donkey [*al-Ḥimār*]." This ought not lead to any misunderstanding about the Caliph. Although he had the misfortune to be the last of his house, Marwān was by any standard an able and energetic figure. Contrary to what one may first surmise, his nickname carried no pejorative meaning. It was intended to signify a man of proud bearing and independent behavior.[59] In this respect he shared a great deal in common with ᶜUmar b. ᶜAbd al-ᶜAzīz. Both men charted an independent course and both were the only Marwānid sovereigns of the Umayyad house who were not the direct descendants of ᶜAbd al-Malik b. Marwān. It is rather ironic that the two able "outsiders" should have been singled out to play critical roles in the apocalyptic texts that predicted the demise of the Umayyad regime and the concurrent resurgence of the Banū Hāshim through their ᶜAbbāsid representatives.

The predictions of a future ᶜAbbāsid triumph were, no doubt, read with keen interest and satisfaction by supporters of the newly established dynasty. For them, the apocalyptic traditions clearly confirmed the legitimacy of ᶜAbbāsid claims and validated ᶜAbbāsid authority. What doubts they may have had concerning their patrons were swept aside by a restructuring of history that anticipated questions of an embarrassing nature and provided evidence for satisfactory explanations. This recording of history *cum* prophecy may have served ᶜAbbāsid needs, but it also obscures the real sequence of events that gave rise to the ᶜAbbāsid revolution and the dynastic line which followed.

[58] See Dennet, "Marwān b. Muḥammad."

[59] Note the following rather piquant incident which reflects on Marwān's name. An opponent of Marwān, who was an Abbysinian, used to climb the wall of his city which was besieged by the Caliph's allies, the Banū Sulaym. He would fasten his penis to that of a donkey and shout: "O Banū Sulaym, you sons of so and so; here is your banner." For this indiscretion he later lost his genitalia and his nose. See Ṭabarī, II/3: 1912. Note the reservations of Azizi on the explanations given for the Marwān's nickname. See *Domination Arabe*, 107–8.

PART THREE: CASE STUDIES

Revolutionaries and the Path to Revolution that Might Have Been

III

PROPOSED TURNING POINTS IN THE HISTORY OF ᶜABBĀSID RESISTANCE: IBRĀHĪM AL-IMĀM AND THE PILGRIMAGES OF 125 AND 126 A.H.

> This profligate of theirs [al-Walīd] wil be killed and his murderer will, in turn, enjoy rule but for a short period until he dies. Then their brutality [i.e., the Umayyads] will turn against them and rule will be taken from them. At that time there wil be internal dissension and the region [i.e., Khurāsān] will rise up in revolt.
>
> Ibrāhīm al-Imām

> Verily the murder of al-Walīd will be one of the critical turning points of Umayyad rule. then will come tribal strife in Khurāsān. . . the Khārijites [will also revolt]. Next will come sweeping pestilence and then the earthquake.
>
> Bukayr b. Māhān

Seen from the later perspective of ᶜAbbāsid apologists, the rise of the new dynasty was nothing less than the expected fulfillment of prophecies deeply rooted in the historic past. The emergence of the Banū ᶜAbbās was therefore inevitable, and for those skilled at recognizing the signs embedded in the apocalyptic visions, it should have been entirely predictable. It would appear, however, that contemporaries of the long clandestine struggle were less certain about political developments. Given the resilience of Umayyad power, the revolutionary agents of the Banū ᶜAbbās were frustrated by constraints placed upon them by a cautious leadership and also divided over a proper course of action. In truth, the transformation of the ᶜAbbāsid *daᶜwah* into a militant movement was a slow and sometimes painful process which began only about the year 120 A.H. Even then, each halting step toward militancy was grudgingly conceded to activist elements. A close reading of the sources reveals that the path to victory over the Banū Umayyah was neither assured, nor even planned in detail, until the open revolt was fully underway. That is to say, the ᶜAbbāsid leadership took no decisive action and had no clear blueprint for victory until some three decades after Muḥammad b. ᶜAlī first embraced the revolutionary cause.[1]

The lengthy delay in challenging the Umayyad regime was dictated by the continuing weakness of the revolutionary movement. The transfer of ᶜAlī b. Abī Ṭālib's authority from his childless grandson, Abū Hāshim, to the latter's Abbāsid kinsman, Muḥammad b. ᶜAlī, gave the ᶜAbbāsid a claim to legitimacy and some measure of support among the Hāshimīyah. But this following, which was rooted in al-Kūfah, represented a parochial splinter group, merely one of many factions seeking an end to Umayyad rule.[2] The early acquisition of a following in Khurāsān expanded the geographical scope of the ᶜAbbāsid effort, but it did not seriously enhance the patriarch's ability to promote an insurrection against the regional authorities, let alone confront the battle-tested armies of the reigning dynasty.[3] Moreover, the support for the ᶜAbbāsids in Khurāsān was highly problematic.[4] Relations between the eastern provinces and the other revolutionary centers became strained when Khidāsh, the head of the ᶜAbbāsid mission to Naysābūr turned out to be an ᶜAlid sympathizer with a dangerously high political profile. The tension persisted after he was killed in 118 A.H., an action which the ᶜAbbāsids may have instigated, if they were not, indeed, more directly involved.[5] Be that as it may, any consideration of a premature revolt in Khurāsān, and/or an ᶜAlid alternative to the ᶜAbbāsid leadership, would have had a chilling effect on the close circle of conspirators that surrounded the patriarch.

The ᶜAbbāsids certainly had cause to worry when the Khurāsānīs sent an important emissary to Muḥammad b. ᶜAlī in 120 A.H.[6] Sulaymān b. Kathīr, an early convert to the ᶜAbbāsid cause, had been chosen to express their concern about the Khidāsh affair and to elicit the patriarch's response to their grievances. The latter cursed the dead Khidāsh and those who subscribed to his views, and sent Sulaymān back to his native province with a sealed letter.[7] When the Khurāsānīs broke the seal, they discovered a document that contained only the salutation, "In the name of God the Compassionate and Merciful." The absence of any text was meant to indicate that no explanation was necessary, for Khidāsh's orders had contravened the imām's wishes, and that response made them swallow hard. It appears that Muḥammad b. ᶜAlī had ruffled their feathers because when, later that year, he sent the Kūfan revolutionary Bukayr b. Māhān to deal with them, the Khurāsānīs treated the patriarch's messenger curtly, forcing him to return empty-handed. Bukayr b. Māhān, a most logical choice to negotiate with the Khurāsānīs, was not

[1] The gist of this argument is suggested by Sharon throughout "ᶜAlīyat" and by Nagel in his *Untersuchungen*, esp. 63–70, 131ff.

[2] See Sharon, "Alīyat," 17–83, esp. 36–43, 75–83.

[3] Ibid., 164–76.

[4] Ibid., 84–116, esp. 92–93.

[5] Ibid., 91–105; *EI*[2] s.v. Khidāsh.

[6] Ṭabarī, II/3: 1639–40; *Akhbār*, 208ff.

[7] Ibid., 1640. *Akhbār*, 212–13 indicates that he sent letters along with Bukayr.

one to be turned aside so easily. His considerable experience in the region went back some twenty years earlier when he converted many leading figures of the revolutionary movement to the ᶜAbbāsid cause.[8] It was no doubt expected that he would be able to put his experience and contacts to good use on behalf of Muḥammad b. ᶜAlī. Seen in this light, Bukayr's initial difficulties may be taken as an indication of how sensitive the ᶜAbbāsid position was in the wake of Khidāsh's death. Undaunted, however, Bukayr came to Khurāsān once more, this time carrying a staff for each revolutionary. He thus indicated, in symbolic fashion, that they were all the imām's servants and were obliged to comply with his wishes. At this, the Khurāsānīs returned to the fold repentant. The chronicler indicates nothing more of these deliberations but one may surmise from another source that before agreeing to Bukayr's overtures (on behalf of the imām) the Khurāsānīs had forced him to review policy and consider changes in the structure and operation of the eastern station, changes which suggested a more active policy of resistance.

A. BUKAYR AND THE CONCLAVE OF 120 A.H.

The most detailed description of Bukayr's delicate mission in 120 A.H. is found in the *Akhbār al-dawlah*.[9] No date is given for the events described, but it is stated that Bukayr gathered a group of revolutionaries (*al-shīᶜah*) at the residence of Sulaymān b. Kathīr "when Khurāsān was thrown into disarray [*lammā iḍṭaraba amr Khurāsān*]." Although this expression, or some variation of it, is often used to indicate the outbreak of tribal warfare in the province, a cataclysmic occurrence which took place in 126,[10] the details of the account, as well as its position in the narrative, are more suited to an earlier event. As it is, the *Akhbār al-dawlah* reports elsewhere that Bukayr was thrown into prison when he was about to leave al-Kūfah for the eastern centers, seemingly in 126 A.H., and that this projected mission was

[8] The list of those received by Bukayr as new converts includes: Mālik b. al-Haytham, ᶜAmr b. Aᶜyan, Ziyād b. Ṣāliḥ, Ṭalḥah b. Zurayq, Abū al-Najm, Khālid b. Ibrāhīm, ᶜAlāʾ b. al-Ḥārith, and unnamed others from the Khuzāᶜah. Some of these had been brought to him by Sulaymān b. Kathīr, who along with Yazīd b. Hunayd and Abū ᶜUbaydah Qays b. al-Sarī al-Muslī were the earliest recruits of the revolutionary movement in Khurāsān. See *Akhbār*, 201–2; Anonymous, 252a. Note Ṭabarī, *Annales*, II/3: 1358 *sub anno* 100 discusses the origins of the ᶜAbbāsid *daᶜwah* in Khurāsān and indicates that Muḥammad b. ᶜAlī sent Abū ᶜIkrimah, Muḥammad b. Khunays and Ḥayyān al-ᶜAṭṭār to Khurāsān. These three recruited a host of Khurāsānīs to the cause. A list of recruits was sent to the patriarch who chose twelve agents (*naqīb*) from among them. It would appear, however, that Ṭabarī confuses two different historic moments. The appearance of Abū ᶜIkrimah in the region occurred only several years later. See Azdī, 26, *sub anno* 107; *Akhbār*, 203ff. explicitly states that Abū ᶜIkrimah followed Bukayr b. Māhān and that the latter had already converted the leading figures in Khurāsān. See also Chapter II, n. 35.

[9] *Akhbār*, 213ff.

[10] See for example, Ṭabarī, II/3: 1825, *sub anno* 126. On the breakdown of Umayyad rule in Khurāsān and its effect on ᶜAbbāsid thinking, see text above.

subsequently undertaken by a lieutenant, Abū Salamah al-Khallāl. Bukayr remained incarcerated in an Iraqi prison until the latter returned and released him by paying off his debts.[11] The ubiquitous Kūfan was surely a man of many accomplishments, but the ability to appear in two distant places simultaneously was beyond even him. The aforementioned text undoubtedly refers to a previous episode, namely Bukayr's earlier trip to the east when the ᶜAbbāsid movement was in disarray following the death of Khidāsh.

As reported in the *Akhbār al-dawlah*, Bukayr, relying on allusions to the past, reconstituted the revolutionary apparatus and created the climate for a more active challenge to Umayyad rule. His meeting with the Khurāsānīs clearly recalls Ibn Isḥāq's description of the Prophet's negotiations with the Medinese at the second (conclave of) al-ᶜAqabah,[12] an historic meeting which led to the hijrah and paved the way for armed conflict against the Umayyad forebears, the oligarchs of Quraysh. A first gathering between Muḥammad and twelve Medinese had taken place the previous year in A.D. 621, when the latter, who were visiting Mecca, pledged allegiance to the Prophet according to an oath that merely invoked broad moral principles (*bayᶜat al-nisāᵓ*).[13] During the pilgrimage of the following year, the Medinese, now numbering some seventy individuals, again met with the Prophet at the wooded area of al-ᶜAqabah. This later meeting, which reportedly was conducted amidst great secrecy, focused on a second oath which explicitly bound the Medinese to the Prophet's cause. Serving as his nephew's spokesman, the Prophet's uncle, al-ᶜAbbās (the great-grandfather of Muḥammad b. ᶜAlī) asks the visitors to make a choice between a more specific commitment to his nephew or severing negotiations. When the Prophet, in turn, asks for their protection, the leader of the Medinese, stressing his people's long and meritorious service in combat, agrees enthusiastically.[14]

According to tradition, this agreement heralded a major change in the policies of the Islamic community. Before the second meeting at al-ᶜAqabah, God had not given the Prophet permission to fight or shed blood. He was thus ordered to endure insults and ignore provocations. His enemies, the oligarchs of Quraysh, persecuted his followers, causing some to abandon their faith and others to choose exile. All this was now changed. The second oath taken by the Medinese was not a restatement of broad moral principles, it was a pledge of war (*bayᶜat al-ḥarb*). God had finally given the Prophet permission to enter into combat, and his Medinese supporters (*anṣār*) were enjoined to help him in this effort, regardless of circumstances.[15]

Abū al-Haytham al-Tayyihān, one of the Medinese, interrupts the proceedings and questions the Prophet about his (that is, Muḥammad's) commitment.[16] He points out that, in answering Muḥammad's call, his people would have to sever their

[11] *Akhbār*, 247–49; also Anonymous, 258b.
[12] Ibn Hishām, I/1: 293ff.
[13] Ibid., 288–89.
[14] Ibid., 296.
[15] Ibid., 288, 296–97.
[16] Ibid., 296–97.

ties with others (an analogue to the ᶜAlids?), and wonders whether the Prophet would continue to remain with his new converts after God grants him victory. The Prophet answers that the new oath will be mutually binding, and asks for twelve leaders (*naqīb*, pl. *nuqabā*ᵓ) to take charge of affairs at al-Madīnah. The *nuqabā*ᵓ in turn arranged for Muḥammad's acceptance among their brethren, paving the way for the hijrah, the event that was to change the course of Islamic history. That is, ensconced at al-Madīnah with growing support, the Prophet was soon able to take the offensive against his long standing opponents, the forerunners of the Umayyad dynasts whom his ᶜAbbāsid kinsmen would later seek to replace.

Any similarities between the two series of meetings (i.e., Muḥammad and the Medinese during the pilgrimages of A.D. 621 and 622, and Bukayr and the Khurāsānīs in 120 A.H.) may strike us as entirely coincidental; but the analogy between the Prophet at Mecca, shortly before the hijrah, and the ᶜAbbāsid patriarch a hundred years later was not lost on Bukayr b. Māhān. The Kūfan leader vividly recalled the second meeting at al-ᶜAqabah during his mission to Khurāsān in 120 A.H. Sent by Muḥammad b. ᶜAlī to revitalize support on behalf of the ᶜAbbāsid leadership, Bukayr proposed a revolutionary apparatus that invoked memories of a glorious past.

He spoke to the Khurāsānīs of how the Prophet had chosen twelve leaders (*naqīb*) to organize his following in al-Madīnah. Then Bukayr gave his listeners (as did al-ᶜAbbās for his nephew) the choice of accepting the imām or breaking off the negotiations.[17] Acceptance in this case meant pledging allegiance to Muḥammad b. ᶜAlī and, following a proposal set forth by Bukayr, establishing an organizational structure similar to the one employed by the Prophet. Like the Medinese before them, the Khurāsānīs responded affirmatively and with enthusiasm. A so-called "charter" of the newly formed revolutionary units (which was dictated by Bukayr b. Māhān) thus recalled that "seventy men of the Aws and Khazraj met with the Prophet on the night of al-ᶜAqabah and pledged allegiance to him; whereupon he appointed twelve leaders [*naqīb*] from among them." The charter affirmed that the tradition (*sunnah*) of the Khurāsānīs was surely the *sunnah* of the Prophet.[18]

The apocalyptic significance of Bukayr's formulation has been treated earlier;[19] the concern here is with the organizational model and the role the ᶜAbbasid leadership had earmarked for the Khurāsānīs in 120 A.H. The groups created by Bukayr b. Māhān were distinguished according to size and region. The first unit, which retained primary control of the entire apparatus, consisted of twelve *nuqabā*ᵓ.[20] These were leaders chosen exclusively from among the various agents in Marw, the major revolutionary station in Khurāsān. The preeminent figures were reportedly part of a more inclusive group of seventy that also contained various operatives from other regional centers.[21] It would appear, however, that the cadres from Marw

[17] *Akhbār*, 214–15; also Anonymous, 253b.
[18] Ibid., 215–16; also Anonymous, 253b–54a.
[19] See Chapter II, Section A.
[20] *Akhbār*, 216–17; also Anonymous, 254a.
[21] Ibid., 217–19; also Anonymous, 254a.

exercised the decisive influence in the eastern provinces, for they dominated the larger group, representing in all fifty-two of the seventy constituents. The other subgroups ranged from six people of Nasā, to single representatives from Marw al-Rūdh, Khuwārizm and Āmul. Replacements were also designated should death overtake any of the twelve members of the inner council. Several of the replacements were drawn from the wider list of seventy, but there were also others who were not part of the original group.[22] There was, moreover, confusion as to whether the replacement pool consisted of twelve, twenty or twenty-one agents.[23] Interestingly enough, the replacement list contained a high proportion of relatives, especially sons of the highest ranking agents.[24] In any case, this group also represented the political circles at Marw.

According to the *Akhbār al-dawlah*, there was another group of seventy called "the propagandists [*dāʿī*, pl. *duʿāt*]."[25] The list of this unit contains the names of various *nuqabāʾ*, particularly those coming from regions other than Marw. One has the impression that the *duʿāt* represented a regional organization consisting largely of operatives who were to recruit support for the ʿAbbāsids at the grass roots level. There was in addition still another group called "the propagandists of the propagandists [*duʿāt al-duʿāt*]," a unit of thirty-six members which may have been analogous to the replacement pool of the *nuqabāʾ*.[26]

Although these lists seem to represent the "who's who" of ʿAbbāsid supporters in Khurāsān, they do not indicate the precise activities of the agents. On this matter the chroniclers seem to represent a conspiracy of silence. One may, nevertheless, speculate how the newly-formed revolutionary apparatus in Khurāsān might have differed from its precursor which had been established about the turn of the century, and which also utilized seventy agents, twelve of whom were labeled *nuqabāʾ*.[27] At the least, the reorganization of the cadres in Khurāsān involved a broadening of support for the ʿAbbāsid effort. The creation of the new revolutionary apparatus in 120 A.H. might, therefore, be considered a major turning point; for it transformed the ʿAbbāsid following in the east from yet another conspiratorial splinter group centered around Marw into a growing movement. Under proper circumstances, such an organization might be expected to attract a broadly-based following. No serious challenge to Umayyad rule would have been possible without this widespread support. The size of this expanded following should not be exaggerated, however, for despite Bukayr's efforts, or more correctly because of his concerns, the movement remained, for the time being, small and highly secretive.

[22] These were the so-called *nuẓarāʾ al-nuqabāʾ*. See *Akhbār*, 219–20.

[23] Ibid., 220.

[24] For example, Muḥammad b. Sulayman b. Kathīr, and Ḥumayd and al-Ḥasan b. Qaḥṭabah.

[25] *Akhbār*, 221–22.

[26] Ibid., 222–23.

[27] See Ṭabarī, II/3: 1358, *sub anno* 100 (n. 8), and 1987–88, *sub anno* 130. Note only one of the *naqībs* had a father who was still alive at the time of the revolution.

Given the state of affairs in 120 A.H.,[28] size could be the enemy as well as the ally of the Banū ᶜAbbās. The inclusion of new supporters in an enlarged revolutionary apparatus risked exposing the entire movement. The ᶜAbbāsid leadership therefore enjoined its adherents to practice secrecy and restraint. The Khurāsān agents, however anxious they might have been for more active resistance, were instructed by Bukayr to exercise extreme caution, to use only the most discreet means of communication, and to limit their recruiting to individuals whose trustworthiness was beyond doubt.[29] Changing circumstances may have created pressures which could no longer be denied; nevertheless, Bukayr b. Māhān was hardly empowered to recommend senseless bravado. There is no evidence in the accounts of this meeting that the ᶜAbbāsid operatives were planning an insurrection for the immediate future. For the time, it was sufficient that the Khurāsānīs concentrate on building support. This involved a major organizational effort, but in addition, the eastern stations were asked to contribute substantial wealth to the new imām, thereby creating a central fund for revolutionary activities. Their agreement to all that Bukayr had requested in 120 A.H. was a sign of their good faith and the skill with which the Kūfan revolutionary cultivated his long-standing relationships in the east despite the initial resistance of his colleagues there.

Bukayr's diplomacy thus avoided a rupture that would have dashed ᶜAbbāsid hopes of displacing the Umayyads from power; for Khurāsān turned out to be the linchpin of ᶜAbbāsid policy. This does not imply, however, that problems did not remain. Although the strained relations with Khurāsān may have been eased, the revolutionary cadres operating in the eastern provinces could not be taken for granted. There was no guarantee that the Khurāsānī links to the ᶜAbbāsid family would survive the death of Muḥammad b. ᶜAlī; whatever ties existed between the ᶜAbbāsid patriarch and his distant supporters were highly personal and did not necessarily extend to his offspring. In any event, he appears to have attracted a rather limited following in Khurāsān throughout the course of his career. Under scrutiny, the sources reveal that Muḥammad b. ᶜAlī's reputation in ᶜAbbāsid historiography exceeds his historical role as a revolutionary. His association with Abū Hāshim and the beginnings of ᶜAbbāsid resistance notwithstanding, Muḥammad b. ᶜAlī was a voice of caution, and to all external appearances, a model of restraint. This is, to be sure, a charitable description of the political course which he steered; there were, no doubt, less favorable explanations for thirty years of acquiescence to Umayyad misrule. Nevertheless, when viewed in retrospect, the ᶜAbbāsid patriarch would seem to have had a better grasp of reality than some of his more spirited detractors. The small and highly secretive group organized by him and his agents was not about to proclaim an insurrection, let alone succeed at it, but neither did it draw the attention of the authorities. One might say that the ᶜAbbāsid patriarch was still waiting for the propitious moment to declare his intentions when death overtook him and presented the ᶜAbbāsid movement with a crisis of decision.

[28] Ibn Hishām, I/1: 256.

[29] *Akhbār*, 215.

The death of Muḥammad b. ᶜAlī, together with political upheavals that suddenly emerged in the Umayyad state, created a new set of realities for a new ᶜAbbāsid leadership. The ᶜAbbāsids, now led by Muḥammad's son, Ibrāhīm al-Imām, once again undertook a cautious but discernible shift to a more activist policy. The guidelines for this change were ratified at one or more extraordinary meetings between Ibrāhīm and various representatives of the revolutionary centers. Such as they are, the details of these conclaves, which took place at Mecca, are extremely elusive. What happened is therefore largely a matter of conjecture based, as is often the case, on a series of highly tendentious accounts. And yet, there would seem to be sufficient evidence to reconstruct the agenda, analyze the deliberations, and draw tentative conclusions about the importance of these events. When carefully examined, the meetings and the discussions which preceded them also appear to be major turning points in the history of ᶜAbbāsid resistance; for agreements of a far-reaching nature were concluded by the various revolutionary factions in attendance. These agreements, coming a few years after the earlier and equally important meeting of 120 A.H., continued to transform the ᶜAbbāsid following from a narrowly defined secretive conspiracy into a more broadly based revolutionary apparatus.

Although at first glance the sources seem to describe but a single meeting between the new ᶜAbbāsid patriarch and his following, there is reason to believe that the accounts of a conclave with Ibrāhīm al-Imām in Mecca actually conflate two different events—a meeting in 125 A.H. and a second meeting the following year. This reading of the texts explains some of the overlapping and confusing details. In any case, the purpose of the meeting or meetings was to validate the authority of the new ᶜAbbāsid patriarch and to establish the basis for future policy within the revolutionary movement.

B. MEETING WITH IBRĀHĪM AL-IMĀM

The inherent need for an extraordinary meeting of the revolutionary leadership has been suggesed by M. Sharon in a detailed and thought provoking analysis of the events leading up to the insurrection in Khurāsān.[30] Based largely on an account in the *Akhbār al-dawlah*, he indicates that various ᶜAbbāsid agents, who had been operating in Khurāsān and Iraq, gathered in Mecca to meet with Ibrāhīm al-Imām during the pilgrimage of 125 A.H.[31] As a rule, the city was crowded during the rites of pilgrimage, making it difficult for the authorities to keep track of individuals or small groups. The occasion therefore suited ᶜAbbāsid purposes because the ever-cautious family leadership preferred anonymity to a high profile at this stage of their effort. One could add that there were excellent precedents for establishing secret liaisons during the holy month; Muhammad b. ᶜAlī may have conducted meetings under similar circumstances,[32] and, as previously noted, the Prophet himself negotiated with the Medinese during the pre-Islamic *ḥajj*. The focus of ᶜAbbāsid propaganda,

[30] "ᶜAlīyat," 123ff.

[31] *Akhbār*, 239–41, 253 (no date).

[32] Kūfī, *Futūḥ*, VIII: 154–55; Ṭabarī, II/3: 1769, *sub anno* 125; also Azdi, 53. Ṭabarī, op. cit., 1726–27, *sub anno* 124 indicates that various Khurāsānī agents went to Mecca but gives

with its heavy emphasis on emulating the behavior of the Prophet and his early followers, may cause some to assume that the accounts of this visit with Ibrāhīm are imaginative reconstructions of the past. Their function would have been to legitimize the new ᶜAbbāsid patriarch by linking him to the ancestor whose mantle he coveted. The references to the meeting in Mecca are, however, not mere literary inventions; the period of the pilgrimage was, for obvious reasons, the most convenient time to arrange a secret rendezvous.

For Sharon, the meeting was occasioned by the death of Muḥammad b. ᶜAlī in al-Sharāt one month earlier; the purpose for gathering was to confer with Ibrāhīm, the new imām, to reaffirm the unity of the movement, and apparently to reconcile various viewpoints on how to proceed with the revolution. One has the impression from Sharon's remarks that the Khurāsānī agents may have been particularly anxious for a conclave. He vaguely refers to renewed links between the eastern (Khurāsān) and western (Iraq) centers of the *daᶜwah* following the death of the ᶜAlid pretender Yaḥyā b. Zayd, but offers no explanation for why these events should be linked.[33] One may infer from his comments, however, that the Khurāsānīs had felt the time was now ripe to inaugurate a more activist phase of revolutionary activity. That is, Yaḥyā's death and the total collapse of the revolt originally begun on behalf of his father, Zayd b. ᶜAlī, left a leaderless ᶜAlid constituency that could now be co-opted in favor of the ᶜAbbāsid cause. It is not clear how Yaḥyā's death might have been known to the ᶜAbbāsids at this particular time. According to the account cited by Sharon, news of the ᶜAlid's execution was not received until shortly after the pilgrimage, that is in 126 A.H.[34] One may suppose, however, that the initial failure of the ᶜAlid revolt would have been sufficient to cause a reassessment of revolutionary policy. In any event, the dramatic circumstances occasioned by the death of Muḥammad b. ᶜAlī alone would have required a full discussion by an important cross-section of the revolutionary leadership, thus explaining the reported attendance of powerful agents from the Kūfah center (Abū Salamah and Bukayr b. Māhān) and various other revolutionaries of the highest rank from Khurāsān and Jurjān.[35]

Given the date accepted by Sharon for the death of Muḥammad b. ᶜAlī (the beginning of Dhū al-Qaᶜdah, 125 A.H.), one must conclude that the arrangements for the crucial meeting at Mecca were made and carried out within barely a month. Such a time schedule seems much too restrictive considering the obvious problems of security and the required presence of political agents from widely dispersed geographical regions. One might counter that a meeting had already been set prior to Muḥammad's death and that it was occasioned by important events which had

no indication that they were meeting with Muḥammad b. ᶜAlī. Ibn ᶜAbd Rabbihi, *Iqd*, IV: 477 indicates Khurāsānī's met with Muḥammad b. ᶜAlī but does not mention that the meeting was in Mecca. The other details are, however, consistent with Ṭabarī, 1769.

33 "ᶜAlīyat," 123.

34 *Akhbār*, 242. For a brief description of the Zaydī revolt, see Jafri, *Origins and Development of Shiʾa Islam*, 265ff.

35 *Akhbār*, 240–41 and text above.

occurred that year; however, the *Akhbār al-dawlah* makes it quite clear that the passing of the ᶜAbbāsid patriarch set into motion complex preliminary discussions between the ranking figures of the revolutionary stations. There is, therefore, reason to believe that the event in Mecca was actually preceded by a number of important meetings involving elements of the revolutionary leadership, including conclaves which took place in al-Kūfah and various districts of Khurāsān. However, if this were indeed so, how could these numerous contacts have taken place between the onset of Dhū al-Qaᶜdah (Muḥammad b. ᶜAlī's death) and the pilgrimage rites the following month?

A careful analysis of the *Akhbār al-dawlah* in conjunction with parallel texts indicates that the chronology should be reordered. In this instance, the testimony of the medieval accounts suggests not one, but two possible scenarios of how the ᶜAbbāsid agents assembled in the regional centers of revolutionary activity, and how, following these gatherings in the eastern provinces and al-Kūfah, they met with Ibrāhīm al-Imām in the Ḥijāz. The first scenario sets the meetings in 125 A.H., but it assumes that Muḥammad b. ᶜAlī died the previous year thus providing the necessary time for preliminary negotiations. The second fixes the death of the ᶜAbbāsid patriarch in 125 A.H., but it postpones the meetings until the following year. In either case, there is a time lag of about a year between the passing of the old leader and the formal acceptance of his son as successor. Both versions suggest that the preliminary encounters in al-Kūfah and Khurāsān were of considerable importance. These early gatherings were not chance meetings, but high level conclaves, necessitated not only by death of Muḥammad b. ᶜAlī in al-Sharāt, but also by dramatic developments taking place elsewhere. Leaving aside the complex issue of ᶜAbbāsid succession, these developments would most certainly have called for an urgent review of policy. Circumstances therefore portended serious changes in the future course of the revolutionary movement.

The key to the chronology of these gatherings and the episodes which occasioned them is the date of Muḥammad b. ᶜAlī's death. There is, however, certainly no consensus, let alone universal agreement as to when he died. In fact, the "official" history of the ᶜAbbāsid family preserves a brief entry under the rubric "The Death of Muḥammad b. ᶜAlī," in which three (and allowing for manuscript variants, four) different dates are offered.[36] It is thus reported (anonymously) that the ᶜAbbāsid patriarch died in 122, the very year in which his grandson (the Caliph Muḥammad) al-Mahdī was born,[37] that he died in 124 during the reign of Hishām (reported on the

[36] Ibid., 239; also Anonymous, 256a–b; Balādhurī, *Ansāb*, III: 80; Ibn Ḥazm, *Jamharah*, 20; Ibn Khallikān (DeSlane), IV: 161–62 also gives 126 A.H. for the death of Muḥammad b. ᶜAlī based on Ṭabarī. The latter reports his death, however, *sub anno* 125. See II/3: 1769. He also reports (p. 1727 according to al-Wāqidī) that Muḥammad b. ᶜAlī died in 124 A.H. to add to the confusion. Note that Balādhurī (ibid.) also quotes al-Wāqidī but indicates that the ᶜAbbāsid died in 125.

[37] Balādhurī, *Ansāb*, III: 80 gives this date on the authority of Hishām b. al-Kalbī who indicates that about five years separated Muḥammad b. ᶜAlī's death from that of his father (d. 118 A.H.). See also n. 36.

direct authority of Abū Nuᶜaym), and finally "it is said [*yuqālu*] that he died at the age of sixty in 125 in the place called al-Sharāt which is located in Syria."[38]

One can discount the earliest date. The tradition linking the grandfather, the architect of the ᶜAbbāsid revolution, to his grandson, the future Caliph, is most certainly a literary invention authenticating the line of Muḥammad b. ᶜAlī vis-à-vis other elements within the ruling family. In particular, it speaks against al-Manṣūr's nephew ᶜĪsā b. Mūsā who at one time stood before the Caliph's son Muḥammad al-Mahdī in the line of succession.[39] The death of the patriarch and the concurrent birth of his grandson and namesake is meant to demonstrate the unbroken continuity of the family line, and to establish the Manṣūrid offspring as legitimate successors to the authority originally vested in the Prophet, the most distinguished Muḥammad of them all.[40] It is no coincidence that the closest parallel to the present text is the tradition that ᶜAlī b. ᶜAbdallāh, the father of Muḥammad b. ᶜAlī and great grandfather of al-Mahdī, was born and named by ᶜAlī b. Abī Ṭālib the very day the latter was assassinated, as if to demonstrate to followers of the ᶜAlid cause that by inheriting the name of his distinguished cousin the ᶜAbbāsid relative was destined to transmit the sacred rights to rule, and not the widely heralded descendants of ᶜAlī's line.[41]

On the other hand, there is reason to believe that the middle date (124 A.H.) may be accurate. It fits conveniently with the chronology of a number of events, but more significant, it is entirely consistent with the most detailed account of circumstances following the death of Muḥammad b. ᶜAlī.[42] It is reported that when the ᶜAbbāsid died (at his estate in al-Sharāt), Abū Hāshim (Bukayr b. Māhān), the director of the revolutionary apparatus in al-Kūfah, remained at the family residence for several days with Muḥammad's successor, Ibrāhīm al-Imām. A visibly shaken Bukayr then stopped off at al-Kūfah, once again en route to the eastern provinces on a delicate mission. According to an eyewitness, he was carrying official letters announcing the death of the patriarch and exhorting the faithful on behalf of the new leader. In Jurjān, Bukayr was received by various revolutionary agents who pledged to continue their efforts for the current leadership in accordance with Muḥammad b. ᶜAlī's last will and testament.

He remained in the province as the imām's representative for a period of about two months, an indication, no doubt, that an extensive political effort was required.

[38] Balādhurī, ibid., gives this date on the authority of al-Wāqidī. The latter indicates that he died at the age of 70 shortly before the death of the Umayyad Caliph Yazīd b. al-Walīd. Ibn Khallikān (DeSlane), III: 161–62 indicates that he died at the age of 63 in 126 A.H. (based on Ṭabarī). See n. 36.

[39] See Lassner, *ᶜAbbāsid Rule*, 322.

[40] Note that the patronymic of grandfather and grandson were also identical. See Balādhurī, *Ansāb*, III: 80. The birth of al-Mahdī was also subject to question. Abū al-Yaqẓān indicates that he died at the age of 38, having been born the same year as Muḥammad b. Sulaymān b. ᶜAlī. Since al-Mahdī died in 169 A.H., that would make the date of his birth 131 A.H., which seems a bit late.

[41] See Chapter I, Section A.

[42] *Akhbār*, 240ff. Note Sharon cites this text but assumes that these events occurred in 125 A.H.

Upon leaving, Bukayr instructed the local partisans to send along several representatives so that they might become personally acquainted with Ibrāhīm and directly express their devotion to him. These representatives apparently became part of a larger party that was formed from operatives in Khurāsān and Jurjān, including Qaḥṭabah b. Shabīb, the future commander of the revolutionary armies.[43] The delegation accompanying Bukayr moved westward, and upon arriving in al-Kūfah, received the dramatic news that the Umayyad Caliph Hishām b. ᶜAbd al-Malik had died and had been succeeded by (his nephew) al-Walīd b. Yazīd. The contingent of revolutionaries then remained in Iraq for an undisclosed period of time before setting off for Mecca accompanied by Bukayr's lieutenant, Abū Salamah al-Khallāl. When they finally met with Ibrāhīm in the holy city, they turned over huge sums of money that had been collected on behalf of the movement. According to an anonymous eye-witness, the new ᶜAbbāsid ruler then launched into an emotional speech with apocalyptic overtones.[44] The imām invoked the memory of past martyrs, and although urging caution for the present, he heralded an end to the quiescent stage of revolution in favor of an open revolt against the Umayyads. The target date for the long delayed uprising was announced as the year 130 A.H.

It is clear from this detailed catalogue of events that the meeting in Mecca was the last stage of a rather long process initiated by the imām and coordinated by the Kūfah leadership. There was a visit of several days in al-Sharāt, two months in Jurjān, an undisclosed period of time in Khurāsān, a similar stay in al-Kūfah, and finally an extraordinary meeting in the holy city. The death of Muḥammad b. ᶜAlī reported for Dhū al-Qaᶜdah, 125, simply does not allow time for all of this to transpire. Moreover, the *Akhbār al-dawlah* makes it explicit that upon reaching al-Kūfah, the coterie of revolutionary leaders received word concerning the death of the Umayyad Caliph.[45] Given the supposition that dramatic news travels quickly, the arrival of the ᶜAbbāsid party in Iraq must be fixed around Rabīᶜ II, 125, that is, several months before the date accepted by some authorities for the death of Muḥammad b. ᶜAlī. The contradiction cannot be reconciled at all with the year 125 A.H., but the sequence of events would be entirely consistent had the ᶜAbbāsid patriarch died the previous year in accordance with the tradition cited earlier.

Under ordinary circumstances, the presence of so distinguished a body in al-Kūfah might have called for some discreet gathering. At the least, the Iraqis would have been obliged to show the usual hospitality to the important guests gathered in their midst. But the circumstances in 125 A.H. were hardly ordinary. The death of the Caliph Hishām after twenty years of energetic and efficient rule must have buoyed the hopes of those who sought to replace the house of Umayyah with a dynasty that could properly represent the interests of the broad Islamic community. Apocalyptic visions reflecting ᶜAbbāsid views call attention to Hishām's successor, his nephew al-Walīd II. They indicate in dramatic fashion that his reign would set into motion

[43] See *EI*² s.v. Ḳaḥṭaba b. Shabīb.

[44] *Akhbār*, 241; also Anonymous, 258a. See also text above.

[45] Ibid., 240.

events hastening the collapse of Umayyad rule. In this context, one may cite the inaugural address allegedly given by Ibrāhīm al-Imām before the revolutionary agents in Mecca. After comparing the short years left to the Umayyads with a fleeting dream, the imām reportedly declared: "This profligate of theirs [al-Walīd] will be killed and his murderer will, in turn, enjoy rule but for a short period until he dies. Then their brutality will turn against them and rule will be taken from them. At that time, there will be internal dissension and the region [i.e., Khurāsān] will rise up in revolt [creating the preconditions for a successful ᶜAbbāsid victory]."[46]

If there is a sense of déjà vu about the imām's address, it is because it was undoubtedly composed with the hindsight of having seen critical events in retrospect. Although the final years of Umayyad rule are described here as a projection of future occurrences, they were most certainly an established fact by the time the author of this particular version set his instrument to writing surface. The allusions are unmistakable: al-Walīd's debauchery and political license, his murder at the hands of his successor Yazīd III, the coup that brought the last Umayyad Caliph, Marwān al-Ḥimār, to power, and finally the great tribal wars in Khurāsān that led directly to the ᶜAbbāsid revolt.[47] As did Abū Hāshim and Muḥammad b. ᶜAlī, the newest leader to hold the sacred authority became a vehicle for expressing the sentiments of ᶜAbbāsid propagandists in the post-revolutionary age. The apologist's task was to imbue the ᶜAbbāsid leadership with a martial spirit that seemed conspicuously lacking throughout the clandestine stages of the revolution. It is true that Ibrāhīm also spoke of caution—there was indeed a strong rationale for continuing a cautious policy even at this late date—but the imām's clairvoyance indicated a significant shift in ᶜAbbāsid thinking. The revolutionaries were certainly led to believe that the internal collapse of the Umayyads was finally at hand, and with the dramatic change in government, the indignities long endured would soon give way to a policy of confrontation.

On the other hand, a politically aware observer of al-Walīd's succession might have safely predicted, although not in precise detail, that the immediate, if not long-range, future of Umayyad rule would be trouble plagued. Such a prediction would have required neither the gift of prophecy nor the benefit of a retrospective glance at history. It was no secret that Hishām was forced to recognize the future claims of his nephew despite a preference for his own offspring.[48] Given the nephew's style and flawed understanding of government administration, it could be anticipated that the second al-Walīd's political behavior might lead to civil strife and the breakdown of political authority. To a group of politically astute revolutionaries, the death of the able Hishām could very well have signaled that a new phase of the revolution was now in the offing. At the least, the Caliph's passing would have called for high-level conferences in al-Kūfah and Khurāsān to discuss various strategies for the future. The substance of these discussions would then have been

[46] Ibid., 241; also Anonymous, 258a.

[47] For a survey of these events, see Wellhausen, *Arab Kingdom*, 356–491.

[48] Ibid., 350–52.

passed on to Ibrāhīm al-Imām at a subsequent meeting already scheduled for the Ḥijāz.

The pivotal event upon which this analysis hinges is the change of leadership among the Umayyads. By fixing a date for the conclave in al-Kūfah, as well as establishing a rationale for the meeting, Hishām b. ᶜAbd al-Malik's death becomes the central fact giving credence to a reconstruction of events based on the years 124–125 A.H. And yet, his death also creates certain difficulties which are not easily resolved. There is no question as to when the Umayyad died, so that any concurrent meeting of ᶜAbbāsid agents in al-Kūfah had to take place in Rabīᶜ II, 125. This, however, places the revolutionaries in Iraq a full five months before their meeting with Ibrāhīm al-Imām. Had the group returned to their native provinces after concluding the business in al-Kūfah, they most assuredly could have journeyed unobserved to the Ḥijāz several months later during the season of the pilgrimage. However, the *Akhbār al-dawlah* indicates that after remaining in al-Kūfah for a short time they went directly to Mecca (in order to meet with the new ᶜAbbāsid patriarch). This sequence of events raises certain troublesome questions. How could the movement have functioned with so many important operatives away from their posts for so extended a period of time, and wouldn't there have been a problem in finding suitable cover for their travels? The hectic period immediately preceding the pilgrimage would have disguised their movements, but the time element in this tradition covers a much longer period. It is, of course, possible, if not probable, that the revolutionaries did not travel as a single group, but instead dispersed into smaller units, moving slowly and using circuitous routes to reach a common destination.[49] Nevertheless, the rigid chronology imposed by the death of the Umayyad Caliph and the concurrent arrival of the revolutionary agents in Iraq is a "fact" not comfortably explained.

Moreover, the aforementioned analysis which focuses on 124–125 A.H. is based in large measure on a single text, the version of the *Akhbār al-dawlah*. There are other accounts that appear to chronicle events between the death of Muḥammad b. ᶜAlī and the meeting in Mecca the following year. The closest parallel to the text of the *Akhbār al-dawlah* is a concise report found in Ṭabarī, where the chronicler reveals that (following the death of Muḥammad b. ᶜAlī) Bukayr b. Māhān was sent off to Khurāsān by the new patriarch.[50] His purpose was to announce the passing of the ᶜAbbāsid leader and to make public his last will and testament. Upon reaching Marw, Bukayr gathered the *nuqabā*ᵓ and other agents, and presented them with letters which had been entrusted to him by Ibrāhīm al-Imām. They received the Kūfan, and then turned over to him a fund which had been collected to support revolutionary activities. He in turn brought the accumulated wealth to the new ᶜAbbāsid leader.

While this account is rather sparse when compared with the rich detail of the *Akhbār al-dawlah*, it seems to echo the very developments portrayed by the latter

[49] See *Akhbār*, 241.
[50] *Annales*, II/3:1770.

source. There is, however, one significant difference; Ṭabarī lists these events *sub anno* 126. One may note that he does not appear to be particularly certain of this fact since the report is prefixed with the formula: "According to the opinion of some authorities." Any doubts which may be implied by this formula are understandable; there are a number of traditions describing meetings between ᶜAbbāsid agents and their leader, be it Muḥammad b. ᶜAlī or his son Ibrāhīm, and these accounts which may, or may not, refer to distinct historical moments are often marked by considerable confusion. Nonetheless, if Muḥammad b. ᶜAlī did, in fact, die in 125 A.H., as some sources state, and if the complex arrangements that reportedly followed his death are an accurate reflection of historical events, then the earliest possible date for the meetings at al-Kūfah and Mecca would have been the following year as Ṭabarī indicates.[51]

Admittedly, the later chronology does not provide for a specific event that might have given rise to the alleged meeting at al-Kūfah. There is no single dramatic occurrence like that of Hishām's death which can be linked with the arrival of the *nuqabā*ᵓ in Iraq. Nevertheless, when taken as a whole, the historic developments of 126 A.H. were even more significant for the future course of the revolutionary movement. Contemporaries witnessed the death of al-Walīd, the murder of Yazīd III, the emergence of Marwān al-Ḥimār, the shock after the ᶜAlid Yaḥyā b. Zayd's execution, the beginning of a widespread Khārijite rebellion and, above all, the emergence of civil strife among the armed tribal units of Khurāsān. With the exception of Yaḥyā's death, all these events are allegedly prophesied by Ibrāhīm al-Imām in his meeting with the revolutionaries.[52] If these circumstances did not bode well for the incumbent regime, they presented unusual opportunities for those striving to replace it. The internal breakdown within the Umayyad house increasingly weakened its ability to cope with problems developing on the periphery of its rule. Concurrently, the total collapse of the revolt led by Yaḥyā b. Zayd left a leaderless ᶜAlid constituency. In the uncertain political climate, the ᶜAbbāsid followers might have thought that the leaderless ᶜAlids could be induced to shift their allegiance to the nameless figure eventually identified with the house of al-ᶜAbbās.

The emergence of tribal warfare in Khurāsān was, however, the critical factor in the ᶜAbbāsid challenge to the existing Caliphate.[53] Without the disaffected tribal armies of the east, the revolutionary apparatus lacked the necessary military component to overcome the large and battle-tested loyalist forces of Nubātah b. Hanẓalah and ᶜĀmir b. Ḍubārah. Before 126 A.H., historical realities dictated clandestine operations conducted by small cadres of trusted agents. The changing circumstances still required caution, but at least conditions were now favorable for contemplating future actions of a bold sort. Reflected in the deliberations at Mecca

[51] One would then have to explain how Bukayr b. Māhān would up in prison in 126 A.H. while his lieutenant Abū Salamah went to Khurāsān. See text below.

[52] See n. 47.

[53] See Sharon, "ᶜAlīyat," 138–54.

was the expressed desire for an activist policy that would lead eventually to open revolt.

Which of those two scenarios is the most plausible, the one which suggests that the meeting between Ibrāhīm and the revolutionaries took place following the death of the Caliph Hishām in 125 A.H., or the second, which places the conclave in Mecca in 126 A.H., the year in which Umayyad rule had begun to unravel? One can argue that paradoxically both versions are essentially correct, and that the accounts of a meeting with Ibrāhīm in Mecca actually conflate two different events that occurred in succeeding years. This last reading of the texts explains some of the overlapping and often confusing details. The first meeting would have taken place during the pilgrimage of 125 A.H., a year following the death of Muḥammad b. ᶜAlī and subsequent to Bukayr b. Māhān's mission to Khurāsān. The purpose of the conclave would have been to validate the leadership of the new patriarch, Ibrāhīm al-Imām, and to consolidate organizational support for him. The second meeting, following a format similar to the first, would have been occasioned by political developments of the following year; that is, the internal disorders of the Umayyad state and the concurrent collapse of the ᶜAlid resistance. Faced with what seemed a unique opportunity in 126 A.H., some ᶜAbbāsid agents would no doubt have perceived that the changed political circumstances dictated abandoning the time-honored policy of restraint in favor of an increased resistance. If proposed, such a change in policy was likely to have become the central issue for discussion at the second conclave at Mecca.

C. DEVELOPING AN AGENDA FOR DISCUSSION

The event which paved the way for the meetings with Ibrāhīm was Bukayr b. Māhān's last mission to Khurāsān in 125 A.H. The Kūfan leader was the obvious choice to negotiate with the local agents on behalf of the new imām. He had had considerable experience in the region even before joining the ᶜAbbāsid effort some twenty-five years earlier.[54] More recently, he had served with great distinction as Muḥammad b. ᶜAlī's special emissary to the eastern center. As before, the ᶜAbbāsid family had reason to be pleased with the performance of one of their oldest and most trusted clients. After lengthy discussions the Khurāsānīs were brought into line, and having made their way to Mecca on the pilgrimage of 125 A.H., they expressed their allegiance to Muḥammad b. ᶜAlī's successor.

The obligations reportedly assumed by the revolutionaries in response to Bukayr's urging seem consonant with the events of 125 A.H. rather than those of the following year. The need to pledge allegiance to the new imām was a matter of great urgency following the death of Muḥammad b. ᶜAlī, whose leadership, such as it was, had been in evidence for a quarter of a century. It is hardly possible that recognition of Ibrāhīm's legitimacy should have remained unsettled among the Khurāsānīs for two years, or even one year after the death of his father. Considering the activist mood of the eastern cadres in the past, and the presence of the ᶜAlid, Yaḥyā b. Zayd,

[54] See n. 8.

who fled to the region, it would have been imperative for the new patriarch to form the local revolutionaries into a cohesive group representing ᶜAbbāsid interests before the vacuum of leadership was filled by another—indeed, by a leader who had already declared his revolt against Umayyad rule.

Prior to the emergence of the ᶜAbbāsid regime, the loosely organized revolutionary factions were not divided along rigid ideological lines.[55] Given the exigencies of the moment, they could shift allegiance to any of several worthy candidates from among the Banū Hāshim. Quite obviously, this arrangement became increasingly less suitable as a larger and more cohesive revolutionary movement was required. Any attempt to widen support on behalf of a declared revolutionary leader was therefore certain to cause shifts in the political alignments of the splintered proto-Shīᶜite groups. To hold his following at this critical juncture, the new ᶜAbbāsid imām would have been forced to compete directly with his kinsmen from the house of ᶜAlī b. Abī Ṭālib. The presence of a militant ᶜAlid in Khurāsān was, in this respect, a more serious threat to ᶜAbbāsid leadership than any intervention on the part of the Umayyad authorities. This was made explicitly clear by Bukayr when he journeyed among the revolutionaries in the east.[56]

In the end, the fortuitous execution of Yayḥā b. Zayd in 125 A.H. enabled Ibrāhīm to preserve his hold on the revolutionaries pledged to his father. But the vacuum caused by the death of this potential rival helped shape a second dilemma for the ᶜAbbāsid leadership. The events of the following year, beginning with the news of Yaḥyā's brutal demise, created demands for his revenge and increased pressures for a change in the long honored ᶜAbbāsid policy of restraint. By declaring his militancy, the imām might seize the opportunity to unite the disparate factions supporting the restoration of the Banū Hāshim. Having invested twenty-five years in keeping a low political profile, the ᶜAbbāsid leadership was not about to shift gears without warning. Any important review of current policy would undoubtedly have called for another gathering of the revolutionaries with Ibrāhīm al-Imām, presumably during the pilgrimage of 126 A.H. when government security officers would have been disconcerted by the throngs of visitors to the holy city.

The theory that a second meeting was convened at Mecca in 126 A.H., this time to discuss active resistance, is supported by an account dealing with the messianic black flags of the revolution. The account is framed within an apocalyptic tradition reported on the authority of Abū Hāshim (that is, Bukayr b. Māhān).[57] It describes a conversation between the Kūfan revolutionary and the ᶜAbbāsid patriarch (following

[55] A critical study of these groups has long been a desideratum. In many respects, Wellhausen's, *Die religiös-politischen Oppositionsparteien im alten Islam* continues to remain a standard work a century after its initial appearance. See also M. Hogdson, "How did the early Shīᶜa Become Sectarian?" Azizi, *Domination Arabe*, 90ff. should be read with caution because of his inclination to see Iranian influences everywhere.

[56] *Akhbār*, 230–31; see also Anonymous, 255a.

[57] Note the admonitions of Bukayr b. Māhān about following Yaḥyā who was bound to fail. See *Akhbār*, 242.

the death of Yaḥyā b. Zayd). After announcing a revolt for 130 A.H., the new leader of the ᶜAbbāsid family orders his loyal agent to carry the black battle flags to the various revolutionary stations. The choice of black, which was to become the official color of the revolution and then the dynasty, was deliberate.[58] The account recalls a long history linking black to the Prophet's grandfather (contesting the ancestors of the Umayyads for leadership in Mecca) and ultimately, to young David when he went against Goliath (an analogue to challenging the current Umayyad leadership), and to the army of David the King (once again linking the ᶜAbbāsid revolutionaries to the Banū Isrāʾīl). The Prophet's supporters at al-Madīnah (*anṣār*) also might have covered themselves in black following the battle of Uḥud where they suffered a serious setback (at the hands of the Umayyad forebears), but they were dissuaded from doing so by the angel Gabriel when he indicated to the Prophet that the (latter day) *anṣār* of the ᶜAbbāsids would be the ones to redeem all the sufferings of the past.[59]

Leaving aside the explanatory notes on the significance of color and politics, the account is essentially the reworking of a familiar story; namely, how in 125 A.H. the ᶜAbbāsid patriarch sent Bukayr b. Māhān to Khurāsān to recruit support among key representatives from the various revolutionary stations. There are, however, certain modifications that distinguish this particular account from the aforementioned descriptions of Bukayr's mission. There is no mention here of letters of introduction, nor is there any soliciting of political and financial support for the new leadership—all that is taken for granted. The subject for discussion is the coming insurrection against the Umayyad authorities and the preparations required for it.

As reported here, Bukayr could not complete his mission, for upon returning to al-Kūfah (from the patriarch's estate in al-Sharāt), he was seized by his creditors and thrown into prison.[60] As a result, Abū Salamah, Bukayr's hand-picked successor, carried on in his stead, bringing the black flags to the revolutionary stations in Marw, Jurjān, and eastern Khurāsān (*mā warāʾ al-nahr*).[61] The flags were entrusted to Abū ᶜAwn (Jurjān), who had been acquainted with Muḥammad b. ᶜAlī as well as Ibrāhīm, to Sulaymān b. Kathīr (Marw) and to Mujāshiᶜ b. Ḥārith al-Anṣārī (eastern Khurāsān). The text explicitly states that while in Marw Abū Salamah witnessed the outbreak of tribal conflict in Khurāsān. It also indicates that the murder of the Umayyad Caliph al-Walīd added to the conditions of near anarchy prevailing in the province. Since these were events that clearly occurred in 126 A.H., Abū Salamah's mission can be dated without question. Bukayr had paved the way for the acceptance of Ibrāhīm al-Imām the previous year, and it was now Abū Salamah's mandate to lay the groundwork for more decisive action. In the favorable circumstances that were developing, Abū Salamah expanded the activities of the revolutionary movement,

[58] On the significance of black for the ᶜAbbāsids, see Omar, *ᶜAbbāsīyāt*, 148–54, which is derived from his lengthier article in Arabic "al-Alwān wa dalālatuhā al-siyāsīyah fī al-ᶜaṣr al-ᶜAbbāsī al-awwal," 827–46.

[59] See n. 71.

[60] *Akhbār*, 245.

[61] Ibid., 245, 247–49; also Anonymous, 257b–58a.

setting into motion thereby an irreversible course that was to lead to open revolt four years hence. The Kūfan remained at Marw for four months before returning to his native city. This would seem to confirm what has been suggested on the basis of other accounts; namely, that any serious missions to the east in 125 and 126 A.H. were likely to have been extended visits and not trips of short duration.

Returning to Iraq, Abū Salamah set Bukayr b. Māhān free by redeeming his debts; however, two months after his liberation, the latter became seriously ill and his illness grew progressively worse.[62] According to a report that is an appendage to this account, Bukayr was near death when he was informed of al-Walīd's murder.[63] He rejoiced to the extent that his strength allowed and proclaimed, "O Abū Salamah get on with your work. God has begun the misfortunes of the Banū Umayyah and the deliverance [*faraj*] of the family of the Messenger of God. Indeed, we used to say: Verily, the murder of al-Walīd will be one of the critical turning points of Umayyad rule [*inna qatl al-Walīd aḥad awqātihim*].[64] Then will come the tribal strife in Khurāsān—it has already manifested itself in the east. The Khārijites [will then revolt].[65] Next will come sweeping pestilence and then the earthquake." His voice then trailed off indistinguishably as death overtook him.

Given the apocalyptic thrust of this tradition, the more skeptical reader will be extremely cautious before accepting Bukayr b. Māhān's parting speech as authentic. Since, to the best of our knowledge, the Kūfan died in 127 A.H. (after the second meeting at Mecca), it is hardly likely that news of al-Walīd's murder, an event which took place the previous year, should only have reached him on his deathbed.[66] And even if Bukayr had, indeed, died in 126 A.H., there is no reason why he should not

[62] Ibid., 248–49; also Anonymous, 258a.

[63] Ibid., 249–50; also Anonymous, 258a.

[64] These apocalyptical "turning points" varied with the times. For an early formulation see Balādhurī, *Ansāb*, III: 82 where Muḥammad b. ᶜAlī is credited with the following statement: "There are three turning points for us, the death of the tyrant Yazīd, the passing of one hundred years [*ra's al-miʾah*] and the religious strife [*fatq*] in Ifrīqīyah. At this, the propagandists [*duᶜāt*] will begin to preach on our behalf, then our supporters [*anṣār*] will come from the east until their cavalry reaches the west. . . ." The author then points out that when Yazīd b. Abī Muslim (the governor) of Ifrīqīyah was killed and the Berbers were out of control, Muḥammad b. ᶜAlī sent a man to Khurāsān to propagandize on behalf of the "chosen one from the house of the Prophet." People responded to him, and when they reached 70 in number he made 12 of them *nuqabāʾ*. Yazīd was killed ca. 102 A.H. (see Ṭabarī, II/3: 1435ff.). This tradition therefore reflects the earliest period of ᶜAbbāsid activities when Muḥammad b. ᶜAlī sent Bukayr to Khurāsān about the turn of the century. For changing of interpretations of *ra's al-miʾah* see Chapter II, Section A. See also Nagel, *Untersuchungen*, 125ff.

[65] Following Anonymous, 258a. The *Akhbār*, 250 reads: "Then will come the tribal strife in Khurāsān. The Khārijites have already appeared in the east [*thumma al-ᶜaṣabīyah wa qad badat bi-l-mashriq al-Ḥarūrīyah* correcting *bi-l-Ḥarūrīyah* to *al-Ḥarūrīyah*]. This reading makes no sense, for the troublesome Khārijite revolts of the late 120s were not in the eastern provinces. See Wellhausen, *Arab Kingdom*, 388–90.

[66] See Ṭabarī, II/3: 1916.

have been told of the change in Umayyad leadership while he was in prison, or at the latest when Abū Salamah set him free two months before his last illness. Be that as it may, the sentiment behind his call for action is entirely genuine and must reflect the appraisal of seasoned revolutionaries who witnessed the times.

The dramatic developments of 126 A.H. presented unusual opportunities which were not to be treated casually, for in the absence of a forceful policy, other contenders might seize the initiative and establish their claims to leadership. Despite their apparent lack of support for the ᶜAlid, Yaḥyā b. Zayd, the eastern stations were probably more anxious than the Kūfans to press for an active stance in accordance with their designated role and the favorable conditions which prevailed in Khurāsān. They could be expected to bring their case before the imām and argue it with considerable vigor. It is no small wonder that Bukayr b. Māhān and Abū Salamah spent the good part of two years in the eastern provinces formulating a new policy and laying the groundwork for the full acceptance of Ibrāhīm al-Imām.[67]

At this juncture of the struggle against the Umayyads (125 through 126 A.H.), the options before the ᶜAbbāsid family were both heady and full of risk. The rapidly changing circumstances, however opportune, presented Ibrāhīm with a critical dilemma. On the one hand, there was pressure for a more pronounced revolutionary stance, but on the other, there was the danger that such a policy might give rise to a premature venture resulting in failure. The willingness of the imām's ᶜAlid kinsmen to risk martyrdom was no doubt embarrassing for the ᶜAbbāsid revolutionaries who, in contrast, exhibited a rather low political profile. Nevertheless, the conspicuous failure of the ᶜAlid pretenders fully justified the clandestine strategy opted for by the ᶜAbbāsid leadership. Once control of the Islamic community was attained, it would always be possible to rewrite history and retroactively establish a prominent role for the ᶜAbbāsid imāms and their following.

Political circumstances had forced the ᶜAbbāsids to declare a virtue of patience and to recognize the wisdom of caution, but such didactic messages left a residue of frustration. One of the agents present at the initial meeting with Ibrāhīm in Mecca reportedly asked, "How long will the birds eat the flesh of your family [that is, the family of the Prophet] and how long will their blood be shed? We left Zayd [the ᶜAlid] crucified at al-Kunāsah,[68] and his son [Yaḥyā] driven in flight to the province [Khurāsān]. Fear has enveloped you while the evil house [of Umayyah] continues beyond the point of toleration [*wa ṭālat ᶜalaykum muddat ahl bayt al-sūʾ*]."[69]

So sharply worded a statement drawing attention to the imām's ᶜAlid kinsmen was capable of arousing dangerous passions. By way of response Ibrāhīm launched

[67] Ibid., 1917 would seem to indicate that Abū Salamah also went to Khurāsān in 127 A.H. It was Abū Muslim, however, who was to be the imām's permanent representative among the Khurāsānīs. The notion of a young client having influence over the old revolutionaries in Khurāsān did not go down easily with some of the local agents. See for example *Akhbār*, 271–73.

[68] That is, in al-Kūfah. See Yāqūt, *Muᶜjam*, IV: 307. The author refers specifically to the death of Zayd b. ᶜAlī.

[69] *Akhbār*, 241; also Anonymous, 257a.

into an address filled with familiar apocalyptic overtones: the cruelties of the Umayyads will be answered in kind. The punishment meted out to them will be merciless. Their downfall is indeed inevitable and the time remaining to them is fleeting. The imām's words thus suggested a new and more active policy. Nevertheless, patience was still necessary if the revolution was to be brought to a successful conclusion. Despite his strident rhetoric, Ibrāhīm made it clear that rebellion against the Umayyad oppressors would have to wait several years until 130 A.H. "One cannot oppose that which is ordained for us. . . ."[70]

These particular words are without doubt a literary invention, but they would seem to echo historical circumstances in 125 A.H. Although the revolutionary underground became increasingly restive in Khurāsān, ᶜAbbāsid policy remained essentially cautious. The justification for this sensible course of action is filtered through an account which was ironically designed to emphasize ᶜAbbāsid boldness the following year. The tradition of the battle flags attributed to Bukayr Ibn Māhān links ᶜAbbāsid black to the color of the Prophet (a notion entirely consistent with ᶜAbbāsid propaganda). It also underscores the military preparations for the open revolt and the prediction of its ultimate success. There is, however, an additional message subtly embedded within the text. One recalls that the *anṣār* were inclined to wear black after the Muslim defeat at Uḥud, but they were dissuaded from doing so by the angel Gabriel. As was customary among the Arab tribesmen, the wearing of black was to have signified sentiments associated with calamitous occasions (*maṣāʾib*). God's angel, nevertheless, suggested that the *anṣār* put aside their garments for some future time when the wearing of black would give them strength, and hence victory. When asked about the black battle flags, he remarked that faith was better (for the present) than fragments of iron. There was no need for Gabriel to add that among the Arabs black was considered the color of revenge. Given this convention, the heavenly visitor was asking the *anṣār* to put aside the public expression of their feelings and delay their gratification (until the ᶜAbbāsid revolt).[71]

Such calls for patience could only have given rise to mixed emotions, particularly when the time seemed propitious to redress old grievances. This ambivalence over a proper course of action is seemingly reflected in Bukayr b. Māhān's commentary on the story of the black flags. After recounting the episode of Gabriel and the *anṣār*, the Kūfan exclaimed to a gathering of revolutionary agents, "Calamities [*maṣāʾib*] have continued to follow the family of the Messenger of God. Nevertheless the wearing of black will ultimately be approved of, so that the [revolutionary] factions [*ashyāᶜ*] supporting the family can attain their revenge."[72] The historical echoes preserved in the accounts clearly illustrate the tension produced by the conflicting strategies of boldness and caution, and further suggest that these tensions were a major source of concern for the revolutionary leader.

In their present form, the accounts of the black flags and Ibrāhīm's inaugural address stem from the post-revolutionary period. The specific references to the

[70] Ibid.
[71] Ibid., 247; also Anonymous, 257b.
[72] Ibid.

chronology of the revolt and other events taking place after 126 A.H. leave no doubt that these traditions represent a retrospective glance at history. They are, in fact, consistent with later traditions designed to deflect criticism of the essentially passive role played by the ᶜAbbāsid leadership throughout most of the Umayyad period. Nevertheless, there is no reason to deny that the texts explicated here reflect concerns contemporary with the events they describe. If the ᶜAbbāsids felt compelled to shore up their image at a time when they had solidified their hold on the community of the Faithful, one can readily imagine the pressures the new imām must have felt upon meeting his revolutionary constituents for the first time in 125 A.H., and when he met with them again following the dramatic events of the next year. Taking stock of the situation after the death of Muḥammad b. ᶜAlī, the ᶜAbbāsid leadership decided to play its hand resolutely but not recklessly. This was surely a prudent decision since they had not yet forged a coalition capable of displacing their enemies from power.

The missing elements required by the ᶜAbbāsids were the disaffected tribal armies of Khurāsān. It was, however, still somewhat premature to solicit their support against the Umayyads. The ᶜAbbāsid mission following the alleged meeting of 125 A.H. was therefore limited to the further expansion of the revolutionary cadres. However, an unexpected event in 127 A.H. threatened to overtake the ᶜAbbāsids just as their path to success seemed clear of major obstacles. In the confused political circumstances which then prevailed, ᶜAbdallāh b. Muᶜāwiyah, the great-grandson of ᶜAlī b. Abī Ṭālib's brother Jaᶜfar, led an insurrection against the established authorities.[73] The dangers implicit in a Jaᶜfarid success should have been obvious. This most recent pretender had the support of a splinter group of the Hāshimīyah and could thus claim the authority that had been originally invested with Abū Hāshim b. Muḥammad b. al-Ḥanafīyah. Such a claim, at this time, would have completely undercut the ᶜAbbāsid position.[74] Moreover, the Jaᶜfarid managed to rally the remnants of the old Zaydī following, and succeeded as well in attracting support from the Khārijites, whose defeated armies nevertheless remained intact as fighting units. With this disparate following, ᶜAbdallāh b. Muᶜāwiyah established his hold over a wide geographical area in western Iran.

The ᶜAbbāsids were faced with an obvious dilemma. There was the possibility that the Jaᶜfarid would make inroads among their supporters in Khurāsān. The expansion of the ᶜAbbāsid effort in the east was concurrent with promises of future action. Such promises were required to defuse the pressure that was building up among the various revolutionary factions. ᶜAbdallāh b. Muᶜāwiyah could offer a revolution without plans for delayed gratification. His brave showing against the Umayyads contrasted rather well with the ᶜAbbāsid propensity for extreme caution. The revival of Zayd b. ᶜAlī's following was therefore both an embarrassment and a danger to the ᶜAbbāsid leadership.

The broadening of ᶜAbbāsid support was predicated, in part if not in large measure, on the total collapse of Zayd b. ᶜAlī's revolt. It was no doubt assumed that

[73] See Sharon, "ᶜAlīyat," 194–205.

[74] See Prolegomena, pp. 6ff.

the leaderless ᶜAlid supporters would soon turn to their ᶜAbbāsid kinsmen as a last resort. ᶜAbdallāh b. Muᶜāwiyah's sudden appearance threatened to short-circuit this process. Moreover, the reemergence of the Zaydīs in his camp could only have underscored the rather sheepish role played by the ᶜAbbāsids during Zayd's unsuccessful revolt. Although the new imām was personally outraged, and, no doubt, genuinely so over the fate of Zayd's son Yaḥyā, the ᶜAbbāsid family did nothing to support Yaḥyā's effort, nor that of his father before him.[75] To the contrary, they advised Zayd b. ᶜAlī not to rebel, and when he chose to ignore this good counsel, the ᶜAbbāsid cadres in al-Kūfah discreetly withdrew to the Umayyad administrative center in al-Ḥīrah, lest they become implicated in what they conceived to be a premature and disastrous venture.[76]

With the Jaᶜfarid revolt in full swing, the policy of extreme caution would seem to have run its course. To remain aloof from this most recent ᶜAlid attempt at overthrowing Umayyad rule would have entailed risking the revolutionary apparatus that had been so skillfully cultivated over the last two years. On the other hand, the ᶜAbbāsids were hardly about to declare themselves in favor of the Jaᶜfarid pretender—certainly not with an open display of enthusiasm. They therefore followed a prudent course. Various members of the ᶜAbbāsid family associated themselves with ᶜAbdallāh b. Muᶜāwiyah only to retreat hastily once his ambitions were checked by the Umayyad authorities.[77] In 129 A.H. the rebellion was completely broken and the Jaᶜfarid pretender fled to Khurāsān. The ᶜAbbāsids, who by then had begun the final stages of their own revolution, were not inclined to be saddled with their unsuccessful Jaᶜfarid cousin. Abū Muslim, who had taken charge of revolutionary activities to the east, seized ᶜAbdallāh b. Muᶜāwiyah and then had him executed, thereby giving his ᶜAbbāsid patrons a free field in which to seek rule.

[75] *Akhbār*, 242. To the contrary, the imām's emissary Bukayr b. Māhān warned against joining the ᶜAlids.

[76] Ṭabarī, II/3: 1679, *sub anno* 121.

[77] Sharon, "ᶜAlīyat," 201–5.

IV

THE ORIGINS OF ABŪ MUSLIM AL-KHURĀSĀNĪ: THE SHAPING OF A REVOLUTIONARY TRADITION

> The story of my deeds will serve you better than my pedigree.
>
> Abū Muslim al-Khurāsānī

Among the *dramatis personae* of early ᶜAbbāsid history there is perhaps no figure with a more compelling story than Abū Muslim al-Khurāsānī.[1] Beginning modestly enough as a courier in Iraq, he in turn became the director of the revolutionary apparatus in Marw, the founder of the ᶜAbbāsid army, the architect of the decisive victory over the Umayyads, and governor of Khurāsān and the vast territories to the east. Totally committed to the ᶜAbbāsid family during the revolution, Abū Muslim continued to demonstrate loyalty to his patrons after the formation of the state. From his sinecure in Khurāsān, he relentlessly pursued and eliminated the external enemies of the new order. When an internal crisis broke out within the ruling family, he propped up the shaky regime by supporting the claims of the Caliph al-Manṣūr against the latter's paternal uncle ᶜAbdallāh b. ᶜAlī. Then, at the height of his power and reputation, Abū Muslim became embroiled in a bitter dispute with the ruler whose cause he had recently championed. When the Caliph proposed to settle the issues dividing them, Abū Muslim reluctantly accepted al-Manṣūr's invitation and guarantees of safe conduct, and made his way to the Caliph's court at al-Madāʾin. In this instance discretion would have served the ᶜAbbāsid client better than trust, for upon entering al-Manṣūr's quarters as an honored guest, a disarmed Abū Muslim was read a list of charges against him and was then brutally murdered by a group of hand-picked assassins.[2]

[1] See Moscati, "Studi su Abū Muslim"; R. Frye, "The ᶜAbbāsid Conspiracy and Modern Revolutionary Theory"; and his "The Role of Abū Muslim in the ᶜAbbāsid Revolt"; J. Mélikoff-Sayar, *Abū Muslim le "porte-hache" du Khurassan dans la tradition épique turco-iranienne*; Daniel, *Khurasan Under Abbasid Rule*, 25–125; Cahen, "Points de vue," 295–338; van Vloten, *Opkomst*, 70–131; Wellhausen, *Arab Kingdom*, index, 568. See also Sharon, "ᶜAlīyat," 117–37; Omar, *Caliphate*, 149–83; Lassner, *ᶜAbbāsid Rule*, 36–37, 50–51, 61–68, 103–6, 129–30, 219–20; Nagel, *Untersuchungen*, 125–62, esp. 151–62.

[2] Lassner, *ᶜAbbāsid Rule*, 62–67.

The sum of Abū Muslim's contributions to the ᶜAbbāsid cause and the ironic turn of events that led to his dramatic and unexpected demise helped to create a political profile of extraordinary stature. This was a case, however, where the enormity of the reputation only served to obscure the historical personality; for in death, the real Abū Muslim, already a legend in his own lifetime, gave way to a figure of mythic dimensions. Various accounts describing his origins indicate that he was respectively: free-born and a descendant of Persian nobility from the family of the legendary statesman Buzurjmihr, if not the Emperor himself, or a slave from Khurāsān, or in other accounts Isfahan or Iraq, who was manumitted only after he had begun his service for the ᶜAbbāsid cause. The southern Arab tribes who provided the manpower for the revolutionary army that he shaped might have regarded him as one of their own, for there is a tradition suggesting that Abū Muslim was sired by a Yamanī warrior who died in Qazwīn. On the other hand, Abū Dulāmah, the popular jester of the ᶜAbbāsid court, contemptuously described him as a Kurd, and for those who prefer the more colorful vagaries of history, there are accounts that Abū Muslim claimed that he was the son of Salīṭ, the alleged offspring of the ᶜAbbāsid patriarch, ᶜAbdallāh b. ᶜAbbās. If this confusion were not enough, the leading client of the dynasty did not even have a proper name that could be agreed upon, but was instead generally known by the *nom de guerre*, which consisted solely of a teknonym and pedigree. When asked about his credentials at the outset of the revolution, Abū Muslim replied somewhat tartly, "My deeds will serve you better than my pedigree [*khabarī khayr lakum min nasabī*]."[3] He was in short a man for all peoples and seasons, the very image that a secretive revolutionary or astute public figure would do well to cultivate in any given age. It is, therefore, quite possible that many of the contradictions couching his origins may be as intentional as they are often difficult to analyze.

A. SOCIAL ORIGINS: SLAVE OR FREE[4]

Was he a freeman, or was he the slave of an ᶜIjlī family who was bought by revolutionary agents and later manumitted by the ᶜAbbāsid patriarch to whom he had been given as a gift? According to one account,[5] when asked about his status, Abū Muslim maintained that he was in fact the slave of the man who offered him in sale (*faqad aqarra annahu ᶜabd liman abāᶜahu . . .*). Despite this explicit statement, the would-be purchaser (identified in this text as the Kūfan revolutionary Abū Salamah) had doubts sufficient to launch a thorough investigation. The story behind this inquiry, which includes Abū Muslim's pointed declaration of servitude, is related by Abū Salamah himself. He indicates that at the time of the sale, one of his companions observed somewhat cryptically that the lad just did not appear to be a

[3] Ṭabarī, II/3: 1965.

[4] See Daniel, *Khurasan Under Abbasid Rule*, 100ff. His conclusions are to be treated with caution.

[5] *Akhbār*, 263; see also 266.

slave (*la arā lihādhā al-ghulām hay'at al-ᶜabīd*), meaning by that, or so I would conjecture, that Abū Muslim lacked the mix of characteristics which one associates with slaves, including physical appearance, bearing, social graces and the like—that is, the body language of servitude. He therefore implied, Abū Muslim's own declaration notwithstanding, that the lad might well be free and the legality of the transaction might thus be in question.[6] A subsequent investigation based on testimony taken from the ᶜIjlīs would seem to have allayed Abū Salamah's concern, because Abū Muslim came to serve his new master before the latter gave him to the patriarch, who in turn manumitted Abū Muslim and made him a client of the ᶜAbbāsid family.[7]

Other sources indicate that the ᶜAbbāsid patriarch also sought to verify Abū Muslim's legal status before accepting him as a gift from his current owner or owners. Indeed, one account maintains that the patriarch actually questioned Abū Muslim about his background.[8] On this occasion the young man replied somewhat evasively that he had obligations to no one save the patriarch; that he was in effect the patriarch's client and his alone, for as a Muslim he was the client of the Prophet from whom the ᶜAbbāsid inherited his authority. Or as Abū Muslim graciously put it: *faanā mawlā Rasūl Allāh*, and then *faanā mawlāka idh kunta wārithahu*. Although it is far from certain that Abū Muslim expressed his loyalty in quite these words, they certainly would have been appropriate to the occasion if indeed there ever was such an occasion. Most likely his words are meant to reflect the strength that bonds of clientage had acquired in Arab Islamic society and perhaps to conjure up memories also of Zayd b. Ḥārithah who refused to be returned to his own brother, preferring instead to be the slave and then later, when manumitted, the client of the Prophet. One thing is sure, Abū Muslim's response is formulated to reinforce the legitimacy of the ᶜAbbāsid line by stressing the link between the patriarch and his legator, the Prophet—or, put somewhat differently, between the pristine Islam of an earlier age and the messianic era about to begin with ᶜAbbāsid rule.

From the perspective of ᶜAbbāsid apologetics, the new era of the Banū ᶜAbbās was analogous to the time when God's messenger presided over the Faithful just as the patriarch Muḥammad b. ᶜAlī al-ᶜAbbāsī was considered an analogue to the original Muḥammad, as were indeed all the ᶜAbbāsids who inherited the Prophet's authority. The discriminating reader is thus forced to conclude that in all likelihood the story of this interview between the patriarch and his future client is a creation of the post-revolutionary period when ᶜAbbāsid propagandists stressed the critical issue of dynastic legitimacy and, to no one's surprise, found sufficient evidence to support the claims of the rulers at whose trough they fed. However thoughtfully conceived and elegantly stated, Abū Muslim's reply in this account sheds little light on his

[6] Note according to Dīnawarī, 337, Abū Muslim described himself as having been considered their slave (*faanā kahay'at al-mamlūk lahumā*). That is, the ᶜIjlīs treated him as though he was their slave, but the truth was not so simple.

[7] Ibid., 263–64. The investigation was carried out by ᶜĀṣim b. Yūnus, himself an ᶜIjlī.

[8] Ibid., 254.

background. As they are reported here, his words are designed to sustain the ᶜAbbāsid claims rather than inform the patriarch, or for that matter the reader, of Abū Muslim's real origins.

Be that as it may, the patriarch's concern with Abū Muslim's origins is a theme that is reported as well in texts that are not vehicles for establishing ᶜAbbāsid legitimacy. It seems, therefore, that the question of Abū Muslim's background was not a minor aside, but a matter of extended discussion, albeit a discussion that is yet to be contextualized adequately, or for that matter even noticed as being important.

According to al-Haytham b. ᶜAdī,[9] certain Khurāsānī agents (who had encountered Abū Muslim in al-Kūfah) met with the ᶜAbbāsid patriarch Muḥammad b. ᶜAlī and informed him about a *ghulām* or young lad of exceptional abilities. They extolled his virtues, pointing out that he was uniquely endowed with a combination of intellect and resourcefulness, and no less important, they indicated that he was filled with love for the house of the Prophet, implying that he was anti-Umayyad and potentially pro-ᶜAbbāsid, in short, an ideal recruit for the cause. The patriarch enquired "Free [*ḥurr*] or slave [*ᶜabd*]? They replied, "As for ᶜĪsā b. Maᶜqil the ᶜIjlī (the alleged owner), he claims that he [Abū Muslim] is a slave. As for him [Abū Muslim], he claims to be free." Given the conflicting claims, Muḥammad b. ᶜAlī seems to have chosen a pragmatic approach. He instructed the Khurāsānīs to purchase Abū Muslim and then set him free. As I understand the account, the ᶜAbbāsid is portrayed as having covered himself before the law, purchasing the lad from the alleged owner in case he were a slave belonging to the ᶜIjlī and setting him free in order to grant Abū Muslim the status he claimed while at the same time obtaining the latter's clientage.

In traditional and highly literate societies conflicting accounts often invite efforts at harmonization. What may be an attempt to reconcile the opposing claims of Abū Muslim and his alleged ᶜIjlī owner is found in a story preserved by the *Akhbār al-dawlah*,[10] a text rich in ᶜAbbāsidiana. We are informed on the authority of impeccable informants that Abū Muslim's owner, ᶜĪsā b. Maᶜqil, had been whipped to death while incarcerated in an Umayyad prison, but according to Abū Muslim, this had taken place only after ᶜĪsā stipulated that he, Abū Muslim, was to be set free after ᶜĪsā's death according to a well-known formula of manumission. That is to say Abū Muslim became an *ᶜabd mudabbir* (*faiddaᶜa Abū Muslim anna ᶜĪsā qad dabbarhu*).[11] Seen in this light, Abū Muslim had indeed been ᶜĪsā b. Maᶜqil's slave as the ᶜIjlī had maintained, but with the fortuitous death of his ᶜIjlī master, his present status would have been changed to that of freedman. The text supplies no further comments, nor does it report any witnesses to this alleged promise or act of manumission. These omissions were likely to have been intentional on the part of the harmonizer and designed for the more reflective reader, who would now have

[9] *ᶜIqd*, IV: 477; see also Ṭabarī, II/3: 1769; *FHA*, 182; Azdī, 49–50.

[10] Op. cit., 260.

[11] That is, the ᶜIjlī stipulated that Abū Muslim was to be freed upon his death. Note, however, Ibn Khallikān (DeSlane), III: 13 where the ᶜIjlīs are said to have escaped.

understood why Abū Muslim's status was confused. The one person most capable of verifying his claim to freedom was his former master, and according to this report, he was now deceased, having been most likely executed on short notice. The reader familiar with all of these accounts would probably have understood why in these confused circumstances, the patriarch gave orders to deal with Abū Muslim as he did—that is, to purchase him (presumably from the heirs) should there be any confusion as to his status, and then to set him free, thus establishing bonds of clientage between the lad and the patriarch.

The conflicting views of Abū Muslim's legal status were, however, not so easily dismissed. Leaving aside still other reports which indicate that the ᶜIjlī made his way to freedom and was not executed, in which case Abū Muslim could not have been manumitted as an *ᶜabd mudabbir*, the basis of this proposed harmonization is completely undercut by a close variant of al-Haytham b. ᶜAdī's account. Responding to the patriarch's query, "free or slave," the Khurāsānīs reportedly answered, "As to the family of Ibn Maᶜqil, they claim he belongs to them. As for him, he claims to be *free and free born* [ḥurr wa ibn ḥurr]."[12]

According to Islamic law, legal status is largely a matter of birth. If Abū Muslim were indeed a freeborn Muslim, there would have been no way the ᶜIjlīs could have acquired him as a slave, and therefore no way he could have been sold to Abū Salamah or the Khurāsānīs, or later presented as a gift to the ᶜAbbāsid patriarch. For no freeborn Muslim could be reduced to servitude. In any event, this would have been impossible according to the law which was later systematized. The composite picture derived from the traditions of Abū Muslim's birth is therefore particularly significant for determining his status.

Despite differences of detail, the various reports are centered on a particular theme; he was in all accounts a posthumous child. A tradition based on anonymous authorities relates that Abū Muslim's father was (an unbeliever?) from among the non-Arabs of Isfahan (*kāna min ᶜulūj Iṣbāhān*).[13] There is a strong presumption that both father and mother were already dead when the child was but an infant, because he was reportedly raised by his maternal grandfather. The two originally lived on the estate of a man of the Khuzāᶜah, but, oppressed by heavy taxation, they fled and sought refuge with Idrīs b. Maᶜqil, the ᶜIjlī (whereupon the stage was set for Abū Muslim's odyssey into the revolutionary cause). A second and very different account reports that his mother was a non-Arab slave who died in childbirth after having been sold by her Arab owner, a certain ᶜUthmān b. Yasār, in order to cover debts amounting to 800 dirhams.[14] The girl was reported to have been pregnant at the time

[12] Kūfī, *Futūḥ*, VIII: 154.

[13] *Akhbār*, 263.

[14] The mother's name is given in various accounts as Washīqah. There is no agreement as to his name or that of his father. The following is maintained: that Abū Muslim was 1) ᶜAbd al-Raḥmān b. Muslim or ᶜAbd al-Raḥmān b. ᶜUthmān; 2) Ibrāhīm b. ᶜUthmān, but he changed it to ᶜAbd al-Raḥmān at the desire of Ibrāhīm al-Imām in order to disguise his identity. The story is probably apocryphal but it reflects the ᶜAbbāsid concern for secrecy

of the transfer, although both parties to the transaction were unaware of this. Upon discovering her condition, the new owner, ᶜĪsā b. Maᶜqil, an ᶜIjlī kinsman of Ibn Yasār, placed her under his wing, prohibiting anyone from having intercourse with her. The original owner, ᶜUthmān b. Yasār, apparently died before the child was born, the mother followed him in death during her delivery, and the orphaned child, a boy, was subsequently raised among the Banū Maᶜqil.[15]

In contrast, a different and more elaborate version of these last events[16] indicates that Idrīs b. Maᶜqil (the brother of ᶜĪsā) met a Yamanī warrior following the rites of pilgrimage. The latter, who was enroute to the frontier in order to serve as a *ghāzī* for the faith, was accompanied by a slave girl (*jāriyah*) who attended to his needs. Idrīs escorted them until they reached Qirmasīn, at which point the Yamanī became seriously ill. The Ijlī extended his hospitality, offering the warrior a home during the period of his expected convalescence; the latter accepted and remained with Idrīs b. Maᶜqil until he was fully recovered. The honored guest, who was now short of funds and required some 700 dirhams, proposed to leave his servant behind as a surety (*rahn*) for that amount.[17] Idrīs b. Maᶜqil indicated that he was prepared to lend him the money without taking the slave girl, of whom he had no need in any case. Nevertheless, he finally agreed to accept the proposed arrangement, and the girl remained behind with the Banū Maᶜqil. It was subsequently discovered that the servant was pregnant. To complicate matters, news arrived from the frontier that the Yamanī had perished, and the woman joined him in death upon giving birth to a son who was later called Abū Muslim. The orphaned child was entrusted to a family serving the ᶜIjlīs who raised him as foster parents until he reached his majority.

When viewed *in toto* the contradictory stories of Abū Muslim's connection to the ᶜIjlīs do not seem reconcilable. One is thus obliged to ask whether the

---

during the clandestine stages of the revolution; 3) Ibrāhīm, but he adopted the name of his teacher, one Abū Muslim ᶜAbd al-Raḥmān b. Muslim; 4) Ibrāhīm b. Khatkān (Khayyakān?); 5) Abū Muslim was called Salm; 6) Zādhān b. Murmuz was his father. See *Akhbār*, 225, 255, 257; Balādhurī, *Ansāb*, III: 85, 120; Ibn Khallikān (DeSlane), III: 130; Khaṭīb, *Taʾrīkh Baghdād*, X: 207; Ibn Ḥazm, *Jamharah*, 20.

[15] *Akhbār*, 257ff. A later and much embellished account of this tradition is found in Ibn Khallikān (DeSlane), III: 130. The author indicates that Abū Muslim's father was a property holder, that he exported cattle to al-Kūfah, and that he was a tax farmer. Unable to meet his quota, he fled the authorities, taking with him a slave called Washīqah whom he had purchased in al-Kūfah. En route to Ādharbayjān, he had a dream that a fire came from his loins and shot up to the sky, illuminating the horizon until it fell to the east. He told this dream to ᶜĪsā b. Maᶜqil who predicted that the slave would give birth to a boy. The troubled father-to-be went to Ādharbayjān where he died. The girl gave birth to Abū Muslim, and he was subsequently raised by ᶜĪsā. The apocalyptic dream, with its reference to Abū Muslim leading the revolt against the Umayyads in the east, indicates this account to be a later development of the tradition.

[16] *Akhbār*, 263–65, based on the testimony of ᶜĪsā b. Idrīs b. Maᶜqil in response to a query of the imām concerning Abū Muslim's origins.

[17] Note that Abū Muslim was reportedly sold for an equal sum before being given as a gift to Ibrāhīm al-Imām. See Balādhurī, *Ansāb*, III: 20.

contradictions are intentional or simply the result of speculation induced by faded historical memories of perhaps the most enigmatic character in all of early Islamic history. And, related to that, what do these traditions ultimately tell us, if anything, about Abū Muslim's legal status?

In the version of Abū Muslim's birth where he is described as the presumed son of a Yamanite *ghāzī*, there is an oblique suggestion that he inherited the religious purpose and martial spirit of his mother's owner as well as a direct link to the Yaman, whose tribal armies Abū Muslim later co-opted to the ᶜAbbāsid cause. Needless to say, these were more impressive credentials than having been sired by a local debtor unable to meet his financial obligations. Moreover, a link to the Yaman, even if it were based on an invented genealogy, would have been useful to Abū Muslim during his delicate negotiations with the various tribal groups in Khurāsān. Historians familiar with the tendentiousness of ᶜAbbāsid historiography may well wonder whether the story of the Yamanī connection may echo an actual attempt by Abū Muslim to ingratiate himself with the tribesmen who served as the backbone of the newly formed ᶜAbbāsid armies or, in any case, an attempt by later writers to endow him with credentials that were worthy of these connections and more generally of his historic mission organizing the revolt against Umayyad rule.

It would appear, however, that there is more to these accounts than ᶜAbbāsid apologetics. Moving from an educated guess to rank speculation, one almost has the feeling that the reports of Abū Muslim's birth may have been literary inventions which explore the finer points of family law as it then pertained to offspring born of concubines. Focusing on a well-known figure about whom people knew little but talked a great deal, various authorities might have woven fact and fiction to explore a wide variety of legal questions. These would have been the kinds of questions prompted by the alleged social upheaval that followed the ᶜAbbāsid revolution.

Scholars currently interested in the historical development of Islamic law are apt to raise a number of questions. Could the status of the slave mother have been clouded by the peculiar circumstances of her pregnancy and the inopportune death of her owner? Did the report that establishes her as a surety to cover her master's debts serve to obscure the issues still further? In any case it is not the woman's status that is the main concern here, but that of her son. The thrust of these stories concerning Abū Mūslim's birth would seem to indicate that he could well have been freeborn.[18]

In the two major accounts of his birth there is a strong presumption that the original owner was responsible for paternity; one source explicitly states that ᶜUthmān b. Yasār had sired Abū Muslim and several other children.[19] Regardless of who the father was made out to be, he (or the grandfather) is pictured as freely

[18] There is, however, the brief note in Balādhurī, *Ansāb*, III: 120 which indicates that Abū Muslim's father was a servant of the family of (*min khawal*) Ibn Maᶜqil. The presumption here is that the father could have been a slave. In this instance, the statement of Abū Muslim's humble origins may be seen as a literary device to give prominence to his self-estimate of future greatness which immediately follows in the account. In general, the sources recognize that there is confusion about his social status. See, for example, Ibn Ṭabāṭabā, 139.

[19] *Akhbār*, 258.

dispensing with property and/or paying taxes, acts that are presumptive signs of a free man.[20] Abū Muslim's claim that he was "free and free born [*ḥurr wa ibn ḥurr*]" is therefore significant. The acquisition of slaves in medieval Islam was no simple matter, at least according to the jurists.[21] As a rule, the child born to a free Muslim enjoyed the father's status and could not be reduced to servitude. The evidence, such as it is, would therefore seem to indicate that Abū Muslim could not have been legally acquired by the ᶜIjlīs, nor could he have been resold subsequently to some operative or operatives of the revolutionary movement.

Might the law prescribed by the jurists have been circumvented under unusual circumstances, particularly in the early period about which relatively little is known? Might earlier practices have been at variance with the law later formulated? The earliest legal discussions which survive in writing describe practices much more diverse than the later systemization of law seems to allow. The circumstances that reportedly surrounded Abū Muslim's birth were certainly peculiar. Given no father, no mother, and possibly a clouded question of paternity and ownership, could the real status of the orphaned child have depended on the good graces of the ᶜIjlīs assuming responsibility for him? And, if there were even a doubt as to who owned Abū Muslim or that he were indeed freeborn, would ᶜĪsā b. Maᶜqil have felt free to sell him, and upon discovering Abū Muslim's clouded history, would others have bought him? One supposes that the options available were determined by the efficacy of the law as it was then understood and practiced. In any case, there is no reason to doubt that Abū Muslim served the ᶜIjlīs and then the ᶜAbbāsid revolutionaries in al-Kūfah, and that he was later sent personally to serve the imām as his client.

Some observers may feel that this serpentine discussion of Abū Muslim's legal status has a certain air of preciosity. To all intents and purposes the distinction between categories of freemen and freedmen would have had little bearing on Abū Muslim's service to the ᶜAbbāsid house. Regardless of the law then operative, all the clients of the ruling family were obliged by historical realities to serve their master in perpetuity and in absolute obedience. The execution of Abū Muslim was ample proof of this. No other client of the ᶜAbbāsids commanded such power or inspired such fear as he did, and yet, when the Caliph al-Manṣūr decided to eliminate him, the matter was taken care of with no more than moderate difficulty. This is quite a contrast to the Caliph's dealings with his uncle ᶜAbdallāh b. ᶜAlī, a declared rebel against the regime. ᶜAbdallāh b. ᶜAlī could hardly be characterized as a quixotic figure, but after he was apprehended it took years to create the necessary preconditions that led to his death, and even this death was far less dramatic than tradition leads us to believe.[22] The execution of Abū Muslim, on the other hand, required only that he be lured away from his army contingents; once his death was a fait accompli, it was an easy matter to calm the passions of key personnel through the distribution of favors. A

[20] See also Ibn Khallikān (DeSlane), III: 130.

[21] For a brief survey see *EI*^{2} s.v. ᶜAbd.

[22] See Lassner, "Did al-Manṣūr Murder His Uncle ᶜAbdallāh b. ᶜAlī?" 66–99; essentially = his *ᶜAbbāsid Rule*, 39–57.

client realistically assessing his circumstances understood only too well the difference between acquired membership in the ᶜAbbāsid house and full standing within the family due to blood ties.[23]

B. SOCIAL ORIGINS: ABŪ MUSLIM, THE SON OF SALĪṬ[24]

The distinction between blood ties and ties of clientage calls attention to another tradition of Abū Muslim's origins. Among the various charges brought against him shortly before his death, there is the rather startling revelation that Abū Muslim claimed descent from Salīṭ, the alleged son of the great traditions scholar and ᶜAbbāsid patriarch, ᶜAbdallāh b. ᶜAbbās.[25] The connection between Salīṭ and Abū Muslim, which is limited to a few terse statements, reflects in every sense the marriage of two enigmas; for the story of ᶜAbdallāh b. ᶜAbbās's alleged issue is itself a highly problematic tale which leaves much to be explained in each of its puzzling versions.

According to the *Akhbār al-dawlah*,[26] ᶜAbdallāh had a promiscuous servant girl. Given the opportunity for numerous sexual liaisons the girl was soon with child and eventually gave birth to a son who was named Salīṭ. To be sure, women in this position were at times faced with a rather vexing problem. Having had numerous sexual partners, it was often difficult to determine which of them was the father. In pre-Islamic times, the mother might establish the child's genealogy by choosing any of her partners, in which case it was quite natural to select the most suitable among them. The failure to make such a choice and have it recognized would have compelled the child to bear the name of the mother with all that this implied concerning his social status. During the Islamic period measures were taken to reduce the stigma that might be attached to such offspring and genealogy was therefore determined by the conjugal bed (*al-walad li-l-firāsh*). But as people continued to observe the older practices, problems of personal status could become rather complicated, particularly in families of rank.

The classic example (if not the model for the Salīṭ story) is the case of Ziyād, the alleged son of the Umayyad patriarch, Abū Sufyān.[27] Originally named after ᶜUbayd, the husband of his prostitute mother, Ziyād was later established by trial to have been the legitimate heir to a more prestigious sire. By legal sleight of hand which rested on some rather suspicious testimony, Ziyād b. ᶜUbayd at once became Ziyād b. Abī Sufyān, the half brother of the Caliph Muᶜāwiyah. The new arrangement proved suitable to all concerned. Ziyād acquired a share of Abū Sufyān's legacy, and the Caliph finally succeeded in co-opting this loyal partisan of the ᶜAlid cause,

[23] See Lassner, *ᶜAbbāsid Rule*, 91–115.

[24] See pp. 44ff. in relation to the imprisonment of ᶜAlī b. ᶜAbdallāh b. ᶜAbbās.

[25] Yaᶜqūbī, *Historiae*, II: 441; Ṭabarī, III/1: 114–15; *FHA*, 183, 222–23; Ibn Khallikān (DeSlane), III: 138–39; Ibn Ḥazm, *Jamharah*, 19–20; Balādhurī, *Ansāb*, III: 79, 205ff.; *Akhbār*, 256; Khaṭīb, *Taʾrīkh Baghdād*, X: 209; Ibn Ṭabāṭabā, 139. See also above.

[26] *Akhbār*, 149ff.

[27] Masᶜūdī, *Murūj* (Beirut), III: 6ff.; Balādhurī, *Ansāb*, IVA: 102 (187, 205, 207: Ziyād b. Sumayyah); Ibn Ṭabāṭabā, 109–10; Ṭabarī, II/1: 133; Yaᶜqūbī, *Historiae*, II: 262.

transforming thereby a former enemy into a valuable ally of the Umayyad dynasty. Although in this case the renaming of Ziyād resulted directly from the perceived needs of state policy, the rather dubious legal foundation upon which the trial decision was rendered left a cynical populace referring to Ziyād b. Sumayyah or the more neutral Ziyād b. Abīhi, that is, Ziyād the son of his anonymous father.

The *Akhbār al-dawlah*[28] goes on to indicate that throughout ᶜAbdallāh's life Salīṭ was known by the name of his mother. That is to say, ᶜAbdallāh b. ᶜAbbās accepted no responsibility for paternity nor were any such claims brought against him. Only when the ᶜAbbāsid patriarch died did the mother intervene on behalf of her son. Seeking ᶜAbdallāh's inheritance (presumably a share of it) from his designated heir ᶜAlī, she lodged a complaint for Salīṭ with the Umayyad Caliph, al-Walīd b. ᶜAbd al-Malik. The Caliph, who was at odds with ᶜAlī b. ᶜAbdallāh over a delicate family matter,[29] was desirous of having a law rule in favor of the claimant, but the latter was murdered before a final judgment was rendered.

In an account which is generally favorable to the ᶜAbbāsids, the historian Balādhurī tells the story of Salīṭ with some noticeable differences.[30] Whereas the *Akhbār al-dawlah* merely suggests that ᶜAbdallāh was not the father, the second version strongly denies that he bore any responsibility for siring the child. The patriarch, who had intercourse with his servant on but one occasion, had no intention of having a child with her—the presumption here, or so it would seem, is that ᶜAbdallāh utilized some method of contraception. Nevertheless, taking full advantage of an opportunity suddenly created, the girl became pregnant by one of the local slaves.

Although unstated, the rationale behind this action seems reasonably clear. Were she to give birth to a son, and were the ᶜAbbāsid patriarch to have a notion that the child was his, he might recognize the boy, thus entitling him to a share of ᶜAbdallāh's inheritance. According to the prescription of the law, the mother would remain in ᶜAbdallāh's household until the patriarch's death, when she would be manumitted. If all this were to happen, she might be able to wield considerable influence among the women of the ᶜAbbāsid household. Given these attractive possibilities, such a scheme would have been considered worth the risk. ᶜAbdallāh b. ᶜAbbās, who was not fooled, castigated his deceitful servant; but despite this, he took in her child, named the boy Salīṭ, and raised him as a slave. The latter, who displayed sterling qualities as he grew into manhood, served the patriarch during their visits to Syria (where Salīṭ was presumably brought to the rulling court). In time the boy became a favorite of the Umayyads, and more particularly he was welcomed by the Caliph al-Walīd. Thus when Salīṭ falsely claimed that he was, in fact, the son of ᶜAbdallāh b. ᶜAbbās, the Umayyad ruler urged him on in contesting ᶜAlī for the ᶜAbbāsid family legacy.

[28] *Akhbār*, 149.

[29] See pp. 41ff.

[30] *Ansāb*, III: 79ff.; see also Ibn Ṭabāṭabā, 139–40.

According to Yaᶜqūbī,[31] whose version of these events presents still another story, ᶜAbdallāh b. ᶜAbbās emphatically denied paternity (*anā aᶜlamu annahu laysa minnī*), but out of the kindness of his heart he instructed his heir ᶜAlī to set aside a portion of the inheritance for Salīṭ. There was, however, a strict provision that the latter should not marry. There is no explanation for this arrangement, but the reason behind it seems self-evident. Salīṭ was not to produce any offspring that might complicate the lines of succession and inheritance within the ᶜAbbāsid family; for as the author casually points out, at this juncture of his life, the future ᶜAbbāsid patriarch was himself without children (meaning he had no one to whom he could leave a legacy). It was only after he was exiled to al-Ḥumaymah following Salīṭ's death that ᶜAlī b. ᶜAbdallāh produced over twenty male descendants. The fact that most of them died while ᶜAlī still lived is an indication of how delicate the question of inheritance could have become.[32] Be that as it may, ᶜAlī had no intention of allowing Salīṭ an honored place among the ᶜAbbāsids. Unlike al-Walīd's kinsman, Muᶜāwiyah b. Abī Sufyān, the new patriarch had neither the intention nor the need to share his genealogy with someone who was not party to it. Salīṭ was invited to ᶜAlī's estate where he died amid mysterious circumstances that indicate foul play.

Several questions come to mind. Why did Abū Muslim claim that he was the son of Salīṭ? What advantage was there to being the offspring of a man of questionable ancestry who had been at odds with ᶜAbbāsid leadership and who had been murdered for it? And if, as seems likely, there is no substance to the story of Abū Muslim's claim, what need was there to forge such a tradition and place it judiciously among the charges brought against him?

It is well to remember that ᶜAbdallāh b. ᶜAbbās was not simply a first cousin of the Prophet and a great traditions scholar. To be sure, the detailed treatment of ᶜAbdallāh's life in ᶜAbbāsid family history reflects the vast number of stories circulating about him as opposed to his less well known successors. But this alone would not explain why roughly one third of the *Akhbār al-dawlah* is devoted to his career.[33] ᶜAbdallāh b. ᶜAbbās's high profile in this "official" tract is clearly a function of his importance to later ᶜAbbāsid claims. An evolving ᶜAbbāsid doctrine maintained that ᶜAbdallāh b. ᶜAbbās was a critical link in the chain of those who possessed the prerequisites for sacred rule. As a child he reportedly received the Prophet's authority and the esoteric knowledge required to guide the community of the Faithful. Moreover, it is implied that he was destined to transmit this authority to his offspring, for he was recognized, and even by ᶜAlī b. Abī Ṭālib, as siring the "Father of [future] Rulers," a not so subtle prediction of the dynasty to be founded by the ᶜAbbāsid's descendants.[34]

After ᶜAbdallāh's death, his youngest son ᶜAlī became the patriarch of the family with all that this implied for events yet to come, and young ᶜAlī, in turn, bequeathed

[31] *Historiae*, II: 347–48.
[32] For a list of ᶜAlī's descendants, see *Akhbār*, 147–48.
[33] Ibid., 25–134.
[34] See p. 40.

the authority to his son Muḥammad, the progenitor of the revolution that overthrew the Umayyad regime. Following the pattern established earlier, three sons of Muḥammad b. ʿAlī, Ibrāhīm (al-Imām), Abū al-ʿAbbās (al-Saffāḥ) and Abū Jaʿjar (al-Manṣūr) were similarly invested with the right to rule.[35] Among those excluded from this chain of authority were the ʿAlid kinsmen of the ʿAbbāsids and, significantly, the other branches of the ruling house. The dynastic ideologues thus made it abundantly clear that any past or future challenges to the line of ʿAbdallāh b. ʿAbbās ran, and would run, counter to a tradition of authority that begins with the Prophet himself.

It is inconceivable that this particular line of succession was clearly articulated before the actual emergence of the ʿAbbāsid dynasty, but for the purposes of the ʿAbbāsid apologists, and our discussion as well, it is sufficient that the stories circulating were regarded as factual by certain political constituencies of the new regime. One may therefore suppose that among various elements of the populace Abū Muslim's alleged claim of descent from Salīṭ gave rise to considerable speculation. From their perspective, Salīṭ's unexpected appearance as a rival heir to the legacy of ʿAbdallāh could very well have threatened the arrangement of family succession. With a case that was likely to be ruled in his favor, Salīṭ might have gone a step further and privately contested ʿAlī's sacred authority as well as the right to his father's possessions. If this were so, Salīṭ could then have passed on this second legacy, or at least the claim of this legacy, to his alleged son Abū Muslim. The latter and not Muḥammad b. ʿAlī and his offspring would therefore have been entrusted with destroying the Umayyad Caliphate and restoring the Prophet's family to its rightful place at the head of the Islamic community.

No single individual inside or outside the ʿAbbāsid family was more closely identified with these last events than Abū Muslim. Muḥammad b. ʿAlī might have been credited with being the progenitor of the revolution, but it was Abū Muslim who coordinated affairs in Khurāsān during the most important phase of the clandestine struggle. And when the ʿAbbāsid revolution was openly declared, it was once again Abū Muslim who skillfully assembled the military apparatus that ended some ninety years of Umayyad hegemony. In effect, it was Abū Muslim who fulfilled the numerous apocalyptic visions which predicted the triumph of the ʿAbbāsids and the onset of the messianic age.[36] If his claimed ancestry to Salīṭ were indeed taken seriously, and if Salīṭ himself had claims that were similarly regarded as authentic, what was to prevent Abū Muslim from formally challenging al-Manṣūr and claiming the Caliphate? As the grandson of ʿAbdallāh b. ʿAbbās he would have been regarded as a blood member of the ruling family and, unlike al-Manṣūr, his activities on behalf of the revolution would have earned him a reputation that was conceived in prophecy and later forged on the anvil of an authentic history.

This imaginative reconstruction of events is not intended to demonstrate that Abū Muslim was actually a descendant of Salīṭ, nor that he claimed that he was, nor

[35] See p. 58.

[36] Some of these visions directly involved him. See for example Ibn Khallikān (DeSlane) III: 130; and the dream of Abū Muslim's mother mentioned above.

that he was a contender for the Caliphate, nor for that matter that the ᶜAbbāsid leadership ever thought he might challenge their rule. It does provide, however, the basis of a subtle argument which explains why al-Manṣūr eliminated the individual most responsible for bringing him and the ᶜAbbāsid family to power. For many apologists of the ᶜAbbāsid cause the treatment meted out to one of their greatest partisans was no doubt a continuing source of embarrassment. When asked by al-Manṣūr to seek peace and settle their differences, an ᶜAlid rebel reportedly said: "What kind of guarantees do you offer me—the likes of which you offered [your captive] Ibn Hubayrah, or [your uncle] ᶜAbdallāh b. ᶜAlī, or [your client] Abū Muslim?"[37]

In each of these cases the historic memories were still vivid; al-Manṣūr had agreed to guarantee safety and then reneged on his initial agreement. Since the rebellious uncle ᶜAbdallāh b. ᶜAlī was a respected blood relative of the ruling family, the Caliph had to be content with placing him under house arrest.[38] On the other hand, Ibn Hubayrah, the last Umayyad governor of Iraq, and Abū Muslim, the first ᶜAbbāsid governor of Khurāsān, were lulled into a false sense of security and were then treacherously murdered in the most brutal fashion. The apologists might have argued that Ibn Hubayrah, who retained a large military force, was a carry-over from the former regime and hence deserved his fate regardless of any guarantees offered him.[39] But what of Abū Muslim? What great crimes of state did he commit that enabled the Caliph to act in so brazen a fashion?

Moreover, the breach of faith represented by Abū Muslim's murder extended beyond the Caliph's client; it affected as well al-Mansūr's nephew and heir apparent, ᶜĪsā b. Mūsā.[40] A long-standing friend of Abū Muslim, ᶜĪsā had personally vouched for his safety during the ill-fated visit to al-Manṣūr's court at al-Madāʾin.[41] In all

[37] The response of Muḥammad b. ᶜAbdallāh al-Maḥḍ during the events of 145 A.H. See Ṭabarī, III/1: 209; *FHA*, 241; Azdī, 158.

[38] See n. 20.

[39] See Ṭabarī, III/1: 66ff., *sub anno* 132. Ironically, it was Abū Muslim who suggested that Ibn Hubayrah was too dangerous and should be killed. Note the negotiations between al-Manṣūr, who served as his brother's representative (i.e., the Caliph al-Saffāḥ), and Ibn Hubayrah were carried on for a long period of time, and many drafts were written before they reached an agreement between them. For the delicate negotiations which led up to Abū Muslim's ill-fated visit to the Caliph's court, see Lassner, *ᶜAbbāsid Rule*, 66–67.

[40] Lassner, op. cit., 50–51.

[41] Ṭabarī, III/1: 112ff., *sub anno* 137; Balādhurī, *Ansāb*, III: 204ff. The meeting presumably took place at one of the ancient cities (al-Madāʾin) situated some 12 miles south of Baghdad along the Tigris. See G. Le Strange, *Lands*, 25, 33–35. Ibn Khallikān (DeSlane), III: 138–39, 140 specifies that Abū Muslim was killed at Rūmiyat al-Madāʾin (Jundīkhusrah). See Yāqūt, *Muᶜjam*, II: 130, 867. Jundīkhusrah was one of the seven cities (*Madāʾin*) built by Sassanian rulers; no specific location indicated. Yāqūt also indicates that Abū Muslim was killed at Jundīkhusrah. See also Balādhurī, *Ansāb*, III: 203. The reference to Rūmiyat al-Madāʾin in Ibn Khallikān's account allows for an additional explanation as to why Abū Muslim accepted the Caliph's invitation despite the seeming danger that faced the governor of Khurāsān. That is, according to the author, Abū Muslim was an avid reader of

probability, the governor of Khurāsān would never have accepted the Caliph's invitation had it not been for the presence of the latter's nephew at court. One account relates that ᶜĪsā attempted to persuade Abū Muslim not to appear before the Caliph without him, the clear presumption being that if al-Manṣūr intended foul play, the presence of the heir apparent would prevent it.[42] When ᶜĪsā tarried, however, Abū Muslim foolishly proceeded by himself and became the victim of the brutal fate that awaited him. A second account of this event indicates that ᶜĪsā b. Mūsā gave his former colleague in arms a verbal commitment of protection.[43] With this understanding, Abū Muslim did not fear to attend his audience with the Caliph, as it was then certain that al-Manṣūr would not betray the word of his would-be successor. The assassination of the recalcitrant governor was, therefore, not simply a question of client-patron relations. By compromising the heir apparent, it directly affected the internal politics of the ᶜAbbāsid house. Al-Manṣūr's distinguished nephew, who does not appear to have been politically ambitious, did not make an issue of how he had been treated by the Caliph; however, ᶜĪsā's failure to protest was most likely based on his instinct for self-preservation, rather than an insensitivity to the murder of his friend and the humiliation which he (ᶜĪsā) had personally sustained.

The Caliph himself could not have emerged untarnished by this sequence of events. That is, his reputation would have suffered if it were generally acknowledged that Abū Muslim was at heart a loyal client of the ruling family and that the conflict between governor and Caliph could have been reconciled short of drastic action. But what if the client claimed blood ties to the descendants of al-ᶜAbbās? The alleged tie to Salīṭ and hence ᶜAbdallāh b. ᶜAbbās would have transformed the Caliph's client into his paternal uncle thereby allowing the populace to believe that Abū Muslim might have been a serious contender for family leadership. Were this his intention, surely the governor of Khurāsān would have had designs on the Caliphate, and with that there would have been no need for al-Manṣūr to honor the guarantees of safe conduct that were extended to his overly ambitious governor. However duplicitous, the murder of Abū Muslim would have been seen in many quarters as entirely justified. When ᶜĪsā b. Mūsā ultimately made his way to the Caliph's tent, it is reported that he first inquired as to the whereabouts of his guest, and he then spoke on Abū Muslim's behalf. The Caliph responded by publicly upbraiding his heir apparent. He called his nephew stupid and pointed out that Abū Muslim was actually

---

apocalyptic works (*malāḥim*) which were then circulating and were widely read. In one of these books, he found a prediction of his own future. He was destined to die in the territory known as Bilād al-Rūm. Thus, when al-Manṣūr invited him to al-Madāʾin, he never suspected that he would meet with foul play. He did not realize that Rūmiyat al-Madāʾin had been intended. Note, Khaṭīb, *Taʾrīkh Baghdād*, X: 209 indicates that Abū Muslim was killed in the (village) Baghdād in 140 A.H., clearly an error.

[42] Ṭabarī, III/1: 112.

[43] Ibid., 114: *taqaddam wa anta fī dhimmatī*. Balādhurī, *Ansāb*, III: 204–5 is even more explicit. Abū Muslim is seen requesting ᶜĪsā's company for he felt evil lurking.

his (ᶜĪsā b. Mūsā's) greatest enemy, a not so subtle implication that Abū Muslim stood between the heir apparent and *his* succession to the Caliphate.[44]

The contention that Abū Muslim might (or indeed did) claim the Caliphate based on his alleged descent from Salīṭ may have served as a convenient explanation for the former's execution; however, this was not a line that could easily be argued by the ᶜAbbāsid, or more correctly by Manṣūrid propagandists. They had to exercise caution so that they did not overstate the case against the Caliph's client. Had they maintained that he actually was a blood relative of the Caliph, it is hardly likely that Abū Muslim could have been treated more harshly than ᶜAbdallāh b. ᶜAlī. The Caliph's paternal uncle had been spared after leading a bloody and dangerous revolt against the regime. Following painstaking negotiations it was agreed that ᶜAbdallāh should be placed in protective custody but nothing more drastic was contemplated. A second uncle who declared against the nascent regime of al-Manṣūr, the long-lived ᶜAbd al-Ṣamad was granted a full pardon and eventually returned to government service.[45] The mild response of the Caliph to the serious challenge of his bold relatives set a pattern that took hold for many years. When faced with internal conflicts, the ruling family consistently attempted to preserve family unity at all costs. It was not until the Caliphate of al-Maᵓmūn (d. 218) that a member of the ᶜAbbāsid household was killed because of state policy.[46]

In any case, the worst that could be said of Abū Muslim was that he was uncooperative and that he contemplated an open challenge to the Caliph's authority at some future time. How then could one explain the disparity between the Caliph's leniency to the paternal uncle who had confronted him on the field of battle, and his brutality to the "uncle" who was yet to throw down the gauntlet? The cruel death of Abū Muslim was in and of itself dramatic proof that he had no blood ties to the ᶜAbbāsid family. Lest any ᶜAbbāsid loyalists have worried that there might be some substance to Abū Muslim's alleged ancestry, they could also be directed to the language of the charge against him. The bill of particulars did not specify that Abū Muslim was, in fact, the son of Salīṭ, only that he claimed (*iddaᶜa*) this to be so. Indeed, Ibn Ḥazm's treatise on the genealogies of the Arabs preserves the following brief entry: "Abū Muslim claimed that he was [Abū Muslim] ᶜAbd al-Raḥmān, the son of Salīṭ, that is [Salīṭ] the son of ᶜAbdallāh b. al-ᶜAbbās; but Salīṭ had no descendants." Seen in this light, Abū Muslim fabricated a genealogy which left him in a position to challenge the Caliph for control of the Islamic community.[47]

This was not a matter that could have been taken lightly, nor was it portrayed by ᶜAbbāsid apologists as an isolated phenomenon. Although there is no explicit accusation in the remaining charges that Abū Muslim claimed descent from the

44 Ibid.: *mā aᶜlamu fī al-arḍ ᶜaduww aᶜdā laka minhu.*

45 See Lassner, *ᶜAbbāsid Rule*, 38, 92–93.

46 Ibid., 46–50. In 209 A.H. al-Maᵓmūn killed and crucified Ibn ᶜĀᵓishah, the great-grandson of Ibrāhīm al-Imām, in whose name the ᶜAbbāsid revolution was first begun. See Masᶜūdī, *Murūj* (Beirut), III: 448–49.

47 *Jamharah*, 20.

ᶜAbbāsids, they generally call attention to a certain presumptuousness as regards his standing with the ruling family. The implication was that Abū Muslim thought himself equal to, if not more worthy than, the recognized blood relatives of the ᶜAbbāsid house. A reconstruction of the indictment based on several sources reveals that the governor of Khurāsān also stood accused of the following transgressions (although not necessarily in this order):[48]

He indiscreetly placed his name above the Caliph's in formal correspondence. In addition, the ᶜAbbāsid client addressed his master by his proper name ᶜAbdallāh rather than his teknonym Abū Jaᶜfar or his formal title Commander of the Faithful. Were this deliberate breach of protocol not sufficiently offensive, he had the audacity to refer to al-Manṣūr as the "son of Salāmah," a rather contemptuous reference to the Caliph's mother who was a humble Berber slave.[49] The reference to Salāmah al-Barbarīyah was no slip of the tongue; the Caliph's genealogy was a sore point that required the convenient rewriting of history by his apologists. Fortunately for al-Manṣūr, the chroniclers of the ruling family found no lack of traditions to support this revisionist enterprise. Even the lowly Berber woman was made to understand that she carried the seed of future greatness. When pregnant with Abū Jaᶜfar, Salāmah dreamt that a lion had dropped between her legs.[50] Turning its head upward, the animal roared while thrashing about with its tail. As might be expected in an apocalyptic dream of this sort, other lions then came forward from every direction, each one prostrating himself before the newborn cub.

Abū Muslim's alleged actions were intended to indicate that a new champion was about to challenge the king of beasts. Indeed, his mother had also experienced a dream which revealed future events.[51] In the last days of her fatal pregnancy she reportedly envisioned giving birth to a vulture that swept the sky, attacking and downing all the other creatures that flew about. The actions of the rapacious vulture telescope Abū Muslim's spectacular career as a bloodletter for the ᶜAbbāsid cause. There were no guarantees, however, that his talent for political assassination would not eventually be applied against the current leadership of the family. It goes without saying that any challenge to the Caliph by his governor was sure to have been considered against the divine order of things; for in the kingdom of the animals, as in the kingdom of man, it is the lion who is destined to rule and not the carnivore that feeds at his behest. There is, to be sure, an unnatural presumption in the actions of a vulture aspiring to become the king of beasts. Similarly, it is against the established conventions of political order for a mere client to present himself as equal to the noble patrons who sustain him.

The arrogance displayed by the governor of Khurāsān calls to mind another accusation, that he had appropriated for himself two sword-blades that had been the

[48] Yaᶜqūbī, *Historiae*, II: 441; Balādhurī, *Ansāb*, III: 205; Ṭabarī, III/1: 115.

[49] This insult is not actually part of the charges levied against the governor of Khurāsān, but it is consistent with the tone of the accusation against him.

[50] Masᶜūdī, *Murūj* (Beirut), III: 282.

[51] *Akhbār*, 264.

property of the Caliph's defeated uncle ᶜAbdallāh b. ᶜAlī, and related to that, that he had sought to acquire a slave belonging to the latter. Although embellished by symbols indicating that Abū Muslim inherited ᶜAbdallāh's ambition as well as his property, the accusation is clearly rooted in an historic fact. After defeating ᶜAbdallāh b. ᶜAlī, Abū Muslim controlled the major elements of the ᶜAbbāsid military apparatus. In addition, he had acquired the Umayyad treasuries that had previously been taken as booty by the Caliph's uncle.[52] The status of this vast wealth soon became a bone of contention between the Caliph and his client. For Abū Muslim the grievance was based on the Caliph's lack of confidence in him: "I am trusted with [spilling] blood, but not with [handling] money."[53] In defense of al-Manṣūr, the issue was not simply whether Abū Muslim could be trusted. The Caliph was being cautious, for he was no doubt well aware that such large sums could easily be diverted to undermine the fragile government that emerged following the civil conflict.

By refusing to relinquish what he had acquired by conquest, Abū Muslim could have been charged with disobeying a caliphal order. At the least this would have been a damaging charge. There was, however, a greater fear that the governor of Khurāsān would turn his new found resources and the army, which was both the symbol and instrument of his independence, against the established regime. It was therefore imperative that the Caliph separate his client from the levers of power which he controlled. Although he normally traveled with a large military retinue for protection, Abū Muslim was persuaded to meet the Caliph without any of his retainers.[54] Moreover, when he arrived at court for what turned out to be a fatal audience, he was also asked to relinquish his personal weapon which, according to one version, was the aforementioned blade of the defeated ᶜAbdallāh b. ᶜAlī.[55] There is reason to believe that the author of this text intended to suggest an analogy between ᶜAbdallāh b. ᶜAlī's swordblades and the military resources at Abū Muslim's command. Shorn of both his weapons (his sword was conveniently placed beneath the Caliph's pillow,[56] and his army was waiting at camp some distance from the Caliph's court), the defenseless governor of Khurāsān met his end shortly after a list of charges was read against him.

When given a less literal reading, this accusation against Abū Muslim suggests that in addition to acquiring ᶜAbdallāh b. ᶜAlī's swordblades, that is, the cutting edge of his power, he also inherited the uncle's pretensions as a contender for rule within the ᶜAbbāsid family. Seen in this light, Abū Muslim claimed credentials that could

[52] Ṭabarī, III/1: 102ff.; Masᶜūdī, *Murūj* (Beirut), III: 305; Balādhurī, *Ansāb*, III: 201ff.

[53] Ṭabarī, III/1: 103.

[54] Ṭabarī, III/1: 87ff., 99–100, 112; *FHA*, 213. It can be argued that when al-Manṣūr became Caliph, the large retinue was actually needed for Abū Muslim's protection.

[55] *FHA*, 223; Khaṭīb, X: 209.

[56] According to the Khaṭīb (see n. 55) it was placed under the Caliph's prayer rug. The pillow is more convenient because it assumes that the Caliph then sat on the pillow, preventing Abū Muslim from trying to gain access to his weapon.

ultimately lead to the Caliphate, and what is more, after the defeat of al-Manṣūr's uncle, he also possessed the resources to promote such claims. This analogue obviously suited the Caliph's apologists; it not only defined the full extent of Abū Muslim's rebelliousness, it also prescribed failure for him as ᶜAbdallāh b. ᶜAlī had indeed failed before him.

The presumption which is evident in Abū Muslim's behavior extended to matters involving the distaff side. Not entirely content with acquiring ᶜAbdallāh b. ᶜAlī's concubine, the governor of Khurāsān aspired to a match that reflected a much higher social status, one that was befitting of a member of the ᶜAbbāsid family, if not a Caliph. For among the remaining charges lodged against him, Abū Muslim stood accused of proposing marriage to al-Manṣūr's aunt Amīnah bt. ᶜAlī.[57] It would have been astounding, if not perverse, for a mere client to seek the hand of a noble ᶜAbbāsid lady. The only recorded case of this sort was the mock marriage arranged by Hārūn al-Rashīd between his client, Jaᶜfar al-Barmakī and his sister ᶜAbbāsah.[58] It could hardly be said that the ᶜAbbāsid family regarded their clients, no matter how well placed, as social equals; al-Rashīd insisted that this be a marriage of convenience which was never to be consummated. A late medieval author could not bring himself to believe that the Caliph might have gone even that far:[59]

> The story is irreconcilable with ᶜAbbāsah's position, her religiosity, her parentage, her exalted rank . . . How could she link her pedigree with that of Jaᶜfar b. Yaḥyā and stain her Arab nobility with a Persian client? His ancestor had been acquired as a slave, or taken as a client, by one of her ancestors, an uncle of the Prophet and noble Qurayshite (that is, al-ᶜAbbās). . . . How could it be that al-Rashīd . . . would permit himself to be related to Persian clients?

In the end, the Caliph's experiment proved to be a failure. The discovery that ᶜAbbāsah had given birth brought an end to the union and to Jaᶜfar al-Barmakī as well.

The last accusation against Abū Muslim works on two levels. It calls attention to this overwhelming presumption, but it also raises the possibility that he was, in fact, related to the ᶜAbbāsids by direct blood ties, in which case he would have had every right to marry within the family. What if Abū Muslim were indeed the son of Salīṭ, as some might have believed within the wider community? The proposal of marriage to Amīnah bt. ᶜAlī serves to underscore the spuriousness of Abū Muslim's invented genealogy. Had the governor of Khurāsān been the son of Salīṭ, he would have been proposing marriage to his first cousin, a union that al-Manṣūr should have looked upon with great favor, for marriage between first cousins was not only acceptable, it was generally prescribed. The Caliph's negative response to the match is evidence that Abū Muslim did not share the family bloodline. The juxtaposition of these two

[57] See n. 8.

[58] See *ᶜAbbāsid Rule*, 47–48, 100. For the ᶜAbbāsids and their clients see 91–102.

[59] Ibn Khaldūn, *Muqaddimah* (Rosenthal), I: 28–29; *K. al-ᶜIbar* (Bulaq, 1284), V: 436ff.; VI: 7.

charges, that is, Abū Muslim's false claim of descent from Salīṭ and his brazen proposal of marriage to al-Manṣūr's aunt, seems deliberately intended. Its purpose was to cast Abū Muslim into the role of a discredited pretender to that which could never be his.

It seems evident that the claim of descent from the alleged son of ᶜAbdallāh b. ᶜAbbās was one of the wilder accusations leveled against Abū Muslim by ᶜAbbāsid writers. The problematic story of Salīṭ, which was no doubt a source of embarrassment to the ruling house, is reported in extant texts that rarely command more than a page. The report of Abū Muslim's link to Salīṭ is further reduced to a few scattered sentences. Had there been any substance to the charge against the Caliph's client, it would most certainly have received wider currency. It would appear that the Manṣūrid apologists never did quite formulate a convincing explanation of why the Caliph had Abū Muslim executed. Instead they built a presumptive case based on an interlocking series of non-events.

If there is no simple and direct explanation why the Caliph murdered the man who put him in power, it is because no particular occurrence gave rise to this act. On the contrary, the death of Abū Muslim must be seen within a wider context—the shift from revolutionary strategies to the process of creating and enduring ᶜAbbāsid state. Abū Muslim was a dangerous anachronism in the process of transforming a revolutionary apparatus into a government of imperial pretensions and capabilities. The Caliph's decision to eliminate him was not a petulant gesture based on a clash of personalities, but a well thought-out act based on sound reasons of state policy. A detailed exposition of the circumstances leading up to Abū Muslim's death is found elsewhere; the concern here is with his origins.[60]

C. ETHNIC AND GEOGRAPHIC ORIGINS: FALSE LEADS

The shortest and most problematic statement about Abū Muslim's ethnic origins is Abū Dulāmah's description of him as a Kurd.[61] The particular reference is found in a celebrated poem which reportedly combines praise for al-Manṣūr with less flattering remarks for his disobedient client. At least that is how the poem is described in the *Kitāb al-aghānī*;[62] for only a few lines, namely those dealing with Abū Muslim, have actually been preserved. The relevant text reads: "Indeed the people of treachery, are they not your ancestors, the Kurds?" It is not entirely clear what universal judgment might have been attached to Kurdish lineage in early ᶜAbbāsid times, but the same tone of condemnation that is evident in this hemistich pervades the entire poem, such as it is. Although the collector of these verses took the poet's genealogical statement at face value (*wa nasabahu Abū Dulāmah ilā al-Akrād*), this singular reference to Abū Muslim's Kurdish ancestry may be more

[60] Lassner, *ᶜAbbāsid Rule*, 63ff.

[61] *Akhbār*, 256; *FHA*, 183; Ibn Khallikān (DeSlane), III: 140; Khaṭīb, *Taᵓrīkh Baghdād*, X: 210.

[62] Isfahānī, *Aghānī*, IX: 121; see also Ibn Qutaybah, *Shiᶜr* (Beirut, 1964), II: 260–61.

literary than historical. The author's Kurds appear to be a poetic exemplar of perfidious behavior and not a fact of Abū Muslim's family history. While the truth of the Kurdish connection seems dubious at best, the Caliph grasped the gist of Abū Dulāmah's *qaṣīdah* only too well. For his effort the poet received 10,000 dirhams and a reputation for pungent verse that was to stand him in good stead. The ability to manipulate poetic language was a weapon much sought after in the political arsenal, and a well turned couplet or two, when delivered with official sanction, was more than worth its weight in good coin.

The claim that Abū Muslim was free born and a descendant of Persian nobility is similarly found in a few terse statements. There are reports linking him to a past emperor, to Jūdharz (Godarz), the hero of a national epic, and to Buzurjmihr, the celebrated public servant of the Sassanian Emperor Anusharwan I (6th cent. A.D.).[63] One should note, however, that these claims are found only in sources of the later middle ages. Furthermore, the historicity of Jūdharz and Buzurjmihr is subject to question, and references tying Abū Muslim to them and the pre-Islamic era may at best reflect dim echoes of a distant past. In all likelihood the various reports of Abū Muslim's noble Persian origins and the tales of Buzurjmihr's gift of statecraft and martial talents were creations of a subsequent historiography, one that was heavily influenced by a resurgent interest in the Iranian national ethos.

Broadly speaking, the connection between Abū Muslim and these personages of the past was an attempt to link the ᶜAbbāsid client to residual Iranian religious and political sentiments. From the perspective of a later period, far removed from the events that brought the ᶜAbbāsids to power, it was not implausible for highly inventive writers to connect Abū Mūslim's mysterious demise with certain presumed anti-Islamic sentiments on his part. The building blocks from which this theory was constructed were a series of local revolts which broke out following his execution.[64] If these revolts invoking Abū Muslim's name are not prominently mentioned by the early chroniclers, it is because they were relatively minor affairs. The most serious of the uprisings, that of a certain Sunbādh, seems to have had no greater effect than the cancellation of the summer campaign routinely scheduled for the year.[65] In later times, however, this insurrection was given an ideological dimension not explicitly found in the chronicles of the classical period.

When thus seen in retrospect, the revolt of Sunbādh was not bracketed by ambitions of some regional autonomy, a rationale which seems eminently plausible for early ᶜAbbāsid times. According to Niẓām al-Mulk,[66] who wrote three centuries

[63] Balādhurī, *Ansāb*, III: 120; Ibn Khallikān (DeSlane), III: 130, 140; Khaṭib, X: 207. For his descent from Jūdharz, see Daniel, *Khurasan Under Abbasid Rule*, 118, n. 7, citing later Persian texts. Note Jūdharz also wore black in battle.

[64] G. Sadighi, *Les Mouvements religieux iraniens*, 111–62; M. Azizi, *Domination Arabe*, 143ff.; Daniel, *Khurasan Under Abbasid Rule*, 125–56. Daniel's ambitious interpretation of this data seems forced.

[65] See Daniel, *Khurasan Under Abbasid Rule*, 126–30; see also p. 148, n. 1, for extensive bibliography.

[66] *Siyāsat Nameh*, 255 (tr).

later, Abū Muslim's name was invoked to restore a fallen Iranian empire, and to substitute a syncretist national religion for that of normative Islam. The substantive expression of these claims was framed by a familiar eschatological conception. The death of Abū Muslim, like that of various Shīᶜite imāms, was regarded as an ophthalmic illusion. In reality he was able to turn himself into a white pigeon and miraculously escape death at the hands of al-Manṣūr's executioners. From his secret hiding place, he was expected to return as the forerunner of the Messiah, an event that was to have resulted in the eagerly anticipated collapse of Islamic rule. Although there is no explicit statement in this late tradition that Abū Muslim himself embraced anti-Islamic or even anti-Arab views, the alleged position of his followers might have implicated him indirectly.

The general effort to link Abū Muslim with residual Iranian beliefs has been treated by others in some detail and with considerable skepticism.[67] Suffice it to say that when seen in the context of these subsequent associations, Abū Muslim's descent from Persian nobility is entirely consistent with the alleged character of his seditious activities. Who would have been given better cause to subvert the ᶜAbbāsid regime than a living link with the pre-Islamic ruling institution? Such a view may very well have served the outlook of later times, but the failure of the early authorities to pay even the slightest lip service to any anti-Islamic accusations leads to serious doubts.

Although Abū Muslim's geographic origins are treated in greater detail than his ethnic background, the conflicting nature of the reports leaves the matter far from settled. Was he indeed an Iraqi, an Isfahani, or as his *nisbah* would seem to indicate, a man of Khurāsān? One should keep in mind that the geographical component of the Arabic name is not always an indicator of native origins. Although Abū Muslim was officially called al-Khurāsānī, there is little doubt that the title accrued to him as a result of his revolutionary activities in that region. This, however, did not prevent various authors from drawing what seemed to be a logical nexus and designating Khurāsān as his place of birth. In two accounts this is mentioned in passing; another version offers a more detailed picture of the Khurāsānian connection, but when examined *in toto*, what appear to be claims for or suggestions of Khurāsānian origins are essentially limited to a few tendentious statements which are in turn linked to a larger text describing Muḥammad b. ᶜAlī's relationship with that region.[68]

Among the accounts suggesting Abū Muslim's Khurāsānian origins is a well known report preserved by the Andalusian litterateur Ibn ᶜAbd Rabbihi (d. 328).[69] In essence, the text describes the transfer of the sacred authority from Abū Hāshim to the ᶜAbbāsid Muḥammad b. ᶜAlī. A previous analysis of this account indicated that, when taken as a whole, it represents a contrived literary effort designed to strengthen

[67] See for example Frye, "The Role of Abū Muslim." On the later traditions concerning Abū Muslim, see Mélikoff-Sayar, *Abū Muslim*.

[68] Ibn Khallikān (DeSlane), III: 130 (Abū Muslim comes from Mākhuwān 3 *farsakh* from Marw, hence placing him at the very location from which he later proclaimed his revolt against the Umayyads); Kūfī, *Futūḥ*, VIII: 154 (serves the ᶜIjlī family of the Banū Maᶜqil in Khurāsān—an evident confusion); Ibn ᶜAbd Rabbihi, *ᶜIqd*, IV: 477; *Akhbār*, 256.

[69] *ᶜIqd*, IV: 475ff.

the claims of the ruling house, and in particular the Caliphs of the Manṣūrid line.[70] In short, the wider contextual setting reveals a familiar pastiche of highly charged themes drawn from a historiography assembled under official patronage. This being the case, what is one to make of the section dealing with the most famous revolutionary of them all? Does it reflect authentic circumstances or, like the larger text which frames it, is the description of Abū Muslim and his historic role similarly marked by tendentious shaping?

The particular segment dealing with Abū Muslim indicates that he was called to the attention of Muḥammad b. ᶜAlī al-ᶜAbbasī after serving various ᶜAbbāsid operatives imprisoned in Khurāsān. They were apparently much impressed by the young saddler (*sarrāj*), for he was exceptionally gifted and had strong political leanings toward the house of the Prophet (*ahl bayt Rasūl Allāh*). When asked by the patriarch if he was a slave or free, the informants responded that he considered himself to be free, but that ᶜĪsā (b. Maᶜqil al-ᶜIjlī, the youth's master) considered him to be a slave. The ᶜAbbāsid leader then issued orders to purchase the youth and have him manumitted, whereupon he served the ᶜAbbāsid family, initially as a courier and later as the head of the revolutionary apparatus in Khurāsān. To be sure, the text does not explicitly state that Abū Muslim was born in Khurāsān; it only indicates that he had served various ᶜAbbāsid agents who had been incarcerated there. But if this brief story is accurate, there is at least a discernible hint of Khurāsānian origins—one that might have been picked up and reported as fact by less critical readers.

Serious doubts remain, however, about the historicity of the events described. Among the problematic elements in the narrative, two are most certainly worthy of attention: Abū Muslim's link to Muḥammad b. ᶜAlī, and more particularly his alleged service to various ᶜAbbāsid operatives while they were imprisoned in Khurāsān. There is no presumption that these "facts" are necessitated by ideological considerations, but since they are consistent with the central focus of the texts, i.e., Muḥammad b. ᶜAlī's claims, and related to that, the ᶜAbbāsid's involvement with revolutionary affairs in Khurāsān, a cautious reading is very much in order.

The actual transfer of authority from Abū Hāshim to the ᶜAbbāsids is reported to have taken place at Muḥammad b. ᶜAlī's estate in Palestine. It is, however, the vast province to the east that is the geographical epicenter of the author's account. Muḥammad b. ᶜAlī is advised to establish his revolutionary cadres in Khurāsān and in particular the region surrounding Marw. The cataclysmic Year of the Donkey will be the signal for the ᶜAbbāsid leader to send his messengers (*rusul*) eastward on their fateful missions. It is in the east that the (messianic) black flags of the new regime will first be unfurled, and it is from the east that they will be carried victoriously to the outer reaches of an empire encompassing all the domains from Ḥaḍramawt to North Africa and from al-Hind to Farghānah.

There is no need to belabor the fact that Abū Muslim became the director of ᶜAbbāsid interests in Khurāsān. It was Abū Muslim who unfurled the black flags in the oases around Marw, therein signifying the onset of the open revolt against the

[70] See Chapter II.

Umayyad regime. It was Abū Muslim who was responsible for assembling and giving political direction to the diverse coalition of military forces which was to destroy Umayyad rule, first in Khurāsān, and then throughout the entire realm. Hence, Muḥammad b. ᶜAlī and his client were inextricably linked by historic memories to the districts of Khurāsān—the former for having built up a secret network of revolutionary agents, the latter for having used it in promoting a successful military campaign against the hated dynasty in power. Given the impact of their historical associations with Khurāsān, it is not difficult to imagine why various traditions view their careers as intertwined, and how in certain sources Abū Muslim could have been given a genealogy presuming Khrāsānian ancestry.

The only explicit references tying Abū Muslim to Khurāsān before his involvement with the ᶜAbbāsids are those which describe his service to the ᶜIjlī family of ᶜĪsā b. Maᶜqil. According to Ibn ᶜAbd Rabbihi, the Khurāsānī agents first met Abū Muslim while they were imprisoned in that province (*ḥubisū biKhurāsān fī al-sijn wa kāna yakhdumuhum ghulām min al-sarrājīn*) and they later purchased him from ᶜĪsā at the behest of Muḥammad b. ᶜAlī.[71] A close variant of this tradition preserved by al-Kūfī simply states that he served the ᶜIjlī family in Khurāsān (*wa kāna yakhdumu qawm min Banī ᶜIjl biKhurāsān yuqālu lahum Banū ᶜĪsā b. Maᶜqil*).[72] There is no specific indication that Abū Muslim actually came from Khurāsān, or indeed that the ᶜIjlīs themselves were native to the region, but relying only on these terse reports, one might very well have drawn such a conclusion.

The story of Abū Muslim's experience in prison together with his subsequent manumission is, however, found in a number of other extended accounts.[73] While they vary in certain details there is unanimous agreement that the aforementioned event took place in a prison situated in Iraq, and not in Khurāsān. Moreover, it is not likely that the upper echelons of the revolutionary apparatus in Khurāsān would have been imprisoned together in the very province of their activities if the charge against them were sedition. Given their importance to the movement, had the likes of Lāhiz b. Qurayẓ, Sulaymān b. Kathīr, and Qaḥṭabah b. Shabīb (to say nothing of the others) been accused of acting against the state on behalf of an ᶜAbbāsid pretender, the revolutionary effort would likely have collapsed in Khurāsān, if not altogether.

If, in fact, the story of Abū Muslim and the Khurāsānīs is an invention, it is most likely derived from an actual event, the incarceration of various ᶜAbbāsid agents in the prison of Asad b. ᶜAbdallāh al-Qasrī.[74] This occurred, however, in 117 , several

[71] ᶜ*Iqd*, IV: 476.

[72] *Futūḥ*, VIII: 154.

[73] *Akhbār*, 253ff., 265–67; Balādhurī, *Ansāb*, III: 118–19; Ibn Khallikān (DeSlane), III: 131; Ṭabarī, II/3: 1726–27, *sub anno* 124; Dīnawarī, 339; Azdī, 52.

[74] Balādhurī, *Ansāb*, III: 116; Ṭabarī, II/3: 1576ff. Some of the accounts concerning the imprisonment of the ᶜIjlīs in Iraq indicate that the governor at that time was Khālid b. ᶜAbdallāh al-Qasrī, perhaps a further source of confusion. Note the seeming confusion in *Akhbār*, 253, where it is indicated that everyone was imprisoned in al-Kūfah by Asad b. ᶜAbdallāh. Note also the apocryphal story of Khālid's (secret?) support for Muḥammad b. ᶜAlī in Balādhurī, *Ansāb*, III: 80–81.

years before Abū Muslim's conversion to the cause. It goes without saying that Abū Muslim is not mentioned in this account describing the imprisonment of the Khurāsānīs. The historian Ṭabarī simply relates that a group of agents (*du*ᶜ*āt*) in Khurāsān were seized by (the governor) Asad b. ᶜAbdallāh. Some were (summarily) executed, some were brutalized in exemplary fashion, and still others were imprisoned. Among those seized were Sulaymān b. Kathīr, Malik b. al-Haytham, Mūsā b. Kaᶜb, Lāhiz b. Qurayẓ, Khālid b. Ibrāhīm and Ṭalḥah b. Zurayq—altogether a very impressive lot. There is no indication of the charges against them, but it is apparent from Sulaymān b. Kathīr's spirited defense of himself and several of the others that they were brought to Asad's prison because of simmering intertribal feuds and not because they were undermining local authority on behalf of an ᶜAbbāsid pretender.[75] The accounts which indicate that Abū Muslim was converted to the ᶜAbbāsid cause by the leading Khurāsānīs, and even in a Khurāsān prison, may therefore juxtapose two discrete events, the jailing of the local revolutionaries in 117 and an incident which took place in Iraq eight years later.

A second and more plausible version of the agents' encounter with Abū Muslim indicates that the Khurāsānīs passed through al-Kūfah on their way to Mecca in 125 A.H.[76] Enroute to the holy city to fulfill their religious obligations (and to meet with Ibrāhīm al-Imām as regards more practical matters), they stopped off at the local prison where the ᶜIjlīs were interned. There they made the acquaintance of Abū Muslim who had already come under the influence of Abū Mūsā al-Sarrāj, a figure described elsewhere as an ideologue among the Kūfan revolutionaries (*min* ᶜ*ulamā*ᵓ *al-shī*ᶜ*ah*) and one of their leaders (*ra*ᵓ*īs min ru*ᵓ*asā*ᵓ . . .).[77] Coincidentally, it is through this association with the Kūfan saddler that Abū Muslim is said to have acquired his occupational title, al-Sarrāj. Be that as it may, Abū Muslim now attended to the needs of the visiting Khurāsānīs who, visibly impressed, reportedly took him along to the Hijāz on their mission to Ibrāhīm al-Imām. In view of Abū Muslim's later career in Khurāsān, it is understandable that according to certain accounts, he was initiated into the revolutionary movement by leading agents from that province; however, a variant of this story circumvents the Khurāsānīs altogether. It indicates that Abū Salamah, the director of the revolutionary station in al-Kūfah, bought Abū Muslim from his ᶜIjlī master and then shared the young lad's services with (Abū) Mūsā al-Sarrāj before sending him off to the imām.[78]

[75] Balādhurī, *Ansāb*, III: 116 simply indicates that the agents had been slandered by one Jabalah b. Abī Rawwād. As a result, their leader Abū ᶜIkrimah was killed, and another agent, Abū Dāwūd, was whipped until he revealed the others. They, however, finagled their way out of further difficulty. There is no indication as to the nature of the charges. A second tradition (ibid., 117) seems to indicate seditious activities, but no particulars are given. Friendly testimony got them released.

[76] See n. 3.

[77] Balādhurī, *Ansāb*, III: 84, 85, 120; *Akhbār*, 254, 266. He is also referred to as Mūsā al-Sarrāj. See also *Akhbār*, 154, 203, 266.

[78] *Akhbār*, 266. The source regards this tradition as correct.

There is, needless to say, much confusion here, and it would be compounded several times over if every variant of this last tradition were given a thorough analysis. It is sufficient to say that from all these divergent views of Abū Muslim's contacts with the revolutionaries in prison, one salient point commands attention. The contacts, such as there were, occurred in al-Kūfah and not in Khurāsān, casting doubt thereby on those statements linking Abū Muslim with the eastern territories before his initial dealings with the ᶜAbbāsids. There is no indication of what the Khurāsānīs themselves thought of Abū Muslim, that is, those individuals who were in a position to know his real origins, and not a general populace taken in by the conflicting and often convenient legends that accrued to him later. It appears reasonable at first thought that a genealogy from Khurāsān would have stood Abū Muslim in good stead given his complex political dealings in that province. The fact that no such claim is articulated in convincing detail seems proof enough that his origins lay elsewhere.

For the historian/litterateur Masᶜūdī, "elsewhere" was in fact Iraq, a province generally distinguished for its history of political turbulence.[79] To be more specific, Abū Muslim was reported to have come from Khuṭarnīyah,[80] a village in the administrative district of al-Kūfah. A descendant of people from the sub-districts of al-Burs and al-Jāmiᶜayn, the future revolutionary had been the steward (*qahramān*) of one Idrīs b. Maᶜqil al-ᶜIjlī when he (Abū Muslim) became involved in the ᶜAbbāsid cause. Abū Muslim thus attached himself to Muḥammad b. ᶜAlī and then to Muḥammad's son Ibrāhīm al-Imām. The latter invested him with great authority and sent him off to Khurāsān, setting into motion the events which were to change the course of Islamic history. This account is echoed in the chronicle of Ṭabarī;[81] however, the chronicler prefaces the claims for Abū Muslim's Iraqi origins, not with the direct testimony of an informant, but with a rather speculative formula in the passive voice (*fīmā zuᶜima*). When Ṭabarī reports, "According to that which has been asserted, Abū Muslim came from the people of Khuṭarnīyah," he creates the impression that Abū Muslim's Iraqi origins are marked by considerable uncertainty. Nevertheless, considering the nature of revolutionary politics in Iraq, the possible connection between this locale and Abū Muslim was bound to draw attention from meticulous scholars.

With his particular eye for detail, J. Wellhausen was led to believe that Khuṭarnīyah produced the original following of al-Mukhtār, an adventurer associated with the fortunes of various ᶜAlid pretenders, including Muḥammad b. al-Ḥanafīyah.[82] One recalls that this ᶜAlid bequeathed his right to rule to his son Abū

[79] *Murūj* (Beirut), III: 239; see also Balādhurī, *Ansāb*, III: 120; Ṭabarī, II/3: 1960.

[80] The reading follows Balādhurī, op. cit., 120, and Ṭabarī, II/3: 1960. Masᶜūdī reads *Khurṭīnah* (?). Yāqūt, *Muᶜjam*, II: 453 lists a Khuṭarnīyah in Babylonia (Iraq). There is no entry for *Khurṭīnah*. Note that al-Burs and al-Jāmiᶜayn were both situated in Babylonia. See Yāqūt, op. cit., I: 565–66; II: 10–11.

[81] Ṭabarī, II/3: 1960, *sub anno* 125.

[82] *Arab Kingdom*, 503ff. Note, however, his reservations concerning the evidence for a link between al-Mukhtār, Abū Muslim and Khuṭarnīyah (p. 505).

Hāshim; however, the latter had no surviving offspring, so that shortly before dying, Abū Hāshim in turn transferred these rights to his ᶜAbbāsid kinsman, Muḥammad b. ᶜAli. Along with credentials to rule, the ᶜAbbāsid inherited those remnants of al-Mukhtār's movement that had remained faithful to the line of Ibn al-Ḥanafīyah. It was this alleged transfer of authority that formed the earliest basis of ᶜAbbāsid claims vis-à-vis the ᶜAlid pretenders, and it was this inherited following that constituted the inner core of the ᶜAbbasid revolutionary apparatus.[83]

The specific attempt by Wellhausen to imbue this following with a variety of anti-Arab sentiments based on the literature of the heresiographers has not stood up well to recent historical inquiry.[84] Nevertheless, the general implications of a possible connection between al-Mukhtār, Khuṭarnīyah and Abū Muslim are self-evident. Seen in this context, Abū Muslim was, at the least, raised in a revolutionary milieu that produced the earliest ideological and tactical support for the ᶜAbbāsid cause. For Wellhausen, the ᶜAbbāsid client was nothing less than a latter day al-Mukhtār or as he put it, perhaps somewhat whimsically, "If the doctrine of *Rajᶜa* (Resurrection) is correct then the Arab of Khutarnia came to life again in the Maula of Khutarnia."[85]

Although he cites no source for linking the village with the following of al-Mukhtār, there does not seem to be any doubt that Wellhausen's thesis is based on a text drawn from the chronicle of Ṭabarī.[86] The general setting of this account finds al-Mukhtār in league with forces sympathetic to the claims of al-Ḥusayn b. ᶜAlī, whose interests in Iraq were represented by his cousin Muslim b. ᶜAqīl.[87] The latter, in fact, used al-Mukhtār's residence in al-Kūfah as a base, and it was through al-Mukhtār's efforts that he was able to recruit wide support among the ᶜAlid-leaning Kūfans. Under the best of circumstances, promoting a revolution can be a rather complicated affair, on which is fraught with obvious perils. In retrospect, the scheme launched on behalf of the ᶜAlid pretender was much too intricate to succeed, as it called for an insurrection in al-Kūfah concurrent with the appearance there of al-Ḥusayn, who was already under surveillance for activities against the Umayyads. The general outline of the plot soon became known to the authorities, so that Muslim, disregarding the delicate timing required by the plan, acted prematurely in declaring for his distinguished relative. In the end, Ibn ᶜAqīl's hasty action brought about his execution and precipitated the death of the ᶜAlid pretender. With failure assured, al-Ḥusayn b. ᶜAlī insisted on playing Don Quixote to his cousin's Sancho Panza, and thus invoked his honor and that of a small band of followers against 4,000 cavalry of the state.

Against this background, al-Mukhtār is pictured as visiting in Khuṭarnīyah. The chronicler, however, does not explicitly state, or even suggest, that the native

[83] See Prolegomena.

[84] See for example Frye, "The ᶜAbbāsid Conspiracy."

[85] *Arab Kingdom*, 506.

[86] Ṭabarī, II/1: 520.

[87] For a brief summary of these events, see *EI*² s.v. al-Ḥusayn b. ᶜAlī.

populace were among his adherents. Indeed a cautious reading produces no firm evidence that the local inhabitants were involved in any sort of revolutionary activity. Fortunately for al-Mukhtār, he was in Khuṭarnīyah when events overwhelmed Muslim b. ᶜAqīl and thus could not be directly implicated in the abortive plot (*ḥattā kharaja Ibn ᶜAqīl yawma kharaja wa al-Mukhtār fī qaryah lahu biKhuṭarnīyah . . .*).[88] Indeed, the chronicler may have interjected this account to show that al-Mukhtār's "innocent" appearance in the village was fortuitous; for undismayed by the earlier failure of the Ḥasanids whom he supported, and now the Ḥusaynids, the one-eyed adventurer would soon pledge his allegiance to still another branch of the family by endorsing Muḥammad b. al-Ḥanafīyah with all that this implied for the future ᶜAbbāsid cause.

Leaving al-Mukhtār aside, the impetus to link Abū Muslim with the administrative district of al-Kūfah assumes a logic of its own. The area was after all a crucible of revolutionary activity, and almost all the sources agree that Abū Muslim found his way to the ᶜAbbāsid cause from the prison in al-Kūfah where he served his ᶜIjlī patrons. His earliest career as a revolutionary is identified with Iraq and the leading agents stationed there, and when he became attached to the service of the imām he served as a courier to the Kūfah station before embarking on his epic mission to Khurāsān.[89] Abū Muslim's ties to Iraq were in this sense no less pronounced than his later associations with the provinces to the east. This is not to say that the ᶜAbbāsid client had no ties at all with Khuṭarnīyah, a village too obscure to conjure any meaningful associations. What need would there have been to link Abū Muslim to such a place if there were not, in fact, a connection of some sort? Regarding this, Balādhurī maintains that Abū Muslim's father, a certain ᶜUthmān b. Yasār, served in Khuṭarnīyah as an agent (*wakīl*) for the ᶜIjlīs and traveled to al-Kūfah with his patron, the ubiquitous ᶜĪsā b. Maᶜqil.[90] To be sure this kind of information is extremely thin and could well be unreliable, but it does raise the possibility that, as his father reportedly did before him, Abū Muslim might have generally supervised matters for the ᶜIjlīs in Iraq, if not in Khuṭarnīyah itself. Indeed, one rather detailed account reports that prior to his imprisonment ᶜĪsā b. Maᶜqil had actually appointed Abū Muslim to be the agent (*wakīl*) for one of his villages.[91]

After collecting monies and documents as required by his position, the dutiful client attached himself to his patron (who had since been incarcerated) at the prison of Yūsuf b. ᶜUmar in al-Kūfah. Abū Muslim did not actually reside in the prison itself (as no charges were brought against him), but stayed instead at a residence belonging to Ibn Maᶜqil in the ᶜIjlī section of that city.[92] From there he made daily

[88] Ṭabarī, II/1: 520.

[89] *Akhbār*, 254, 256: Ibrāhīm al-Imām indicates that Abū Muslim had already been a courier for Muḥammad b. ᶜAlī. This account may, however, be confused. The sources are not clear as to whether Abū Muslim had already entered the imām's service in the time of Muḥammad b. ᶜAlī, or only after Ibrāhīm succeeded him.

[90] *Ansāb*, III: 120.

[91] *Akhbār*, 260.

[92] *Akhbār*, 260; see also Ibn Khallikān (DeSlane), III: 131.

trips bringing food and drink to his patron. There is very little information here, even if one were to accept this last account at face value; but it is conceivable that men of wealth like the brothers ᶜĪsā and Idrīs b. Maᶜqil had business interests and properties in Iraq as well as in their native Isfahan. In any event, there is certainly no reason to doubt that the family maintained a residence in the ᶜIjlī section (or inn) of al-Kūfah. Abū Muslim therefore could have spent some time in Iraq, even before the ᶜIjlīs were imprisoned. If so, one can readily imagine how various traditions came to portray him as an Iraqi, especially in view of his early service to the ᶜAbbāsid cause in that province.

D. FROM ISFAHAN TO REVOLUTION: THE ORIGINS OF INVOLVEMENT

Were it not for the existence of many accounts indicating Abū Muslim to be a native of Isfahan, the case for Iraq might very well be compelling. His career would therefore be seen against the background of those local clients who embraced diverse revolutionary causes in al-Kūfah and the surrounding area. The Isfahan traditions are, however, not only the most numerous of those dealing with Abū Muslim's origins, they are also the most detailed.[93] Moreover, there would have been no reason to associate him with Isfahan if the facts of the situation did not actually warrant it. The city was never a dominant center of the ᶜAbbāsid effort, nor for that matter did it play an important role for any of the early Shīᶜite groups.

With numbers there is often confusion; being no exception, the Isfahan traditions are marked by considerable variation. One report has it that Abū Muslim was kidnapped there as a youth and then brought to al-Kūfah;[94] another maintains that he made his way to al-Kūfah with his ᶜIjlī master in order to serve him while he was in prison for aiding criminals—a rather ironic turn of events which reportedly took place during the governorship of Khālid b. ᶜAbdallāh al-Qasrī (105–120 A.H.).[95] According to Dīnawarī, the incarceration of the ᶜIjlīs from Isfahan actually occurred during the tenure of Khālid's successor, Yūsuf b. ᶜUmar al-Thaqafī, and while he is supported by all the other sources in this matter, Dīnawarī is nevertheless alone in placing this prison in Wāsiṭ.[96] The various traditions which deal with other particulars of Abū Muslim's road from Isfahan to the ᶜAbbāsid house are similarly obfuscated by conflicting testimony.

Perhaps the most detailed and internally consistent account of his origins and later conversion to the cause is a tradition preserved by the *Akhbār al-dawlah*,[97] a text unavailable to Wellhausen, Moscati, Frye and others who grappled with the vexing problems of Abū Muslim's identity and his subsequent role in ᶜAbbāsid

[93] *Akhbār*, 225 (a *dihgān*), 257ff.; 263, 265; Balādhurī, *Ansāb*, III: 120; Ibn Khallikān (DeSlane), III: 131, 134; Khaṭīb, X: 207.

[94] Balādhurī, *Ansāb*, III: 120.

[95] *Akhbār*, 257.

[96] Dīnawarī, 338.

[97] *Akhbār*, 257ff.

affairs. The account is transmitted through a friend of the aforementioned ʿIjlī family, a man whose business dealings frequently took him to their home where he would stay for a year or two. This informant, who was no less than the qāḍī of Abrashahr (Naysābūr) derived his information in turn from one Sābiq, a client of Banū Maʿqil. The latter was not simply a household servant dispensing local gossip; he was considered an expert informant on matters pertaining to Abū Muslim. That is to say, he had impeccable credentials of his own.

According to this account, which has been cited earlier,[98] a certain ʿUthmān b. Yasār, a client of the Banū ʿIjl in Isfahan, found himself unable to overcome the burden of his tax quota. Given the resourcefulness that must have been a prerequisite for dealing with property owners like ʿĪsā b. Maʿqil, he first played upon the sympathies of his fellow tribesman, and then sold him a non-Arab (*aʿjamīyah*) concubine (in order to settle accounts). The transaction, which involved some 800 dirhams, was marked by an unexpected complication, for the girl was with child, a fact which was unknown to ʿUthmān b. Yasār and the prospective buyer. Were this not enough, the pregnant girl died upon giving birth.

God's justice and compassion are, however, infinite; the surviving infant named Salm was raised by his ʿIjlī patron. Along with other children in the ʿĪsā b. Maʿqil household, the boy entered the class of one (Abū Muslim)[99] ʿAbd al-Raḥmān b. Muslim, and received training in the scribal arts. A variant of this account indicates that the young novice assumed both the patronymic and proper name of his teacher, and thus acquired for himself a lasting identity (if not surrogate father). However, the latter source is somewhat less than certain of this attribution; appended to it is the formula "and God knows best [*wa Allāh aʿlam*]." After all has been said, one would probably conclude that Abū Muslim's name will forever remain an enigma since in all likelihood his patronymic was a *nom de guerre* designed to mask his true identity.

After completing his studies, the young client served his master, ʿĪsā b. Maʿqil, by administering the latter's estates in the vicinity of Isfahan, a task which prepared Abū Muslim for the revolutionary career that awaited him. Circumstances suddenly made it necessary for Abū Muslim to take up residence in Iraq. It is reported that ʿĪsā b. Maʿqil was tainted by corruption and complaints were lodged against him by the governors of Isfahan, Hamadān and the Māhān.[100] As a result he was brought to al-Kūfah and imprisoned by the governor of Iraq, here identified as Yūsuf b. ʿUmar al-Thaqafī. One should keep in mind that the incarceration of men of influence and means did not signify an end to all the amenities of life. As fate may have it, Abū Muslim joined ʿĪsā b. Maʿqil in order to serve him.

Under proper circumstances incarceration has sometimes proven to be spiritually uplifting. It is in this prison that Abū Muslim reportedly made contact with those ʿAbbāsid agents who later had him purchased and brought to the head of the family

[98] See p. 103.

[99] Bracketed name added from *Akhbār*, 265.

[100] That is, the two Māhs, Māh al-Kūfah (Dīnawar) and Māh al-Baṣrah (Nihāwand). See Le Strange, *Lands*, 189, 197.

(in this text Ibrāhīm al-Imām).[101] There is a wide divergence among the various traditions regarding this last sequence of events, and given the available evidence, it is simply not possible to choose the most accurate account. If one were to form a composite picture on the basis of all these reports, it would seem that Abū Muslim could have been brought into the fold by any number of revolutionary agents drawn from the upper echelons of the movement. The candidates he reportedly came into contact with at this prison included no less than Sulaymān b. Kathīr, Qaḥṭabah b. Shabīb and Lāhiz b. Qurayẓ, all from the Khurāsān apparatus, Bukayr b. Māhān, the director of the Kūfah station, the latter's successor Abū Salamah (Ḥafṣ b. Sulaymān) al-Khallāl, and Ḥafṣ al-Asīr, an early follower from Khurāsān who was by chance a prisoner in al-Kūfah.[102] It is also indicated that Abū Mūslim's political, if not practical, education took place outside the prison. In his spare time he frequented the saddlers (*sarrājīn*) and thus came under the influence of one (Abū) Mūsā al-Sarrāj, a leading Shīᶜite ideologue in al-Kūfah who eventually shared the youth's services with Abū Salamah.[103] In any event, it was through one or several of these individuals that Abū Muslim eventually was brought to the attention of the ᶜAbbāsid patriarch, be he Muḥammad b. ᶜAlī, or what is more likely, his son Ibrāhīm.

What circumstances, if any, could have brought this impressive collection of leading revolutionaries together and even in the same prison? It is noteworthy that in the account of Dīnawarī,[104] a source generally marked by unique and highly problematic traditions, the ᶜIjlī patrons Idrīs and ᶜĪsā b. Maᶜqil were not imprisoned for some minor indiscretion such as aiding criminals or improperly using their authority. On the contrary, the author invests their misfortune with a rather dramatic interpretation. They were themselves deeply committed revolutionaries who actually had been in contact with the hidden imām and were consequently rounded up and imprisoned with other presumed subversives during an extensive security sweep. The report suggests that various suspects were arrested in the diverse districts that came under the jurisdiction of the governor in Iraq, and that they were later sent to him and detained at his prison. Since most of those who are mentioned in the various accounts as having been arrested continued to play an active, indeed decisive part in the struggle to come, it is clear that nothing serious resulted from any such measures.[105]

[101] *Akhbār*, 261.

[102] According to *Akhbār*, 265, the imprisoned revolutionary ᶜĀṣim b. Yūnus brought Abū Muslim to the attention of Bukayr b. Māhān who then converted Abū Muslim to the ᶜAbbāsid cause. Only later did Abū Muslim enter into direct contact with Abū Salamah and others. Ḥafṣ al-Asīr was allegedly sent to prison in al-Kūfah from Khurāsān along with other revolutionaries by Asad b. ᶜAbdallāh. See n. 74 on the possible confusion between Khālid al-Qasrī and Asad al-Qasrī. See *Akhbār*, 253, 259, where Abū Salamah is also listed as a prisoner.

[103] See p. 122.

[104] Dīnawarī, 339.

[105] Indeed, the account of Dīnawarī gives the impression that the governor (Yūsuf b. ᶜUmar) had no specific knowledge of any plot against the regime. The roundup seems to have been precautionary. See p. 121 for accounts indicating that leading Khurāsānīs had been imprisoned, albeit in Khurāsān.

The descriptions of political prisoners might be more plausible if one were dealing with isolated individuals or agents from the least significant elements of the ᶜAbbāsid apparatus. But the success of the revolutionary effort required the utmost secrecy, so that very few operatives actually knew the identity of the imām, let alone had direct contacts with him. A key element in ᶜAbbāsid strategy was to eschew a high profile and above all to avoid involvement in various revolutionary schemes that were ill-conceived and ill-timed. Under these circumstances, it would have been incredible had any roundup netted the inner core of the revolutionary movement, even if only through an unforeseen stroke of luck.[106] For it would imply that the authorities had infiltrated the most clandestine cells of a highly secretive conspiracy, and as a result had detained the very operatives required to keep the revolutionary effort active. At the least, one could expect a continuing surveillance of those individuals who were later released. How then could they have continued to risk contact with the hidden imām on a regular basis, let alone prepare for an active military campaign against the authority of the state? One might argue (without much conviction) that the entire episode was a perfunctory search and seizure operation designed to weed out potential troublemakers. But if this were the case, why would it have been necessary to transport the Khurāsānīs to Iraq?[107] The local prisons would certainly have done just as well. If indeed all these operatives were located in a Kūfan prison, albeit briefly, the circumstances must have been a good deal more innocuous and easily explained.

To be sure, the rather dramatic interpretation of Dīnawarī leads to a more sympathetic view of the ᶜIjlī brothers—given the climate of the times, political prisoners of a certain persuasion were preferable to out and out thieves. Indeed, a rather oblique reference in Ṭabarī[108] seems to support the view that the ᶜIjlīs themselves influenced Abū Muslim (who cried upon hearing their deliberations). In another report, the author indicates that Idrīs b. Maᶜqil and his servant were both converted to the ᶜAbbāsid cause while in prison together with ᶜĀṣim b. Yūnus al-ᶜIjlī, and that it was Bukayr b. Māhān that brought them around to his views.[109] However, the more detailed accounts of Abū Muslim's revolutionary education indicate that this matter did not concern them. Were they, in fact, active revolutionaries, they would have been more directly involved with his ultimate conversion to the cause. It is of course possible that the ᶜIjlīs were generally sympathetic to anti-Umayyad sentiments, and that Abū Muslim was party to their thoughts, but that is a far cry from having direct familiarity with the hidden imām. As for the others, the evidence, such as it is, seems to rule strongly against their having been incarcerated for suspicion of seditious activities. Wherever charges are delineated against those

[106] According to Dīnawarī, 339, the Khurāsānī's arrived at the prison in Wāsiṭ as pilgrims and were not among the detained. *Akhbār*, 253, indicates that twelve agents were imprisoned in Iraq but does not name any of them other than Abū Salamah and Ḥafṣ al-Asīr.

[107] *Akhbār*, 253.

[108] Ṭabarī, II/3: 1727.

[109] Ibid., 1726.

detained, and there are preciously few examples, they point to indiscretions of a far less serious nature.

Perhaps the most significant prisoner among those mentioned was Bukayr b. Māhān, for many years the director of the revolutionary station in al-Kūfah and at the time possibly the most valued operative in the entire revolutionary apparatus outside of the imām himself. It appears, however, that it was not a dossier filled with revolutionary credentials that brought Ibn Māhān to these unfortunate circumstances, but his failure to pay his debts. The more cynical may assume that this was a small moral failing on the part of an otherwise sterling revolutionary; it seems that Bukayr, who had acquired a small fortune in al-Sind, was moved by conscience and the high operating costs of subversion to turn it over to the ᶜAbbāsid *daᶜwah*, thus providing the party loyalists with a more satisfactory explanation for his financial embarrassment and subsequent imprisonment. In any case, he still possessed the necessary moral stature to convert Abū Muslim to the cause; so that when Abū Salamah, the revolutionary heir apparent at al-Ḳūfah, bought off Bukayr's debts in order to free him, he acquired the latter's new protegé as well.[110]

The only other mention of specific accusations are those leveled against one ᶜĀṣim b. Yūnus, a client of the Banū ᶜIjl. In this case, a nondescript ᶜAbbāsid sympathizer was committed to prison on a general charge of corruption (*fasād*) seemingly related to a capital offense (*ḥubisa bidam*).[111] The spilling of blood, even if unintentional, was of course a serious matter; but there is no firm indication that this act was connected with any activities against the state. An account in Ṭabarī *sub anno* 124 does report that ᶜĀṣim b. Yūnus was actually under suspicion for supporting the ᶜAbbāsid cause,[112] but any charge specifically mentioning the ᶜAbbāsids in this context is hardly plausible, since it implies that the governor of Iraq was aware, already at this time, of the family's involvement in revolutionary affairs. In all likelihood, the ruling authorities had no inkling of ᶜAbbāsid intentions until al-Saffāḥ was proclaimed Caliph of the new dynasty in al-Kūfah eight years later. As to the others, even the question of imprisonment becomes extremely cloudy. It does seem that Ḥafṣ al-Asīr, who had been an important ᶜAbbāsid agent from the outset, was brought from Khurāsān to al-Kūfah and incarcerated by Yūsuf b. ᶜUmar.[113] Abū Salamah (Ḥafṣ b. Sulaymān) is mentioned among the interned,[114] but he was also said to have been in Khurāsān, and upon his return to Iraq he allegedly paid off

[110] *Akhbār*, 248, 265; Anonymous, 258a. Note, however, Ṭabarī, II/3: 1726, which seems to indicate that Bukayr was imprisoned for attempting to influence some people from al-Sind (to join the revolutionary cause?) while they were in al-Kūfah. The text of Ṭabarī seems corrupt.

[111] *Akhbār*, 255, 259; Balādhurī, *Ansāb*, III: 118–19.

[112] Ṭabarī, II/3: 1727. Note, however, that this contradicts a previous account given by the author which indicates that ᶜĀṣim was converted by Bukayr b. Māhān after he had been incarcerated (see p. 1726).

[113] *Akhbār*, 191, 253, 259.

[114] *Akhbār*, 259. The text indicates that twelve revolutionaries had been imprisoned, surely a literary invention to correspond to the twelve *nuqabāᵓ*. See below, p. 64.

the debts of Bukayr b. Māhān in order that the latter be released.[115] It thus appears that Abū Salamah's place in prison might have been that of visitor and not occupant, or that he simply might have been confused with "the prisoner" whose proper name he shared.

The jailed Khurāsānīs reportedly included the top leadership from the eastern branch of the movement, that is to say, Sulaymān b. Kathīr, Qaḥṭabah b. Shabīb, and Lāhiz b. Qurayẓ. As was previously noted, it is unlikely that operatives bearing credentials such as those held by the Khurāsānīs could have been interned concurrently. The movement's clandestine structure precluded their joint exposure. To be sure, this is only an assumption, but it is seemingly validated by the substantive political role which the Khurāsānīs and their Kūfan allies later played. There is simply no plausible explanation how the Umayyad authorities could have suspected all these important agents of subversion, let alone why they later released them and then allowed them sufficient latitude to plan and carry out an armed rebellion against the state. If there is any truth to the imprisonment of the Khurāsānīs and the others, then their appearance in jail was probably a good deal less dramatic than the sources indicate.

This rather skeptical reading of the narratives leads to a larger historiographical question. If the inmate population of the Umayyad prisons were somewhat less distinguished than the sources reveal, what need was there to formulate traditions that indicate otherwise? What purpose was served by placing so many leading ᶜAbbāsid operatives in the prisons of Umayyad provincial governors and without any clear indication of the charges brought against them? In this instance, the artfully composed narratives of Abū Muslim and the imprisoned revolutionaries were intended to suggest, among other things, a sense of martyrdom and suffering that had no substance in fact. There was no ᶜAbbāsid equivalent to the early and visible ᶜAlid resistance against the Umayyad regime, and despite certain "innovative" accounts to the contrary, the historic martyrdom of al-Ḥusayn and his relations was without parallel in the house of al-ᶜAbbās. It would be difficult to underestimate the impact of the dramatic, albeit unsuccessful, ᶜAlid resistance to Umayyad rule. What cynical witnesses may have taken for misplaced bravado was recast by the ᶜAlid faithful as courageous defiance born of total commitment to traditional Islamic ideals. Historical failures occasioned by premature ventures were in this fashion restyled to suit more positive images, and these images of heroic ᶜAlid martyrs in turn had a marked effect on the formation of political ideology.

To be sure, the pragmatic ᶜAbbāsid strategy of clandestine operations bore more positive results since it created preconditions for the actual overthrow of the entrenched regime; however, once in power the new dynasty was not about to rest its case solely on its recently established military successes. It plunged into ideological combat with an officially sanctioned historiography that subtly reshaped events in accordance with ᶜAbbāsid needs. To proclaim an ᶜAbbāsid martyrology in bold face where none existed would have been too artificial for an alert audience, and hence

[115] For his activities in Khurāsān, see pp. 85ff.

self-defeating. The requisite tactic was to describe the incarceration of the ᶜAbbāsid agents without reference to substantive charges, diffusing the distinction between legend and history. Without any clearly defined reasons for the collective imprisonment of so well defined a group, the reader was likely to consider their common revolutionary background and draw the obvious political conclusion: the ᶜAbbāsid leadership was no less active or courageous than their kinsmen from the house of Abū Ṭālib.

If demonstrating fortitude were indeed the essential rationale for these highly embellished accounts, it still does not preclude chance meetings in and out of Yūsuf b. ᶜUmar's prison in Iraq. There is no reason to doubt that Abū Muslim served his ᶜIjlī masters while they were incarcerated, or that he could have made the acquaintance of various revolutionary operatives as a consequence of this activity. It is therefore possible that a meeting involving Abū Muslim and certain Khurāsānī agents might have taken place in al-Kūfah, traditionally a focal point of subversive activity against the Umayyad state. However, the ᶜAbbāsid need to emphasize an activist profile comparable to that of their ᶜAlid rivals did not specifically require Ibn ᶜUmar's prison; and although the tradition calls for various Khurāsānīs in order to link the leading operatives, the revolutionary stations and the open revolt, no apparent reason comes to mind why certain *nuqabāᵓ* should have been singled out to the exclusion of others. These specific details seemingly point to distant echoes of an historic event long since forgotten.

Somewhere within the highly complex system of coding utilized by the chroniclers there are allusions, however vague, to particular historical circumstances. The speculation here is that Abū Muslim's revolutionary conversion was but one element of a complex drama that began with Muḥammad b. ᶜAlī's death in al-Sharāt in 125 A.H. and came full cycle when the revolutionary leadership met the following year with his son Ibrāhīm in Mecca.[116] For the village agent turned revolutionary, the critical moment was a gathering of the leadership in al-Kūfah, an occurrence of unusual significance whose contemporary meaning was largely forgotten because the event itself was completely reshaped by the subsequent needs of ᶜAbbāsid propaganda.

The meeting in Iraq was but one of several important gatherings that were undertaken in response to dramatic political changes.[117] Between the passing of the patriarch and the conclave with the new imām in the Ḥijāz there were various developments of historic importance: the death of the profligate Caliph, al-Walīd, the murder of his successor Yazīd III, the ascension of the last Umayyad, Marwān al-Ḥimār, the total collapse of an ᶜAlid rebellion led first by Zayd b. ᶜAlī and then by his son Yaḥyā, the beginning of a widespread Khārijite rebellion, and above all the emergence of a civil war which enveloped the armed tribal units of Khurāsān. It is no wonder that in those heady times, the loosely connected elements that identified with

[116] See Chapter III.
[117] See pp. 89ff.

the ᶜAbbāsid cause held a critical series of meetings to chart their future course of action. It was at these meetings, which almost certainly included an important gathering in al-Kūfah, that the grand strategy of the ᶜAbbāsid revolution was first formulated, and the coalition of forces that was to carry out the long-awaited military phase was first envisaged.

Given the clandestine structure of the revolutionary apparatus, any conclave that would have necessitated the presence of many operatives was likely to have been somewhat unusual and certainly full of risk. Such a situation would have called for extensive security precautions. Suitable cover would have to be found in order to mask the arrival of travelers from diverse locations whose presence in a single place was bound to attract curiosity, if not attention. A meeting in the governor's prison hardly seems a proper setting for an event requiring sensitive arrangements. The actual deliberations were most probably attended by a group of intimates and kept intentionally small. It is suggested here that Abū Muslim, despite his humble status and recent association with the Kūfan agents, was considered sufficiently trustworthy to be present at these proceedings, and as a result he became generally acquainted with key elements of the Khurāsānī leadership. In addition to his widely acclaimed talents, this familiarity with the Khurāsānīs would later serve him well, as the imām himself handpicked Abū Muslim to act as a courier to the revolutionary stations, and then chose him to coordinate the rebellion that was scheduled to break out in the east. The meeting could thus be considered Abū Muslim's real introduction to a broad cross-section of the decision-makers and the process by which the important decisions were made.

POSTSCRIPT

The mere declaration of a rebellion against the ruling dynasty did not guarantee success for the ᶜAbbāsids and their followers. Marwān, who was destined to be the last of the Umayyad sovereigns, was an able if not innovative warrior and the veteran of many hard-fought and successful campaigns. Moreover, he commanded the allegiance of a large and seasoned army, led by experienced generals of first rank. As the battleground shifted from the turbulent province of Khurāsān to Iraq, hard fighting was required to settle the outcome of the conflict between the rebels and the government forces. The preliminary victories of the *ahl Khurāsān*, impressive as they had been, were merely preparation for the decisive struggle that was to take place along the Zāb river in 132 A.H. There, in the month of Jumādā I, tens of thousands of fighting men engaged in a momentous struggle. When the fighting had ceased, the Umayyad army, shattered as an effective fighting force, withdrew to Syria with the Caliph fleeing before them.

Defeat was contagious. One after another, the garrisons of fortified towns and cities displayed the ᶜAbbāsid colors, and having changed allegiance, they denied the defeated Marwān safety and rest. Syria, the heartland of the Umayyad state, lay open to the rapidly advancing rebel armies. In fact, one could no longer call the *ahl Khurāsān* rebels, for even before the victory at the Zāb, the new patriarch of the ᶜAbbāsid house, Abū al-ᶜAbbās, had been proclaimed Caliph in the mosque at al-Kūfah, thus signifying the return of the Prophet's family to its position of leadership among the Faithful. Abandoned by most of his following, and incapable of launching any meaningful defense, even in the traditional centers of Umayyad rule, Marwān retreated, first to Palestine and then to Egypt. Throughout his sojourn he was actively pursued by forward elements of the ᶜAbbāsid army. Finally, a squadron of Khurāsānī cavalry caught up with the Caliph in a village called Būṣīr. There, he made his last stand, fighting valiantly and alone, until he was overcome by sheer numbers.

The death of Marwān was paralleled by a series of bizarre events taking place at different locations. Leading members of the old ruling family were assembled in various regional centers and brutally put to death. In Damascus itself, the graves of the Umayyad cemetery were exhumed as part of an effort to erase all traces of the recently deposed regime. These measures taken against the Umayyads were unprecedented in the history of the Islamic community. There had been assassinations, random killings, and executions, but never before had it been the declared policy of an Islamic ruler to exterminate an extended Muslim family. It was as though the new dynasts wished to wipe the slate clean and start again.

This was a revolution true to the word describing it. The ᶜAbbāsid *dawlah* was a great victory, signifying a turn in fortune as well as a return to the pristine Islam of their ancestor, the Prophet. By returning to the ethos of an earlier age, a new order had been created, one which was to be led for eternity by the descendants of Muḥammad b. ᶜAlī, the progenitor of the revolution. More specifically, it was the line of his son Abū Jaᶜfar ᶜAbdallāh al-Manṣūr that was to guide the fortunes of the Faithful. All this had been ordained long before the first ᶜAbbāsid dynast ascended the pulpit in al-Kūfah to receive the oath of allegiance. It was simply a question of actors adapting to roles that had been intended for them. In any case, this was how the ᶜAbbāsid triumph was proclaimed by apologists for the new dynasty, and how it came to be understood by generations of Muslims.

APPENDIX A

PROTO-SHĪᶜITE CONTENDERS

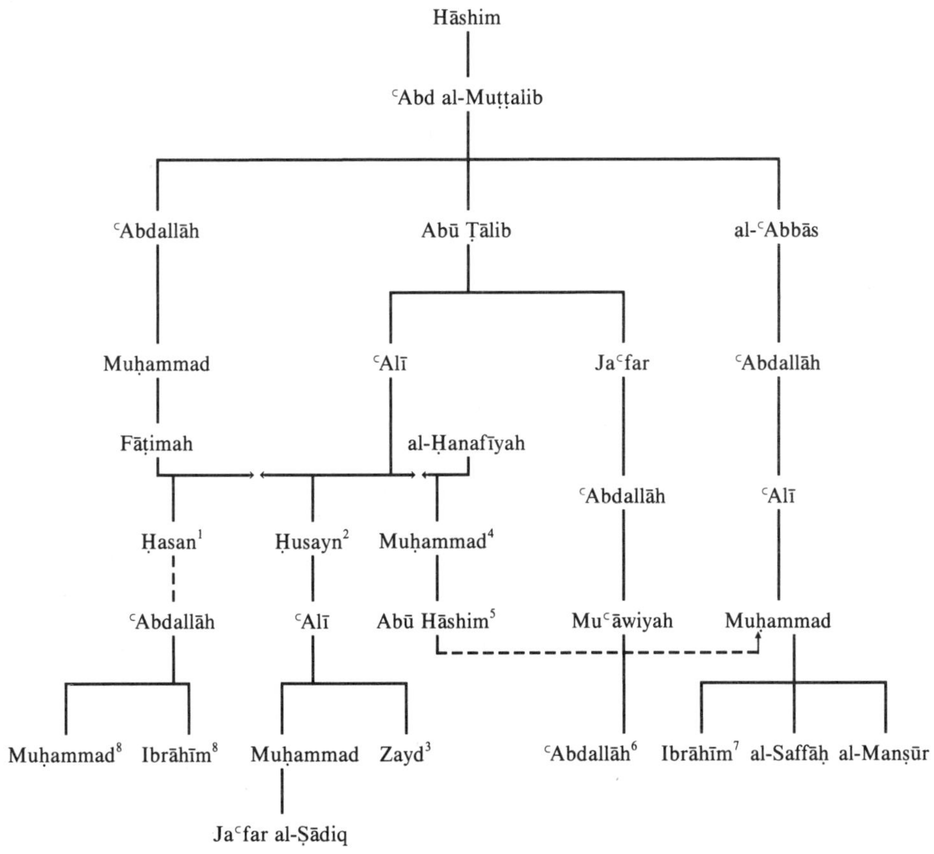

[1]Resigned (661 A.D.)
[2]Killed at Karbalāʾ (680 A.D.)
[3]Killed during revolt at al-Kūfah (740 A.D.)
[4]Imām of al-Mukhtār's revolt at al-Kūfah (685–87 A.D.)
[5]Transferred authority to ᶜAbbāsids (ca. 716 A.D.)
[6]Killed by Abū Muslim following the revolt against the Umayyads (747 A.D.)
[7]Allegedly killed by the Umayyads (749 A.D.)
[8]Killed in the widespread ᶜAlid revolt of 762 A.D.

APPENDIX B

THE EARLY ʿABBĀSID CALIPHS

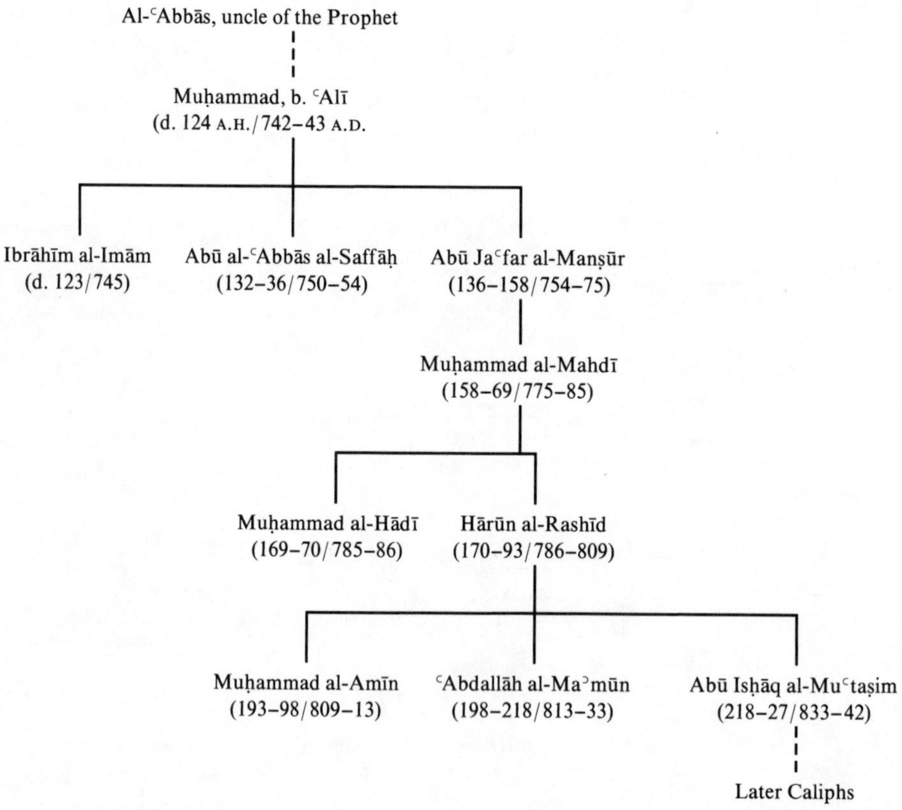
Al-ʿAbbās, uncle of the Prophet
Muḥammad, b. ʿAlī
(d. 124 A.H./742–43 A.D.
Ibrāhīm al-Imām
(d. 123/745)
Abū al-ʿAbbās al-Saffāḥ
(132–36/750–54)
Abū Jaʿfar al-Manṣūr
(136–158/754–75)
Muḥammad al-Mahdī
(158–69/775–85)
Muḥammad al-Hādī
(169–70/785–86)
Hārūn al-Rashīd
(170–93/786–809)
Muḥammad al-Amīn
(193–98/809–13)
ʿAbdallāh al-Maʾmūn
(198–218/813–33)
Abū Isḥāq al-Muʿtaṣim
(218–27/833–42)
Later Caliphs

APPENDIX C

THE MANṢŪRID FAMILY

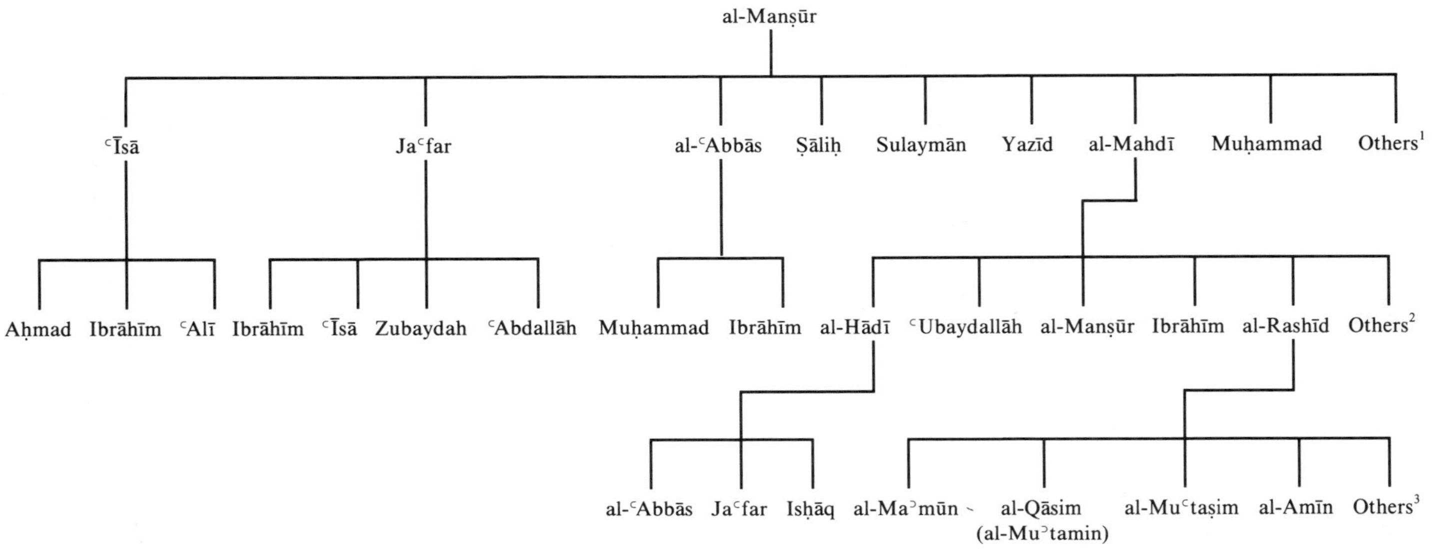

[1] Al-Qāsim, Yaᶜqūb, ᶜAbd al-Azīz: obscure and leave no record of offspring.

[2] Yaᶜqūb, Alī, Isḥāq and four daughters.

[3] ᶜAlī, Ṣāliḥ, Muḥammad (Abū ᶜĪsā), Muḥammad (Abū Yaᶜqūb), Muḥammad (Abū al-ᶜAbbās), Muḥammad (Abū Sulaymān), Muḥammad (Abū ᶜAlī), Muḥammad (Abū Aḥmad), Abū Muḥammad.

APPENDIX D

THE FAMILY OF MUḤAMMAD B. ᶜALĪ[1]

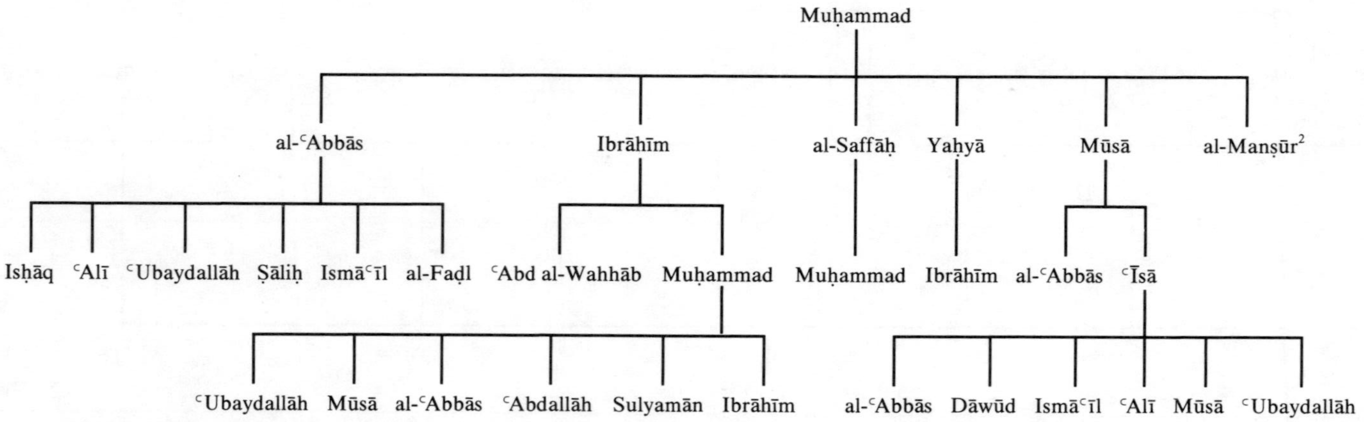

1. Limited to three generations.
2. See Manṣūrid Family.

APPENDIX E

THE ᶜ*UMŪMAH*

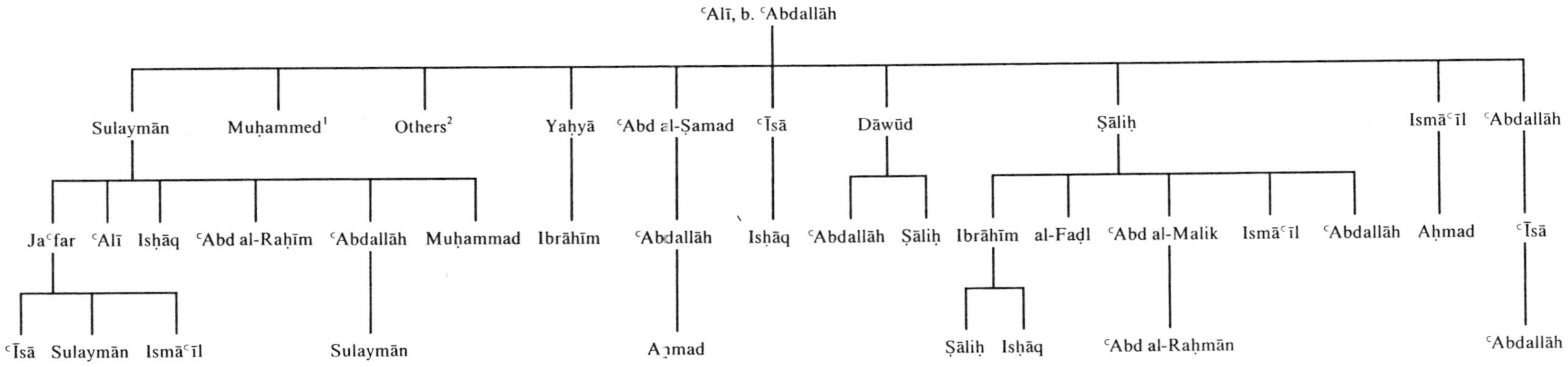

[1]Gives rise to ᶜAbbāsid Caliphs. See Appendix B.
[2]Bishr, Aḥmad, Isḥāq, Mubashshir and others. Obscure and leave no offspring.

APPENDIX F

THE UMAYYAD CALIPHS

41/661	Muʿāwiyah b. Abī Sufyān	60/680
60/680	Yazīd b. Muʿāwiyah	64/683
64/683	Muʿāwiyah b. Yazīd (II)	64/684
64/684	Marwān b. al-Ḥakam[1]	65/685
65/685	ʿAbd al-Malik b. Marwān	86/705
86/705	al-Walīd b. ʿAbd al-Malik	96/715
96/715	Sulaymān b. ʿAbd al-Malik	99/717
99/717	ʿUmar b. ʿAbd al-Azīz[2]	101/720
101/720	Yazīd b. ʿAbd al-Malik (II)	105/724
105/724	Hishām b. ʿAbd al-Malik	125/743
125/743	al-Walīd b. Yazīd II	126/744
126/744	Yazīd b. al-Walīd (III)[3]	126/744
126/744	Ibrāhīm b. al-Walīd[4]	127/744
127/744	Marwān b. Muḥammad (II)[5]	132/750

[1]Cousin of Muʿāwiyah b. Abī Sufyān.
[2]Nephew of ʿAbd al-Malik.
[3]That is, Yazīd b. al-Walīd b. ʿAbd al-Malik.
[4]That is, Ibrāhīm b. al-Walīd b. ʿAbd al-Malik.
[5]Cousin of ʿAbd al-Malik's offspring by way of Muḥammad b. Marwān, brother of ʿAbd al-Malik.

BIBLIOGRAPHY

The bibliography is alphabetically ordered, but no consideration is given to the Arabic definite article *al-*, which is often prefixed to a given name. Thus, the chronicler al-Ṭabarī appears as though his name were written Ṭabarī. Works are listed under the name of the author, with the exception of compilations and editions of anonymous works, which are entered by title. When an author is known by two names, for example, Ibn al-Ṭiqṭaqā, who is also referred to as Ibn Ṭabāṭabā, the name is cross-listed. The bibliography is limited essentially to those works cited in the text and is therefore not to be considered all-inclusive. It is divided into primary and secondary sources; translations of the original texts that are copiously annotated are listed among the primary sources.

AO	Acta Orientalia
ArO	Archiv Orientální
BAHG	Bibliothek Arabischer Historiker und Geographen
BGA	Bibliotheca Geographorum Arabicorum
BI	Bibliotheca Islamica
BSOAS	Bulletin of the School of Oriental and African Studies
EI	Encyclopedia of Islam
EI^2	Encyclopedia of Islam, New Edition
FHA	Fragmenta Historicorum Arabicorum
GAL	C. Brockelmann, Geschichte der Arabischen Litteratur
GAS	F. Sezgin, Geschichte des Arabischen Schrifttums
GMS	Gibb Memorial Series
IC	Islamic Culture
IOS	Israel Oriental Studies
IJMES	International Journal of Middle East Studies
JAOS	Journal of the American Oriental Society
JESHO	Journal of the Economic and Social History of the Orient
JNES	Journal of Near Eastern Studies
JQR	Jewish Quarterly Review
JRAS	Journal of the Royal Asiatic Society
MW	Muslim World
PIEO	Publication de l'Institut d'Études Orientales
PIFAO	Publications de l'Institut Fran*çais d'Archéologie Orientale du Caire*
PIFD	Publications de l'Institut Français de Damas
RAAD	Revue de l'Academie Arabe (Majallat al-majma^{c} al-ilmī al-^{c}arabī)
REI	Revue des Études Islamiques

RSO Rivista degli Studi Orientali
TLS Times Literary Supplement
WZKM Wiener Zeitschrift für die Kunde des Morgenlandes
ZA Zeitschrift für Assyriologie
ZDMG Zeitschrift der Deutschen Morgenländischen Gesellschaft

PRIMARY SOURCES

Akhbar al-dawlah al-ʿAbbāsīyah. Edited by ʿA.ʿA. Dūrī and ʿA. J. al-Muṭṭalibī, Beirut, 1971.

Anonymous: see *Taʾrīkh al-Khulafāʾ*.

al-Azdī, Yazīd b. Muḥammad. *Taʾrīkh al-Mawṣil*. Cairo, 1387/1967.

al-Baghdādī, ʿAbd al-Qāhir b. Ṭāhir. *al-Farq bayn al-firaq*. Edited by M. Badr. Cairo, 1910; translated and annotated as *Moslem Schisms and Sects*. 2 vols. K. Seelye, vol. 1. N.Y., 1920 and A. Halkin, vol. 2. Tel-Aviv, 1935.

al-Balādhurī, Aḥmad b. Yaḥyā. *K. ansāb al-ashrāf*. Vol. 3. Edited by ʿA. ʿA. Duri. Beirut, 1398/1978; v. IV A. Edited by M. Schloessinger, revised and annotated by M. J. Kister. Jerusalem, 1971.

al-Bayhaqī, Ibrāhīm b. Muḥammad. *K. al-maḥāsin wa al-masāwī*. Edited by F. Schwally. Giessen, 1902.

al-Dhahabī, Muḥammad b. Aḥmad. *K. tadhkirat al-ḥuffāẓ*. 5 vols. Hyderabad, 1915–16.

al-Dīnawarī, Aḥmad b. Dāwūd. *K. al-akhbār al-ṭiwāl*. Edited by V. Guirgass. Leiden, 1888; indices by I. Kratchkovsky (1912).

Fragmenta Historicorum Arabicorum. Edited by M. J. De Goeje. 2 vols. Leiden, 1869.

Ibn ʿAbd Rabbihi, Aḥmad b. Muḥammad. *al-ʿIqd al-farīd*. Edited by A. Amīn, A. al-Zayn, I. al-Abyarī. 6 vols. Cairo, 1965.

Ibn al-Athīr, ʿAlī b. Muḥammad. *al-Kāmil fī al-taʾrīkh*. Edited by C. J. Tornberg. 12 vols. Leiden, 1851–76.

______. *al-Lubāb fī tahdhīb al-ansāb*. 3 vols. Cairo, 1357/1938.

Ibn Ḥawqal, Abū al-Qāsim al-Nāṣibī. *K. al-masālik wa al-mamālik*. Edited by M. J. De Goeje. Leiden, 1897, *BGA* 2.

Ibn Ḥazm, ʿAlī b. Aḥmad. *K. al-faṣl fī al-milal*. Cairo, 1317/1903; translated and annotated by I. Friedlander. "The Heterodoxies of the Shiites." *JAOS* 28 (1907):1–80; 29 (1908):1–83.

Ibn Hishām, *K. sīrat Rasūl Allāh*. Edited by F. Wüstenfeld. 3 vols. Göttingen, 1858–60. Reprinted Frankfort a. Main, 1961. Translated by A. Guillaume, *The Life of Muhammad*. London, 1955.

Ibn al-Jawzī, ʿAbd al-Raḥmān b. ʿAlī, *Manāqib Baghdād*. Edited by M. M. al-Atharī. Baghdad, 1923; partially translated and annotated by G. Makdisi. *Arabica* 6 (1959):185–95.

______. *al-Muntaẓam fī al-taʾrīkh al-mulūk wa al-umam*. Edited by F. Krenkow. Vols. 5^2–10. Hyderabad, 1938–39.

Ibn Kathīr, Ismāᶜīl b. ᶜUmar. *al-Bidāyah wa al-nihāyah*, 14 vols. Cairo, 1932–40.
Ibn Khallikān, Aḥmad b. Muḥammad. *K. wafayāt al-aᶜyān wa anbāᵓ abnāᵓ al-zamān*. Cairo, 1881; translated and partially annotated by M. G. DeSlane. Ibn Khallikan's Biographical Dictionary. 4 vols. Paris and London, 1843–71.
Ibn Khayyāṭ, Khalīfah al-ᶜUṣfurī. *Taᵓrīkh*. Edited by A. al-ᶜUmarī. 2 vols. Najaf, 1967.
Ibn al-Muqaffaᶜ, *Risālah fī al-ṣaḥābah*. Edited by ᶜUmar Abū al-Naṣr in *Āthār b. al-Muqaffaᶜ*. Beirut, 1966.
Ibn Qutaybah, ᶜAbdallāh b. Muslim. *K. al-maᶜārif*. Edited by F. Wüstenfeld. Göttingen, 1850.
Ibn Rustah, Aḥmad b. ᶜUmar. *K. al-aᶜlāq al-nafīsah*. Edited by M. J. De Goeje. Leiden, 1892. *BGA* 7.
Ibn Ṭabāṭabā, Muḥammad b. ᶜAlī. *al-Kitāb al-fakhrī fī al-ādāb al-sulṭānīyah wa al-duwal al-islāmīyah*. Edited by H. Derenbourg. Paris, 1895; Beirut, 1386/1966; translated and annotated by E. Amar. *Histoire des dynasties musulmanes depuis la mort de Mahomet jusqa'à la chute du Khalifat ᶜAbbāside de Baghdadz*. Paris, 1910. Beirut edition is cited.
Ibn Taghrī Birdī, Yūsuf. *al-Nujūm al-zāhirah fi mulūk Misr wa al-Qāhirah*. Edited by T. G. S. Juynboll and B. F. Mathes. Vol. 1. Leiden, 1855–61; Cairo, 1929.
Ibn Ṭāhir al-Baghdādī: see al-Baghdādī, ᶜAbd al-Qāhir.
Ibn al-Ṭiqṭaqā: see Ibn Ṭabāṭabā.
al-Iṣfahānī, ᶜAlī b. al-Ḥusayn. *K. al-aghānī*. 20 vols. Beirut, 1390/1970. Vol. 21. Edited by R. Brünnow. Leiden, 1888.
______. *Maqātil al-Ṭālibiyīn*. Teheran, 1365/1946.
al-Isfahānī, Ḥamzah b. al-Ḥasan. *Tawārīkh sinī mulūk al-arḍ wa al-anbiyāᵓ*. Edited by J. M. E. Gottwaldt. 2 vols. Leipzig, 1844, 1848.
al-Iṣṭakhrī, Ibrāhīm b. Muḥammad. *K. al-masālik wa al-mamālik*. Edited by M. J. De Goeje. Leiden, 1870. *BGA* 1.
al-Jāḥiẓ, ᶜAmr b. Baḥr. *K. al-bukhalāᵓ*. Edited by A. Bak and ᶜA. Bak. 2 vols. Cairo, 1938–39.
______. *Risālah ilā al-Fatḥ b. Khāqān fī manāqib al-Turk wa ᶜāmmat jund al-khilāfah* in ᶜA. M. Hārun, *Rasāᵓil al-Jāḥiẓ*. Cairo, 1964–65; *Tria Opuscula*. Leiden, 1903: 1–56.
al-Jahshiyārī, Muḥammad b. ᶜAbdūs. *K. al-wuzarāᵓ*. Edited by M. al-Ṣafā et al. Cairo, 1357/1938.
al-Khaṭīb al-Baghdādī. Aḥmad b. Thābit, *Taᵓrīkh Baghdād*. 14 vols. Cairo, 1931; topographical introduction edited, translated and annotated by G. Salmon as *L'Introduction topographique à l'histoire de Baghdadh*. Paris, 1904.
K. al-ᶜuyūn: see *Fragmenta*.
al-Maqrīzī, Aḥmad b. ᶜAlī. *K. al-nizāᶜ wa al-takhāsum fīmā bayna Banī Umayyah wa Banī Hāshim*. Edited by M. ᶜArnūs. Cairo, 1937 (?).
al-Masᶜūdī, ᶜAlī b. al-Ḥusayn. *Murūj al-dhahab wa maᶜādin al-jawāhir*. Edited and translated by C. Barbier de Meynard and P. de Courteille as *Les prairies d'ôr*. 9 vols. Paris, 1861–77; edited by Y. A. Dāghir. 4 vols. Beirut, 1385/1965.

———. *K. al-tanbīh wa al-ishrāf*. Edited by M. J. De Goeje. Leiden, 1894. *BGA* 8.

al-Mubarrad, Muḥammad b. Yazīd. *al-Kāmil*. 3 vols. Edited by M. A. Ibrāhīm and S. Shaḥātah. Cairo, 1956.

al-Muqaddasī, Muḥammad b. Aḥmad. *K. aḥsan al-taqāsīm fi maᶜrifat al-aqālīm*. Edited by M. J. De Goeje. Leiden, 1877. *BGA* 3.

al-Nawbakhtī, al-Ḥasan b. Mūsā. *Firaq al-Shīᶜah*. Edited by H. Ritter. Isanbul, 1931. *BI* 4.

Ps. Ibn Qutaybah. *al-Imāmah wa al-siyāsah*. Edited by T. M. al-Zarīnī. 2 vols. in 1. Cairo(?), n.d.

Qazwīnī, Ḥamdallāh Mustawfī. *Nuzhat al-qulūb* (Persian). Edited by G. Le Strange. London, 1915. *GMS* 23 Part 1; translated by G. Le Strange, *The Geographical Part of the Nuzhat al-Qulūb of Qazwīnī*. London, 1919. *GMS* 23 Part 2.

al-Ṣābiᵓ, Hilāl b. al-Muḥassin. *K. al-wuzarāᵓ*. Edited by A. Farrāj. Beirut, 1958.

———. *Rusūm dār al-khilāfah*. Edited by M. ᶜAwad. Cairo, 1963.

al-Sakhāwī, Muḥammad b. Aḥmad. *al-Iᶜlān bi-l-tawbīkh liman dhamma ahl al-tawārīkh;* translated by F. Rosenthal in *A History of Muslim Historiography*. Leiden, 1952; 2nd ed. 1968.

al-Samᶜānī, ᶜAbd al-Karīm b. Muḥammad. *K. al-ansāb*. Edited by D. S. Margoliouth. London, 1912. *GMS* 20.

al-Shahrastānī, Muḥammad b. ᶜAbd al-Karīm. *K. al-milal wa al-nihal*. Cairo, 1317/1899–1321/1903.

al-Ṭabarī, Muḥammad b. Jarīr. *K. akhbār al-rusul wa al-mulūk* (*Annales*). Edited by M. J. De Goeje et al. 13 vols. Leiden, 1879–1901.

Taᵓrīkh al-khulafāᵓ. Facsimile reproduction. P. A. Gryaznevich. Moscow, 1967.

al-Yaᶜqūbī, Aḥmad b. Abī Yaᶜqūb. *K. al-buldān*. Edited by M. J. De Goeje. Leiden, 1892. *BGA* 7; translated and annotated by G. Wiet. *Les Pays*. Cairo, 1937. *PIFAO* 1.

———. *Mushākalat al-nās lizamānihim wa mā ᶜalayhim fī kull ᶜaṣr*. Beirut, 1962; translated and annotated by W. Millward. "The Adaptation of Men into Their Time: an Historical Essay by al-Yaᶜqūbī." In *JAOS* 84 (1964):329–44.

———. *Taᵓrīkh* (*Historiae*). Edited by M. Th. Houtsma. Leiden, 1883.

Yāqūt, Yaᶜqūb b. ᶜAbdallāh. *Irshād al-arīb ilā maᶜrifat al-adīb* (*Muᶜjam al-udabāᵓ*). Edited by D. S. Margoliouth. London, 1907–31. *GSM* 6.

———. *Muᶜjam al-buldān*. Edited by F. Wüstenfeld. 6 vols. Leipzig, 1866–73.

al-Zubayrī, Musᶜab b. ᶜAbdallāh. *K. nasab Quraysh*. Edited by A. Lévi-Provençal. Cairo, 1953.

SECONDARY STUDIES

Abbot, N. *Two Queens of Baghdad*. Chicago, 1946.

Ayalon, D. "Preliminary Remarks on the Mamluk Military Institution in Islam," *War Technology and Society in the Middle East*. Edited by V. Parry and M. Yapp. Oxford, 1975.

______. *The Military Reforms of al-Muᶜtaṣim. Their Background and Consequences.* Private Circulation. Jerusalem, 1964.
Azizi, M. *La domination arabe et l'épanouissement du sentiment national en Iran.* Paris, 1938.
Barthold, W. *Turkestan to the Mongol Invasion.* Translated by H. A. R. Gibb. 2d ed., London, 1948.
______. *Mussulman Culture.* Calcutta, 1934.
Bergsträsser, G. and Schacht, J. *Gründzüge des islamischen Rechts.* Berlin, 1935.
Biddle, D. "The Development of the Bureaucracy of the Islamic Empire During the Late Umayyad and Early ᶜAbbasid Period." Ph.D. dissertation, University of Texas/Austin, 1972.
Cahen, C. "Points de vue sur la révolution abbāside." *Revue Historique.* 230 (1963):295–338.
Chejne, A. *Succession to the Rule in Islam.* Lahore, 1960.
Cook, M. and Crone, P. *Hagarism, the Making of the Islamic World.* Cambridge, 1977.
Crone, P. "The Mawālī in the Umayyad Period." Ph.D. dissertation, University of London, 1973.
______. *Slaves on Horses.* Cambridge etc., 1980.
Daniel, E. "The Anonymous 'History of the Abbasid Family' and its Place in Islamic Historiography." *IJMES* 14 (1982):419–34.
______. *The Political and Social History of Khurasan Under Abbasid Rule.* Minneapolis and Chicago, 1979.
Dennet, D. "Marwān b. Muḥammad; the Passing of the Umayyad Caliphate." Ph.D. dissertation, Harvard University, 1939.
Dietrich, A. "Das politische Testament des zweiten ᶜAbbāsiden Kalifen al-Manṣūr." *Der Islam* 30 (1952):33–65.
Dixon, A. A. *The Umayyad Caliphate* 65–86/684–705. London, 1971.
Donner, F. *The Early Islamic Conquests.* Princeton, 1981.
Duri, A. A. "The Iraq School of History to the Ninth Century—a Sketch." *Historians of the Middle East.* Edited by B. Lewis and P. Holt. London, 1962.
Fahd, T. "The Dream in Medieval Islamic Society." *The Dream and Human Societies.* Edited by G. von Grunebaum. Berkeley and Los Angeles, 1966.
Forand, P. "The Governors of Mosul According to al-Azdī's *Taʾrīkh al-Mawṣil.*" *JAOS* 89 (1969):88–106.
______. "The Relation of the Slave and the Client to the Master or Patron in Medieval Islam." *IJMES* 2 (1971):59–66.
Friedlander, I. "Jewish-Arabic Studies." *JQR,* n.s. 1 (1910–11):183–215; 2 (1911–12):482–516; (1912–13):225–300.
Frye, F. "The ᶜAbbāsid Conspiracy and Modern Revolutionary Theory." *Indo-Iranica* 5/3 (1952):9–14.
______. "The Role of Abū Muslim in the ᶜAbbāsid Revolt." *MW* 37 (1947):28–38.
Fück, J. *Muḥammad ibn Isḥāq.* Frankfort/a.M., 1925.

Gabrieli, F. "La 'Risāla' di al-Ǧaḥiẓ sui Turchi." *Scritti in onore di G. Furlani.* Rome, 1957 (equals *RSO* 32):477–83.

______. "La successione di Hārūn al-Rashīd e la guerra fra al-Amīn e al-Maᵓmūn." *RSO* 11 (1926–28):341–97.

Gibb, H. A. R. *The Arab Conquests in Central Asia.* New York, 1970.

Ginsberg, L. *The Legends of the Jews.* 7 vols. New York, 1963.

Goitein, S. D. "A Turning Point in the History of the Muslim State, à propos of Ibn al-Muqaffaᶜ's Kitāb aṣ-Ṣaḥāba." *IC,* 23 (1945):120–35; reprinted in his *Studies in Islamic History and Institutions.* Leiden, 1971.

Goldziher, I. *Muhammedanische Studien.* 2 vols. Halle, 1895–90; analytical translation by L. Bercher. *Études sur la tradition islamique.* Paris, 1952. English translation and annotation by S. M. Stern. *Muslim Studies.* 2 vols. Chicago, 1966. London, 1971.

Grabar, O. "Al-Mushatta Baghdād and Wāsiṭ." *The World of Islam: Studies in Honor of P. K. Hitti.* Edited by J. Kritzek and R. B. Winder. New York, 1959.

Guillaume, W. "A Note on the Sīra of Ibn Isḥāq." *BSOAS* 18 (1956):1–4.

______. Trans. *The Life of Muhammad.* London, 1955.

Hamidullah, M. "Nouveaux documents." *Arabica* 7 (1960):293–97.

Herzfeld, E. and Sarre, F. *Archäologische Reise im Euphrat und Tigris Geibit.* Vol. 2. Verlin, 1921.

Hinds, M. "Kufan Political Alignments and Their Backgrounds in the mid-7th Century A.D." *IJMES* 2 (1971):346–67.

Hodgson, M. "How Did the Early Shīᶜa Become Sectarian?" *JAOS* 75 (1955):1–13.

Hoenerbach, W. "Zur Heeresverwaltung der ᶜAbbāsiden. Studie über Abulfarağ Qudāma: Dīwān al-ğaiš." *Der Islam* 29 (1950):257–90.

Horovitz, J. "The Earliest Biographies of the Prophet and Their Authors." *IC* 2 (1928):22–50, 164–82, 495–526.

Jafri, S. H. M. *The Origins and Early Development of Shiᵓa Islam.* London and New York, 1979.

Jones, J. M. B. "Ibn Isḥāq and al-Wāqidī: the Dream of ᶜĀtika and the Raid to Nakhla in Relation to the Charge of Plagiarism." *BSOAS* 22 (1959):41–51.

Juynboll, G. ed. *Studies on the First Century of Islamic Society.* Carbondale and Edwardsville, 1982.

Juynboll, T. W. *Handbuch des islamischen Gesetzes.* Leiden, 1910.

Kennedy, H. *The Early Abbasid Caliphate.* London, 1981.

Kister, M. "The Battle of Ḥarra. Some Socio-Economic Aspects." *Studies in Memory of Gaston Wiet.* Edited by M. Rosen-Ayalon. Jerusalem.

______. "The Interpretation of Dreams." *IOS* 4 (1974):67–103.

Kohlberg, E. "Some Imāmī Shīᶜī Interpretations of Umayyad History." *Studies in the First Century of Islamic Society.* Edited by G. Juynboll. Carbondale and Edwardsville, 1982.

______. "The Development of the Imāmī Shīᶜī Doctrine of *Jihād.*" *ZDMG* 126 (1976):64–86.

______. "The Term *Muḥaddath* in Twelver Shīᶜism." *Studia Orientalia Memoriae D. H. Baneth Dedicata*. Edited by J. Blau, S. Pines, M. J. Kister, S. Shaked.

Kritzeck, J. and Winder, R. B., ed., *The World of Islam: Studies in Honor of P. K. Hitti*. New York, 1959.

Lapidus, I. M. "The Separation of State and Religion in the Development of Early Islamic Society." *IJMES* 6 (1975):363–85.

Lassner, J. "Did the Caliph Abū Jaᶜfar al-Manṣūr Murder his Uncle ᶜAbdallāh b. ᶜAlī and Other Problems within the Ruling House of the ᶜAbbāsids." *Studies in Memory of Gaston Wiet*. Edited by M. Rosen-Ayalon. Jerusalem, 1979.

______. "Some Speculative Thoughts on the Search for an ᶜAbbāsid Capital. Part 1." *MW* 55 (1965):135–41; part 2: 203–10.

______. "The Caliph's Personal Domain: The City Plan of Baghdad Reexamined." *The Islamic City*. Edited by A. H. Hourani and S. M. Stern. Oxford, 1970.

______. *The Shaping of ᶜAbbāsid Rule*. Princeton, 1980.

______. *The Topography of Baghdad in the Early Middle Ages: Text and Studies*. Detroit, 1970.

______. "Why did the Caliph al-Manṣūr Build ar-Ruṣāfah—A Historical Note." *JNES* 24 (1965):95–99.

Le Strange, G. *Baghdad During the ᶜAbbāsid Caliphate*. London, 1900.

______. *Lands of the Eastern Caliphate*. Cambridge, 1905.

______. *Palestine Under the Moslems*. London, 1890.

Lewis, B. *History—Remembered, Recovered, Invented*. Princeton, 1975.

______. *Islam in History*. London, 1973.

______. "Islamic Concepts of Revolution." *Revolution in the Middle East*. Edited by P. J. Vatikiotis. London, 1972. Reprinted in his *Islam in History*.

______. "On Revolutions in Early Islam." *Studia Islamica* 32 (1970):215–31. Reprinted in his *Islam in History*.

______. "The Regnal Titles of the First ᶜAbbāsid Caliphs." *Dr. Zakir Musain Presentation Volume*. New Delhi, 1968.

Lewis, B. and Holt, P., eds. *Historians of the Middle East*. London, 1962.

Løkkegard, F. *Islamic Taxation in the Classic Period with Special Reference to Circumstances in Iraq*. Copenhagen, 1950.

L'Orange, H. P. *Studies in the Iconography of Cosmic Kingship in the Ancient World*. Cambridge, 1953.

Madelung, W. "Das Imāmat in der frühen ismailitschen Lehre." *Der Islam* 37 (1961):43–135.

Marquet, Y. "Le šiᶜisme an IXe siecle a travers l'histoire de Yaᶜqūbī." *Arabica* 19 (1972):1–44, 101–48.

Melikoff-Sayar, I. *Abū Muslim le "porte-hache" du Khurassan dans la tradition épique turco-iranienne*. Paris, 1962.

Millward, W. "The Adaptation of Men into Their Time: an Historical Essay by al-Yaᶜqūbī." *JAOS* 84 (1964):329–44.

Moscati, S. "Il testamento di Abū Hāshim." *RSO* 27 (1952):28–46.

______. "Le Califat d'al-Hadī." *SO* 13/4 (1946):1–28.

______. "Le Massacre des Umayyades dans l'histoire et dans les fragments poétiques." *ArO* 18 (1950):88–115.

______. "Nuovi studi storici sul califatto di al-Mahdī." *Orientalia* 15 (1946):155–79.

______. "Studi storici sul califatto di al-Mahdī." *Orientalia* 14 (1945):300–354.

______. "Studi su Abū Muslim." *Rendiconti Lincei*, ser. 8, 4 (1949–50):323–35, 474–95; 5 (1950–51):89–105.

Nagel, T. "Ein früher Bericht über den Aufstand des Muḥammad b. ᶜAbdallāh im Jahre 145h." *Der Islam* 46 (1970):227–62.

______. *Untersuchungen zur Entstehung des abbasidischen Kalifates*. Bonn, 1972.

Noeldeke, T. *Orientalische Skizzen*. Berlin, 1892; translated by J. S. Black. *Sketches from Eastern History*. London, 1892.

Noth, A. "Der character der ersten grossen Sammlungen von Nachrichten zur frühen Kalifenzeit." *Der Islam* 47 (1971):168–99.

______. *Quellenkritische Studien Zur Themen, formen und Tendenzen Frühislamischer Geschichtsüberlieferung*. Bonn, 1973.

Omar, F. "A Note on the Laqab (i.e., Epithet) of the Early ᶜAbbāsid Caliphs" in his *ᶜAbbāsīyāt*, pp. 141–47.

______. *Al-ᶜAbbāsīyūn al-awāʾil:132–70/750–86*. 2 vols. Beirut, 1380/1970.

______. *ᶜAbbāsīyāt: Studies in the History of the Early ᶜAbbāsids*. Baghdad, 1976.

______. "Alwān wa dalālatuhā al-siyāsīyah fī al-*ᶜaṣr al-ᶜAbbāsī al-awwal." Bulletin, Faculty of the Arts*. Baghdad University 14 (1971):827–36.

______. "Aspects of ᶜAbbāsid Ḥusaynid Relations." *Arabica* 22 (1976):170–79.

______. "Politics and the Problem of Succession in the Early ᶜAbbāsid Caliphate." *IC* 48 (1974):31–43.

______. *The Abbāsid Caliphate, 132–70/750–86*. Baghdad, 1969; a slightly shortened version of his *al-ᶜAbbāsīyūn*.

______. "*The Nature of the Iranian Revolts in the Early Islamic Period*." *IC* 48 (1974):1–9.

______. "The Significance of Colors and Banners in the Early ᶜAbbāsid Period" in his *ᶜAbbāsīyāt*, pp. 148–54.

Parry, V. and Yapp, M. *War Technology and Society in the Middle East*. Oxford, 1975.

Pellat, C. "Ǧāḥiẓ à Baghdād et à Sāmarrā." *RSO* 27 (1952):48–67.

______. *Le milieu basrien et la formation de Ǧāḥiẓ*. Paris, 1953.

Pinto, O. "Al-Fatḥ b. Ḫāqān favorito di al-Mutawakkil." *RSO* 13 (1931–32):133–49.

Pipes, D. *Slave Soldiers and Islam*. New Haven, 1981.

Richter, G. *Das Geschichtsbild der arabischen Historiker des Mittelalters*. Tubingen, 1933.

______. *Studien zur Geschichte der älteren arabischen Fürstenspiegel*. Berlin, 1932.

Robson, J. "Ibn Isḥāq's Use of the Isnād." *Bulletin of the John Rowlands Library* 38 (1955–56):449–65.

Rosenthal, F. *A History of Muslim Historiography*. Leiden, 1952; 2d ed. 1968.

______. "The Influence of the Biblical Tradition on Muslim Historiography."

Historians of the Middle East. Edited by B. Lewis and P. Holt.

Rubin, U. "Prophets and Progenitors in the Early Shī^{c}a Tradition." *Jerusalem Studies in Arabic and Islam* 1 (1979):41–65.

Sachedina, A. A. *Islamic Messianism*. Albany, 1981.

Sadighi, G. *Les mouvements religieux Iraniens au IIe et au IIIe siècles de l'hégire*. Paris, 1938.

Salmon, G. *L'Introduction topographique à l'histoire de Baghdadh*. Paris, 1904.

Santillana, D. *Istituzioni di diritto musulmano malichita con riguardo anche al sistema sciafiita*. 2 vols. Rome, 1926–38.

Schacht, J. *An Introduction to Islamic Law*. Oxford, 1964.

______. *The Origins of Muhammadan Jurisprudence*. Oxford, 1950.

______. "A Revaluation of Islamic Traditions." *JRAS* (1949):143–54.

Scholem, G. *The Messianic Idea in Judaism*. New York, 1971.

______. *Sabbati, Şevi, the Mystical Messiah*. Princeton, 1973.

Shaban, M. *Islamic History: A New Interpretation*. 2 vols. Cambridge, 1971, 1976.

______. *The ^{c}Abbāsid Revolution*. Cambridge, 1970.

______. "The Social and Political Background of the ^{c}Abbāsid Revolution in Khurāsān." Ph.D. dissertation, Harvard University, 1960.

Sharon, M. "^{c}Alīyat ha-^{c}Abbāsim la-sh-shilṭōn." Ph.D. dissertation, Hebrew University, Jerusalem, 1970.

______. "The ^{c}Abbāsid Da^{c}wa Re-examined on the Basis of the Discovery of a New Source." *Arabic and Islamic Studies*, Bar-Ilan University 1 (1973).

______. *Black Banners From the East*. Jerusalem, 1983.

Shoufani, E. *Al-Riddah and the Muslim Conquest of Arabia*. Toronto, 1973.

Sourdel, D. "La biographie d'Ibn al-Muqaffa^c d'après les sources anciennes." *Arabica* 1 (1954):307–23.

______. *Le Vizirat ^{c}Abbāside de 749 à 936*. 2 vols. Damascus, 1959–60.

Speyer, H. *Die biblischen Erzählungen im Qoran*. Hildesheim, 1961.

Tuqan, F. "^{c}Abdallāh b. ^{c}Alī, A Rebellious Uncle of al-Manṣūr." *Studies in Islam* 6 (1967):1–26.

Van Vloten, G. *De Opkomst der Abbasiden im Khurasan*. Leiden, 1890.

______. *Recherches sur la domination arabe, le chiitisme et les croyances messianiques sous le khalifat des Omayyades*. Amsterdam, 1894.

______. "Zur Abbasidengeschichte." *ZDMG* 52 (1898):213–26.

Vollors, K. "Über Rassenfarben in der arabischen Literatur." *Centenario della nascita di Michele Amari*. Palermo, 1910, 1:84–95.

Von Grunebaum, G. "The Cultural Function of the Dream as Illustrated in Classical Islam" in his *The Dream and Human Societies*.

______. *The Dream and Human Societies*. Berkeley and Los Angeles, 1966.

Von Kremer, A. *Culturgeschichte des Orients unter den Califen*. 2 vols. Vienna, 1875–77.

Von Soden, W. "*Muškenum* und die Mawali des frühen Islam." *ZA*, n.f. 22 (1964):133–42.

Waldman, M. *Toward a Theory of Historical Narrative: A Close Study in*

Perso-Islamicate Historiography. Columbus, 1980.

______. "Semiotics and Historical Narrative." *Papers in Comparative Studies* 1 (1981):167–85.

Watt, W. M. *The Formative Period of Islamic Thought*. Edinburgh, 1973.

______. "The Materials Used by Ibn Isḥāq." *Historian of the Middle East*. Edited by B. Lewis and P. Holt.

Wellhausen, J. *Das Arabische Reich und sein Sturz*. Berlin, 1902; translated by M. G. Weir, *The Arab Kingdom and Its Fall*. Calcutta, 1927. The translation is cited throughout this work.

______. *Die religiös-politischen Oppositionsparteien im alten Islam*. Berlin, 1901. Translated by R. C. Ostle and S. M. Walzer as *The Religio-Political Factions in Early Islam*. Amsterdam, 1975.

______. "Prolegomena zur ältesten Geschichte des Islam" in his *Skizzen und Vorarbeiten*, vol. 6. Berlin, 1899.

Wendell, C. "Baghdad: *Imago Mundi* and Other Foundation Lore." *IJMES* 2 (1971):99–128.

Zambauer, E. *Manuel de genealogie et de chronologie pour l'histoire de l'Islam*. Hanover, 1927.

Zotenberg, H., trans. *Chronique de abou Djafer Mo'hammad ben Djarir ben Yazid Tabari*. 4 vols. Nogent-le-Rotrou, 1867–74.

NOTE: It is not unusual that after a manuscript is completed for press, materials of importance become available. Regrettably, it is not always possible to integrate these materials within the body of the text. Of these works, special notice should be taken of M. Sharon's *Black Banners from the East*. Jerusalem, 1983. The work is an expanded version in English of the first part of his Hebrew doctoral dissertation, "ᶜAlīyat ha-ᶜAbbāsim la-sh-Shilṭōn."

INDEX

I have tried to limit the index to personal names and place names. It may seem odd, given the title of the study, that there are no entries for revolution, apologetics, historical writing or even ᶜAbbāsids. The choice to omit these and similar entries is deliberate. The sub-topics are so interlocked with the fortunes of the ᶜAbbāsids and with one another than any attempt to establish discrete entries for them are highly artificial and will in the end not be of much benefit to the reader. One further note: The definite article (*al-*) in Arabic and the genealogical designations (*b.*) and (*bt.*) are not considered in the alphabetical arrangement.